12.30.72

Siberia and the Pacific

Paul Dibb
foreword by
T. H. Rigby

The Praeger Special Studies program—
utilizing the most modern and efficient book
production techniques and a selective
worldwide distribution network—makes
available to the academic, government, and
business communities significant, timely
research in U.S. and international economic, social, and political development.

Siberia and the Pacific

A Study of
Economic Development and
Trade Prospects

Praeger Publishers   New York   Washington   London

PRAEGER SPECIAL STUDIES IN INTERNATIONAL ECONOMICS AND DEVELOPMENT

PRAEGER PUBLISHERS
111 Fourth Avenue, New York, N.Y. 10003, U.S.A.
5, Cromwell Place, London S.W.7, England

Published in the United States of America in 1972
by Praeger Publishers, Inc.

Library of Congress Catalog Card Number: 71-186194

Printed in the United States of America

1732041

For Joyce and Martin

FOREWORD
T. H. Rigby

The regional study is a well-tried device in
several human sciences, and one that has special apt-
ness for research on the USSR.

The combination of highly standardized and cen-
trlized institutions with sharply differing natural
and human conditions spread over a vast area enables
us to observe the same policies and structures in
operation under a variety of conditions, and conversely, to pinpoint and measure the impact of local
circumstances. This helps to account for the interest
in regional case studies among economists, geographers,
and political scientists specializing in the USSR.

Nevertheless, broad-gauge regional studies remain a rarity, and this is notably the case, as Mr.
Dibb points out, with respect to the East Asian half
of the Soviet Union. Yet the close study of this
particular area holds special interest and promise,
for nowhere else in the Soviet Union does the contrast between immense developmental potential and
daunting impediments to their realization stand out
so starkly, and in no other region are the problems
of development so fraught with international implications.

When we consider that the region under study
borders on the historically powerful, advanced, and
populous civilizations of the Far East, it may seem
anomalous that it is inhabited predominantly by Euro-
peans and forms part of a state with its capital
thousands of miles to the west. The situation appears
analagous to one in which Chinese settlers and the
jurisdiction of Peking had advanced to the borders of
Poland. Yet this situation has deep historical roots
and is by no means the consequence merely of recent
imperialist expansion or great power politics.

Although Chinese civilization and the Chinese state originated on the North China Plain, their historical movement lay almost exclusively towards the south and southeast, so that until recent times the northernmost bounds of settlement and effective rule extended only a few miles beyond Peking. The Japanese, for most of their history, have had their faces no less firmly turned towards the south, and the large-scale settlement not only of Hokkaido but even of the northern part of the 'home' island of Honshu had to wait till modern times. By contrast the Russian advance first to the Volga region, then to the Urals and beyond, and finally to the Pacific was a largely spontaneous process extending over more than a millenium, with peasants, traders, and trappers usually preceding each eastward extension of the Russian state. When from the seventeenth century the Russians entered the area that Dibb has aptly termed 'Pacific Siberia', it is not surprising that they were no more deterred by the scattered aboriginal population or the vague suzereinty claimed by the Chinese Empire over part of the territory than at much the same period the English colonists in North America were deterred by the Indians or the earlier papal allocation of this area to Spain. By the time the Chinese and Japanese began to show a real interest in Pacific Siberia, the region had already long been settled and administered by the Russians.

Since the late nineteenth century the environs of Pacific Siberia have repeatedly been the scene of political confrontation or military conflict between the three powers, with the bordering lands of Mongolia, Manchuria, and Korea passing under the control of now one and now another. In our own day the consolidation of China under the Communists and the spectacular resurgence of Japan have cast long shadows over Soviet East Asia. It is clear that the conditions that allowed the Russians to settle and inhabit the area, as it were by default of interest and capacity on the part of adjacent powers, no longer exist. It is not difficult to imagine what might happen should Moscow's capacity to defend and administer the region be drastically reduced; indeed a preview of this was provided by the Japanese intervention during the Russian Civil War.

A new significance and a new urgency has thus been imparted to the question of what the Russians have done, are doing, and can do in this region, and to the region's relations with its powerful neighbors and other lands of the Pacific Rim farther afield. This is the theme of Paul Dibb's book.

T. H. Rigby
Chairman
Committee on Soviet and
    East European Studies
Australian National
    University

America has in one century reached a degree
of development of which we never dared even
to dream. . . . Australia has likewise during this century progressed with gigantic
strides and can now rejoice in a material
and spiritual development the like of
which we in Siberia have perhaps never even
heard. . . . And Siberia...?*

This book was prompted by a keen awareness of
the poor state of knowledge in the West about the
economic development of Siberia. A great deal has
been written about other regions of the U.S.S.R. in
various geographic and economic publications, but
Siberia, stretching from the Urals to the Pacific
Ocean, has not been the focus of nearly so much
attention.

One of the main reasons for this unsatisfactory
state of affairs is the paucity of official statistical and other data on the economy of Siberia compared
with most of the Union republics. Regional newspapers for several republics are accessible to Western
researchers in comprehensive library collections but
such is not the case for Siberia. Moreover, whereas
Soviet economic statistics frequently give a breakdown by republics, often they treat the huge mass of
the Russian Soviet Federated Socialist Republic
(R.S.F.S.R.) as a single undivided unit.

Another disability that we in the West labor
under is our own cavalier attitude to Siberia.
Fleeting impressions of salt and gold mines, forced

---

*J. S. Gregory, <u>Russian Land Soviet People</u> (Lon-
don: Harrup, 1968), p. 622, from a resolution passed
by the Yeniseisk city council at the tercentenary
jubilee of Siberia in 1883.

labor camps, the Trans-Siberian railway, and those
notorious Siberian winters have encouraged us to
pass off Siberia as something of a joke. More recently, the border conflicts with China along the
Amur and Ussuri rivers, articles in the Western press
on Siberia's vast mineral wealth and the construction
of gigantic hydro-electric power stations there, the
presence of Soviet fishing fleets in the north Pacific, and the development of Soviet Far Eastern trade
with Japan have made us increasingly aware of the
eastern regions of the U.S.S.R.

Unfortunately, some of the assessments of new
developments in Soviet Siberia have been marred by a
lack of understanding about the problems faced.
Many commentators look at Siberia with a vision im-
paired by the horizons of Europe. Not living themselves in large, sparsely settled countries, they lack
the essential rapport that comes from a knowledge
that in some parts of the world it is nature, not
man, that sets the limits to economic progress and
that the cost of such progress may be high by European
standards. The Japanese, on the other hand, are ob-
serving economic developments in Siberia from a very
close range; Japan has a long history of trade contacts with the Soviet Far East, and Siberia is of
immense potential value to Japan as a nearby raw materials base.

The region of this study comprises the eastern
three-quarters of Siberia extending from the Pacific
seaboard inland to the Yenisei River and including
the two economic planning regions of the Soviet Far
East and Eastern Siberia. Neighboring West Siberia
is excluded because it is relatively well developed
industrially and agriculturally, it has a reasonably
good transport network, and it is comparatively
densely settled. The Far East and Eastern Siberia,
on the other hand, have weakly developed industries
and agriculture, poor transport facilities, and a
very sparse population. West Siberia has little interest in trade opportunities through the Soviet
Pacific seaboard (mainly because of the great distances involved), but Eastern Siberia and especially
the Far East have begun to show an interest in trade

with countries of the Pacific region. It is for this reason the study territory is here called "Pacific Siberia."

The main body of the book presents a systematic analysis of the Pacific Siberian economy sector by sector. Particular difficulties were experienced in examining the demand aspects of the regional economy, especially in assessing real living standards compared with the rest of the U.S.S.R. Even greater problems were encountered in assigning orders of magnitude to the proportion of regional demand being met by local production and commenting on the prospects for trade with countries in the Pacific region. Trading relationships in the Pacific are generally undergoing a process of fundamental change in response to protectionism in Europe and the United States and the emergence of Japan as an economic superpower. The traditional border trade between the Soviet Far East and China has reached a low ebb, and Soviet trade interest is being diverted to Japan and North Korea. A more complete diversion may occur in the future to other countries in the Pacific that can supply manufactures, consumer goods, and foodstuffs in exchange for Siberian timber, fish, or minerals. This thesis is examined in detail in the latter part of the book.

The author wishes to acknowledge the generous financial support given to this project by the Ford Foundation. I am also indebted to V. D. Ogareff, research assistant at the Australian National University, for his very considerable assistance with the entire work. I thank Dr. T. H. Rigby, professorial fellow in Political Science at the Australian National University, for his encouragement, and my wife for her patient understanding. The late Professor Leon Vstovsky, Director of the Laboratory of Export-Import Specialization, Khabarovsk Research Institute, Siberian Branch of the U.S.S.R. Academy of Sciences, was especially helpful in providing me with books from regional publishing houses. In Australia I received assistance when I needed it from the Department of Trade and Industry and the Department of Foreign Affairs.

The author accepts full responsibility for the contents of this book but wishes to thank Dr. Violet Conolly, Professor Rigby, and Mr. Ogareff for their helpful comments.

Australian National University
February, 1972

CONTENTS

LIST OF TABLES

METRIC CONVERSION TABLE

1 meter	=	3.281 feet
1 kilometer	=	0.621 miles
1 square meter	=	10.764 square feet
1 square kilometer	=	0.386 square miles
1 hectare	=	2.471 acres
1 cubic meter	=	35.315 cubic feet
1 kilogram	=	2.205 pounds
1 metric ton	=	0.984 tons
1 kilowatt-hour	=	3,415 B.T.U.

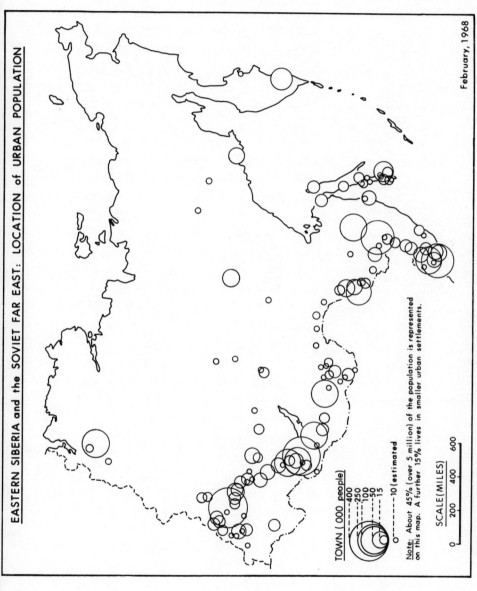

EASTERN SIBERIA and the SOVIET FAR EAST: LOCATION of URBAN POPULATION

February, 1968

TOWN (000 people)
————— 400
————— 250
————— 100
————— 50
————— 15
————— 10 (estimated)

Note: About 45% (over 5 million) of the population is represented on this map. A further 15% lives in smaller urban settlements.

SCALE (MILES)
0   200   400   600

Source: "Itogi Vsesoyuznoi Perepisi Naseleniya goda-RSFSR." TsSU MOSCOW, 1963.

A veil of uncertainty, even of mystery,
obscures the picture of development that
is taking place in the Asiatic part of
the USSR. . . . We have at best only a
dim picture of the actual changes introduced throughout vast areas of Siberia in
the last two decades.[1]

The study region (see map at frontispiece) extends inland, from the Pacific seaboard, for a distance of about 2,000 miles and embraces an area of
almost 4 million square miles. It includes about
one-half of the total territory of the U.S.S.R. but
contains only 13 million people, mostly located in a
narrow belt in the south close to the Trans-Siberian
railway and the border with China and Mongolia. The
distribution of population is about 3.3 persons per
square mile, which may be compared with a sparsely
populated country such as Australia with over 4 persons per square mile. In the northern areas there
are vast stretches of country with hardly any people
at all; the whole of Yakutia, for instance, has only
665,000 settlers in an area larger than India.

Some geographers will object both to the term
"Pacific Siberia," used here to describe the Soviet
Far East and Eastern Siberia as one region (see pref-
ace), and to the delineation of the westward boundary
as being too convenient in terms of Soviet adminis-

5

trative units. D. J. M. Hooson states, "It seems un-
necessarily timid for geographers to cling to . . .
administrative units just on statistical pretexts,"
and goes on to suggest that "true accuracy" should
be centered about the proper geographic definition
of a region rather than the formal precision of a
relatively meaningless statistical unit or area.[2]
Although the validity of this premise is acknowledged,
mention also must be made of the lack of a useful
time series of data resulting from such an approach
precisely because the Soviets rarely present regional
economic data on a krai or oblast' level but more
often on the level of the larger economic raiony.*
Industrial developments around Krasnoyarsk and the
upper Angara, for instance, could justify their in-
clusion in a Central Siberian region including the
Kuzbass and Novosibirsk of West Siberia; but, if we
look at the stage of economic growth and the degree
of development, we should not compare West and Eastern
Siberian industries. Conversely, there is a great
deal to be said for considering the southern "developed" parts of Siberia separately from the northern
underdeveloped parts; wherever possible, there has
been an attempt to highlight this fundamental difference.

----

*Krai, oblast', Autonomous Soviet Socialist Re-
public (A.S.S.R.), Autonomous Oblast' (A.O.), and
National Okrug (N.O.) are administrative units that
are grouped together to form economic regions or
raiony. A.S.S.R.'s, A.O.'s, and N.O.'s contain ethnic
groups and they may, as they develop, be promoted
from an N.O. to an A.O. and from an A.O. to an
A.S.S.R. and from an A.S.S.R. to a Soviet Socialist
Republic. Oblast' and krai are not created on ethnic
principles; the former usually include well-developed
economic regions whereas the latter embrace thinly
populated or frontier areas. Raiony often contain a
great mixture of these administrative units; as the
Soviet economy develops, so the boundaries of the
raiony change.

THE ENVIRONMENT

The physical environment a settler in Pacific
Siberia has to face is, with few exceptions, one of
the most harsh in the world. The only zone of relatively mild climate is in the Ussuri region between
Vladivostok and Khabarovsk. Elsewhere, the climate
becomes progressively harsher the further northward
one goes; except for the relatively well-populated
south, most of Pacific Siberia is typified by "permafrost," or permanently frozen subsoil. This phenomenon is unknown in West Siberia except in the very
northernmost parts and, consequently, has not affected
settlement there to such a great degree. Something
like two-thirds of Pacific Siberia is affected by
permafrost, with a depth varying from 15 to 35 feet
in the south to 650 feet or more elsewhere. In the
permafrost zone agriculture is impossible on a large
scale, soil drainage is impeded, ploughing or culti-
vating the soil is very difficult, tree growth is
stunted, excavating foundations for houses or trenches
for cables or sewers is expensive, and mining and
drilling are impeded. The supply of drinking water
in the long winter, when most rivers and streams are
frozen solid, is also a problem. Transportation is
made difficult and costly because the rivers are not
navigable; with the spring thaw, the dirt roads become impassable.

The cost of settling people in the permafrost
zone is very considerable, and the provision of an
infrastructure and community services is expensive
compared with more climatically favorable parts of
the Soviet Union. The provision of piped water supplies to houses is a major engineering undertaking.
Stall feeding of livestock for prolonged periods and
the problems of generating power in the winter neces-
sitate feverish activity in the brief summer period
to set aside stocks of commodities such as fodder
and coal against the winter.

At practically every location north of the Trans-
Siberian railway the winter lasts for over six months.
Almost 90 percent of the entire territory has 100 or

more days with a mean temperature of -10° C. (14° F.);
in the tundra of the Far North this period extends
to more than 200 days. East of the Lena River, some
of the coldest temperatures on earth are experienced;
and at Verkhoyansk and Oimyakon, temperatures of
-70° C. (more than 125° F. of frost) have been recorded. Yet, at these same locations temperatures
in the brief summer period can be quite hot with ab-
solute maxima in the region of 35° C. (95° F.), even
though night temperatures can fall to zero in the
middle of summer. Dryness makes the Siberian winters
"tolerable" for human settlement. So little rain
falls in the northeast of Yakutia or along the Arctic
coast of Siberia that the area would have the proper-
ties of a desert if it were not for the presence of
water-conserving permafrost subsoils.

Adequate heat and moisture are lacking in the
Siberian agricultural environment except in the
southern parts of the Far East where the problem is
excessive rainfall, caused by the summer monsoons,
which hampers the work of agricultural machinery and
causes the growth of rust and fungi among crops.
Another problem in the farming sector is the prolonged
period of enforced semi-idleness in the long winters;
some state and collective farms are able to turn to
seasonal work in lumbering, sawmilling, hunting furred
animals, and so on; but for many others the "winter
recess" is just another factor adding to the already
great difficulties of lifting labor productivity and
retaining the rural labor force.

In building construction and large capital works
projects, outside working conditions in the winter
pose special problems for men, machinery, and building materials. Mortar carried to bricklayers on a
multistory building will freeze solid in the hods in
a matter of minutes. Pouring cement for dams is accomplished by warming the mixture at the concrete
plant and then conveying it to the work site in dump
trucks insulated against the cold; laying operations
are then carried out in overall housings equipped
with air stoves. The builders of the giant Krasnoyarsk
Dam on the Yenisei River abandoned this laborious
method of transporting and pouring the concrete mix,

which had been used earlier on the Bratsk Dam. Instead, a continuous line process was used to pour
some 141 million cubic feet of concrete. An automated plant produced up to 7 million cubic feet of
mixture a month, which was delivered to the construction site on a conveyor belt running inside a heated
casing. Each block of the dam was poured, packed,
and leveled while protected by a heated housing; when
the layer set, the housing was raised by hydraulic
jacks and another protected layer was poured.

Problems also are associated with the brittleness
of metal under work loads (e.g., bulldozer blades and
excavator buckets) and the need to design special
trucks and locomotives to deal with harsh operating
conditions. According to the Siberian Branch of the
U.S.S.R. Academy of Sciences, 600 to 700 million rubles* have been lost annually owing to machines not
being adapted to northern conditions.[3] Fuels, lubricants, and rubber compounds have yet to be designed
specifically to withstand very low temperatures.

When the outside temperature falls below about
-20° C. (36° F. of frost) there is a very real danger
of frostbite. Special felt boots, quilted or padded
clothing, and furs must be worn so that the entire
body, with the exception of slits for the eyes, is
adequately protected. This adds to the expense of
living in Siberia as does the need to build houses
with extremely thick walls, double windows, and efficient central heating systems. The supply of fresh
fruit and vegetables is a serious problem for the more
remote areas, and the long winters and lack of sun-
light can be psychologically depressing. Violent winter snow storms and blizzards (purga) are common in
the north of Eastern Siberia and the Far East where
they usually last a whole week and disrupt all economic
activity, especially transport and communications.

---

*The ruble is an inconvertible currency. It may
be convenient for the reader to think of the ruble as
being approximately equal to one U.S. dollar. In
purchasing power equivalents it is worth much less,
perhaps as little as 25 to 30 U.S. cents for consumer
goods. There are 100 kopecks to the ruble.

COLONIZATION AND ECONOMIC GROWTH

Russian exploration of Pacific Siberia occurred
in the mid-1600s, but colonization on a significant
scale did not take place until well into the 1800s.
In the early days the occupancy of Siberia was largely
a matter of forcing the indigenous tribes to submit
to Russian rule and then extracting a fur tribute
(yasak) from them.   There was some fierce resistance
from the Buryat Mongols in the south, but the nomadic
tribes of northern Siberia submitted relatively easily
to Russian dominance.   Bands of Cossacks, some of
them outlaws, established forts (ostrog) that later
became the nuclei for settlements and towns.

As the Russian explorers and early colonizers
pushed into the interior toward the Pacific, they had
the advantage of encountering no opposition from any
foreign power.   The colonization process was pressed
to the Pacific seaboard and beyond to Alaska and even
to California, but the lines of communication and food
supply with the metropolitan base became attenuated.
Withdrawal from North America took place, and eventually the Alaskan possession was sold to the United
States in 1867 for $7.2 million primarily because the
lack of communications, naval power, and a dependable
supply route made it impossible to hold and consolidate these far-flung territorial gains.

By the end of the seventeenth century the conquest of Siberia was largely accomplished.   The only
setbacks experienced had been in the Amur River region in what was nominally Manchu territory.   The
Cossack forces were too small to defeat the Chinese
and annex the Amur, and in 1689 the Treaty of Nerchinsk, the first to be signed by China with a foreign
power, effectively halted Russian territorial ambi-
tions for almost 170 years.

The peopling of Siberia was very slow.   In 1709
there were 230,000 Russians in all Siberia; by 1790
this had grown to only 700,000.   Most of the progress
in the 1700s took place in the fertile southern
steppes of West Siberia; the lands further to the
east were agriculturally inferior, and it was not until after 1800 that positive attempts were made to

settle immigrants in Eastern Siberia. Siberia became
the destination of large numbers of political and
criminal exiles,* and runaway serfs and religious
dissenters sought escape in the vast Siberian wilderness while free settlers occupied the rich black
earth (chernozem) soils of the steppes. The relative
freedom in Siberia and the absence of a ruling landed
gentry attracted free settlers in ever-increasing
numbers, especially after the emancipation of the
serfs in 1861, when the shortage of farming land in
European Russia led to a veritable flood of land-
hungry peasants into Siberia. As a result, the population of all Siberia increased from less than 1.5
million in 1811 to almost 5.8 million in 1897.[4]

It was not until the construction of the Trans-
Siberian railway, between 1891 and 1904, that the influx of settlers and mining investment and the development of industries became important. The section
of track up to Lake Baikal carried 1.5 million passengers in 1900, compared with a mere 200,000 five years
previously. On the eve of World War I the population
of Greater Siberia had reached 10 million. Access to
the eastern regions of Russia was now easy, no longer
a prolonged trek of several months by cart or sledge
over unmade roads. The inflow of foreign capital,
particularly in gold, silver, lead, and zinc mining
as well as in the dairying industry, now began to
influence the rate of economic development. With improved communications, coal mines and railway repair
shops were established; sawmills, flour mills, dairy
factories, tanneries, and distilleries also were
built close to the railway line.

Under the Soviets the center of gravity of population in Siberia has shifted eastward. A great deal
of the initial impetus came from the infamous corrective labor camps of the 1930s. The impact of forced
labor on the development of the gold- and coal-mining,
lumbering, and construction industries was very sig-
nificant--particularly in the northern wastelands,
which came under the jurisdiction of Dal'stroi (Far
Eastern Construction Trust). In the southern, more

---

*Between 1825 and 1862 over 55,000 people were
sent to forced labor in Siberia.

favorable, areas, exiles were sent to the more lenient
labor settlements where they were compelled to work
in agriculture or factories.

It was not until World War II, however, that
the Krasnoyarsk-Irkutsk industrial region received
much attention and investments in the Far East were
boosted. In 1940, for example, Pacific Siberia accounted for almost 11 percent of Soviet State and
cooperative investments, compared with 4 percent for
West Siberia and 8.3 percent for the Urals.[5] Per
capita investment in the Far East at that time was
almost five and one-half times the Soviet average,
reflecting the military and strategic preparations
being made because of Japan's warlike presence in
Manchukuo. After the Japanese occupation of Manchukuo
in 1931 the Soviets had made determined efforts to
increase the population of the Far East and, also,
to build up local agriculture as a food supply base.
Double-tracking of the Trans-Siberian railway was
completed in 1937, and this served to strengthen the
Far East's links with the rest of the Union.

During World War II, Pacific Siberia benefited
from the transfer of both industrial equipment and
workers out of the occupied or threatened areas of
European Russia. Thus, whereas in the period 1940-45
the U.S.S.R. as a whole experienced a 13 percent decline in the number of industrial workers, the Far
East experienced an increase of 11 percent and Eastern
Siberia gained 15 percent.[6]

Since the war, a modicum of progress has taken
place in the important timber and fishing industries,
and much more impressive results (but not without
considerable infrastructure costs) are occurring in
the mining and power sectors of the economy away from
established cities. Agriculture and manufacturing
industry proper are still weak in this part of the
U.S.S.R., and transportation facilities are lagging
behind the accelerated rate of economic growth. The
most promising area of all is the growing industrial
axis between Irkutsk and Krasnoyarsk.

For the future, Soviet theoretical concern with
the uneven development between developed and under-

developed regions ("characteristic of capitalist but not of socialist economies")[7] will bear careful watching in relation to attitudes toward regional development in Siberia. A decree of the Communist Party of the Soviet Union (CPSU) and the Council of Ministers in July of 1967 about the development of the Far East and Chita oblast' in the period 1967-75 called for, among other things, self-sufficiency in the production of major foodstuffs.[8] At present the whole of Pacific Siberia produces less than two-fifths of the food needs of its 13 million people, and the development of the Krasnoyarsk-Irkutsk industrial zone will make heavy calls on future food supplies. Under these circumstances, lopsided regional development is certain unless the structure, administration, and approach to agriculture is changed.

Essentially, the postwar problem of most significance has been the unwillingness, or inability, of the central authorities in Moscow to provide sufficient numbers of volunteer workers to develop Pacific Siberia rapidly and evenly. In a federal, multinational state occupying a huge and diverse physical environment it may be inevitable that some areas are relatively neglected and others relatively favored.[9] Pacific Siberia falls into the "relatively neglected" category, and there may exist a correlation in the U.S.S.R. between the distance away from the seat of central bureaucratic power and the degree of neglect.

GEOPOLITICS

One factor likely to promote a noneconomic rationale for an accelerated rate of economic growth in Pacific Siberia, especially the Far East, involves geopolitics and considerations of national security. A frontier of about 6,000 miles is shared by China and the U.S.S.R., including the Soviet-dominated buffer state of Mongolia. Almost one-quarter of that border runs along the republics of Soviet Kazakhstan, Kirgizia, and Tadzhikistan through exceedingly rugged and mountainous terrain. In the Soviet Far East, however, there is a 2,000-mile border with relatively open approaches to the Amur and Ussuri rivers and the Lake Khanka lowland. This border terminates at the

Pacific and for a very short distance shares a frontier with North Korea. From Chita oblast' in the
west through the Amur, Khabarovsk, and Primor'ye regions, the Soviet border with China is highly vulner-
able to conventional attacks across rivers that are,
during the winter months, frozen and capable of sup-
porting half-tracks and armored personnel carriers.
Several Far Eastern cities of major importance, such
as Blagoveshchensk, Khabarovsk, Ussuriisk, and Vladivostok, are located either on or within a few miles
of the border.

From near the big bend in the Amur River to the
Pacific Ocean the vital communications link of the
Trans-Siberian railway runs within 30 to 50 miles of
the frontier; along the Ussuri Valley to Lake Khanka
the Chinese border is only 12 miles away on average
(at places such as Iman or Vyazemskii the line is
little more than 6 miles from the frontier patrols).
When it is realized that this double-tracked railway
link carries over one-half the total freight traffic--
by all modes of transportation--in the Far East, its
strategic importance is apparent.[10]

Most of the Far Eastern population, and two-
thirds of its industry, is located either along or
within a relatively short distance from this railway;
it is estimated that perhaps 3 million people live
within 50 miles of the border.

To the east there is a very different geopolitical relationship with the islands of Japan. Only a
few miles separate Soviet from Japanese territory across the Straits of Laperouse (between Hokkaido and
the island of Sakhalin) or across the Kunashir Straits
(between Hokkaido and the south Kurile Islands).

Japan and China have had territorial conflicts
with the U.S.S.R. in the past, and both still maintain
some territorial claims. Japan's former territories
of south Sakhalin and the southern Kuriles were taken
by the U.S.S.R. at the end of World War II. Sakhalin
and the Kuriles were divided between Russia and Japan
as early as 1854, the southern sections becoming
Japanese and the northern ones, Russian. In 1875 the

Kuriles passed to Japan and Sakhalin became Russian,
but as a result of her defeat in the Russo-Japanese
War of 1904-5 Russia ceded the southern part of Sakhalin to Japan. This was reincorporated into the
U.S.S.R., together with the Kuriles, in 1945. (Japan
still claims the southern Kuriles--Kunashir, Shikotan,
Habomai, and Etorofu.) The U.S.S.R. inherited 40
years of Japanese settlement and development when it
took over southern Sakhalin in 1945. The railways,
pulp and paper mills, and coal mines still owe very
much to Japanese initiative. The Kurile Islands,
however, have progressed little economically and contain only fishing ports with processing facilities.
On both the Kuriles and Sakhalin the U.S.S.R. has
now established extensive defense facilities to protect the population of around 640,000.

With China, conflict centers on the Amur and
Ussuri river provinces. These territories were recognized as Chinese (Han) under the Treaty of Nerchinsk
(1689) when Russia was a comparatively weak colonizing
power.[11] But in 1858, after a very long period during
which the Chinese made no attempt to settle the Amur
lands, the Russians effectively annexed them, with
the Treaty of Aigun, from a China distracted by domestic problems. This is the "unequal treaty" to which
the Communist Chinese now refer. Under that treaty
China ceded the left bank of the Amur from the Argun
to its confluence with the Ussuri. Two years later,
at the Treaty of Peking in 1860, it also ceded the
maritime province of Manchuria to the Russians, with
the border following the Ussuri from the Amur upstream
to Lake Khanka via the Sungacha and thence to the
Pacific along a series of mountain crests.

In recent years, particularly in 1969, there
have been a series of border conflicts over the possession of islands in the Amur and Ussuri rivers.*
The Chinese claim that the border runs down the

_____

*On March 2 and 15, 1969, Damansky Island (Us-
suri); July 8, 1969, Goldinsky Island (Amur); and
July 20, 1969, Kirkinsky Island (Ussuri) were the
scenes of armed conflicts.

middle course, or the main navigable channel (<u>thal-</u>
<u>weg</u>), of the Ussuri River whereas the Soviets say
that in some places the border, marked out in the
1861 protocols to the Treaty of Peking, runs along
the Chinese bank. The Russians cite the 1858 treaty
between Nicaragua and Costa Rica as a precedent in
international law and also the Sino-Soviet agreement
of 1951 as confirming that the border line does not
necessarily run down the main river channel.[12] The
Chinese retort that if the border runs down any one
bank of a river this must be specified in the enabling treaty. Late in 1971, the Soviets were reported
to have offered a border agreement with China by ac-
cepting "the international doctrine" on river borders,
but China rejected this proposal as insufficient--
presumably because it seeks greater territorial ad-
justments under the "unequal treaties."

What is involved here is more than just a border
squabble over some river islands. These rivers are
subject to flooding in the spring and summer and
freezing during the winter months. In the winter a
river changes its fundamental character to become a
road of ice, and when in flood its course is likely
to change radically. In the mid-1950s a joint Sino-
Soviet project for the Amur was agreed upon to control
flooding and to exploit hydro-power and develop natural resources and industries in the Amur basin
(which is bisected by the frontier).[13] Such a development scheme would have had far-reaching economic
consequences for both the Soviet Far East and northern
Manchuria, but it has now been quietly shelved.

If we accept the thesis that territorial units
are primarily successful in extending their authority
into regions where resistance is the weakest (e.g.,
Japan in Manchukuo in the 1930s), we can understand
Soviet concern about its long and permeable frontier
with a potentially aggressive China. Soviet thinking
on this matter is undoubtedly colored by its experience with Japanese (and American) occupation of Siberia and the Allied intervention of the early 1920s
and the bitter experience of land invasion in Europe
during World War II. It is perhaps difficult for
the Anglo-Saxon mind, protected as it is by seas and
oceans, to grasp this simple point.

The emergence of the U.S.S.R. as a superpower
has not seen a concomitant buildup in the population
and industrial base of the Far East or Eastern Siberia. There is thus some pressure on the Soviets,
as a result of their conflict with China, to develop
their sparsely populated territories. This may account for the establishment in Siberia of some industries of doubtful national value in comparison to
the output that could be obtained from alternative
investments elsewhere in the country.

The geopolitical importance of Siberia today is
that it is a forward base for the U.S.S.R.'s strategic strength in the Pacific and Asia. It has its
complement of nuclear submarines, missile sites, and
Red Army divisions. One defensive principle, and
this goes back perhaps 70 years to Sir Halford Mackinder,[14] is that for any given amount of nuclear de-
struction the dispersion of people and resources in
Siberia demands a larger number of successful strikes
than for an equivalent area of, say, the Midwest of
the United States. The lack of compactness of the
U.S.S.R., its great longitudinal extent, and the
disparate location of population and industry in
Siberia are positive strategic assets. The dangers
of a conventional invasion across permeable land
frontiers from neighboring China, which ironically
the U.S.S.R. itself helped to industrialize in the
1950s, may thus be of more real concern to Moscow
than the theoretical implications of nuclear attack.

This has implications for the rate of economic
development and location of industrial plants in
Pacific Siberia. Relations with China may have a
much greater economic impact on the region than the
balance of nuclear deterrence with the United States.
The expenditure of about 20 Red Army divisions in
the Far East Military District in the last few years
must have boosted the local economy but it is likely
to have imposed strains on the supply of food and
consumer goods to the detriment of the living standards of the populace.

THE PACIFIC

Russian, and later Soviet, involvement in the
Pacific region from the Far Eastern base has been
slow and very limited in scope.[15] The Far East and
Eastern Siberia have been dependent for capital investments, essential manufactures, and foodstuffs,
and for marketing outlets for local raw materials,
on the centers of population in European Russia,
which in both Tsarist and Soviet times have exerted
a controlling influence.

The main foreign contacts were initially through
China with the establishment of a regular caravan
and fair trade in the early 1700s, which was not dis-
placed by maritime trading until about 1900. Border
trade with Manchuria was enhanced by the creation of
a Russian sphere of influence there, which culminated
in the occupation of northern Manchuria in 1904 after
the Boxer Rebellion. At this time the Chinese Eastern
Railway, granted by Chinese concession in 1896, provided Russia with its sole outlet to the Pacific at
Vladivostok. The Amur railway, completing the Trans-
Siberian trunk line on Russian territory, was not
completed until 1916; it is 600 miles longer than
the route via China.

Another Russian outlet to the Pacific was obtained with the leasing of the Kwangtung territory
(Dairen and ice-free Port Arthur) from the Chinese
between 1898 and 1905 and again between 1945 and
1955. Port Arthur was connected to the Chinese Eastern Railway at Harbin by the South Manchurian Railway.
These railways were run by Russians, and the major
cities of Harbin and Port Arthur were, in effect,
Russian colonies.

Despite the close trade relationships that
evolved between Manchuria and the Far East, there was
no move on the part of the Russians, or later the
Soviets, to encourage Chinese immigration. Indeed,
both the Russians and the Soviets, until the early
1930s, preferred to use Japanese seasonal labor in
the Far Eastern fish canneries and Korean settlers
for rice cultivation in the cis-Ussuri plain.

The deterioration in political relations between the U.S.S.R. and China has reduced the previously important trade between the Soviet Far East and Manchuria to a trickle. This seems to have caused a heightened awareness of the possibilities of beneficial commercial contacts with some of the countries in the Pacific, especially Japan, as well as North Korea. Japanese trade relations with the Far East date back to the Tsarist-established timber trade and particularly to the export of coal, oil, and fish to Japan in the 1920s and early 1930s. Soviet awareness of Japan as a potential supplier of consumer goods, manufactured products, and capital equipment in return for raw materials and minerals has developed quickly in recent years.

Trade contacts with other countries in the Pacific, such as Australia, New Zealand, or Canada, are not yet substantial. Soviet diplomatic and trade initiatives in the Pacific region generally, however, are gathering some momentum that may herald a future change in policy toward the potential of the Pacific region in relation to the economic needs of the Far East and Eastern Siberia.

NOTES

1. S. G. Prociuk, "The Manpower Problem in Siberia," Soviet Studies, October, 1967, p. 190.

2. D. J. M. Hooson, A New Soviet Heartland? (Princeton, N.J.: Van Nostrand, 1964), p. 15.

3. G. I. Chiryayev, First Secretary of the Yakutsk Regional Committee of the CPSU, Ekonomicheskaya Gazeta, No. 12, 1971.

4. A. G. Rashin, Naselenie Rossii za 100 let (Moscow, 1956), p. 68.

5. Kapital'noe Stroitel'stvo SSSR, pp. 116-18.

6. E. J. Stanley, Regional Distribution of Soviet Industrial Manpower: 1940-60 (New York: Praeger, 1968), p. 62.

7.   N. T. Agafonov and S. B. Lavrov, <u>Vestnik</u>
<u>Leningradskogo Univerziteta</u>, No. 6, 1966, pp. 80-87.

8.   <u>Izvestiya</u>, July 30, 1967.

9.   R. Hutchings, "Geographic Influences on Cen-
tralization in the Soviet Economy," <u>Soviet Studies</u>,
January, 1966, pp. 293-94.

10.   Almost 60 percent of the total freight turnover of the Far East is carried by rail, including
the short lines in Sakhalin, the line from Khabarovsk
to Sovetskaya Gavan', and the line to Chegdomyn, as
well as the Trans-Siberian artery. F. V. D'yakonov
<u>et al.</u>, <u>Dal'nii Vostok, ekonomiko-geograficheskaya</u>
<u>kharakteristika</u> (Moscow: AN SSSR, 1966), p. 240.

11.   I. O. Lattimore, <u>Manchuria: Cradle of Con-</u>
<u>flict</u> (New York: Macmillan, 1932), pp. 10-16, dis-
cusses Peking's traditional policy of maintaining a
vast forest wasteland between the Manchus and the
Russians and the effect this had of minimizing frontier incidents.

12.   <u>Soviet News</u>, No. 5483 (April 1, 1969), and
No. 5494 (June 17, 1969), quoting statements by the
Soviet Government to the People's Republic of China
on March 29, 1969, and June 13, 1969, respectively.

13.   <u>Tass</u>, March 19, 1957, and April 9, 1960;
aggregate hydro capacity was proposed at 5 to 6 million kilowatts.

14.   H. J. Mackinder, "The Geographical Pivot of
History," <u>The Geographical Journal</u>, 23 (1904), 421-37.

15.   See L. Symons, <u>Russia and the Pacific: The</u>
<u>Geography of Involvement</u>, proceedings of the Fifth
New Zealand Geography Conference (Auckland, 1967),
pp. 25-31.

The transport problem is . . . of the highest importance in Siberia and determines
the order of priorities, the scale, and
the rate of industrial development of any
given region.[1]

There are two major factors retarding the economic development of Pacific Siberia. One is the
shortage of labor, especially skilled tradesmen, and
the disruptive effects of the high turnover of migrants on the region's economy (see Chapter 9). The
other is the sparse transportation network and the
extremely high cost of freighting goods long distances into and out of the region. An associated
problem is the large amount of capital investment
needed to build transport facilities in Pacific Siberia because of the distances involved and the difficulties of construction in permafrost in a predominantly mountainous terrain.

The sparse population and weak economic development of Pacific Siberia make it difficult to justify
transcontinental transportation links in comparison
to the alternate uses to which the large amounts of
capital involved could be put in developing transportation in the densely populated and industrialized
parts of European Russia. H. Hunter suggests that,
in purely economic terms, the sparse development of
the Soviet east, especially its northern parts, "is

a credit to Bolshevik common sense."[2] What is implied
here is that high transport and extraction costs (also
related to difficulties of access) have retarded the
development of Siberia's rich natural resources and
relegated the growth of the economy to a relatively
modest role. An area of 4 million square miles containing scarcely 13 million people dependent on extractive industries such as forestry, fishing, and
mining hardly justifies a comprehensive transport
network on economic grounds. There are, of course,
social factors (such as the need to service remote
rural settlements) as well as strategic considerations (such as the Chinese threat to the border zone
and Soviet military requirements for road, rail, and
airport facilities) to be taken into account.

Transportation in Pacific Siberia can be summed
up in a phrase: the Trans-Siberian railway. It is
the most heavily worked railway line in the U.S.S.R.,
carrying 9 percent of all Soviet railway freight,[3]
and it transports an estimated 80 percent of all
freight movements in Eastern Siberia and at least 50
percent of those in the Far East.[4]

The carriage of bulk cargoes in Pacific Siberia
has been organized on a continuous basis only in the
last 60 or 70 years. Before that it was largely a
matter of using the northward-flowing Siberian rivers
for five or six months in the year when they were
navigable and at other times using the thin network
of dirt roads, which were impassable in the spring
and autumn. The railway introduced the transportation of bulk freight on a continuous basis, and the
use of diesel and electric trains has given it a high
degree of efficiency. The construction of branch
lines into the interior to exploit new resources
(e.g., Taishet-Ust'-Kut and Achinsk-Abalakovo for
timber) or industries (e.g., Taishet-Abakan) has enhanced its importance. Trucks are used for short
hauls and for intracity freight, but the absence of
a linked system of all-weather surfaced roads pro-
hibits their use for long distances. Since World
War II a fairly comprehensive system of air services
for passengers and high-value/low-weight commodities,
such as gold, diamonds, and furs, has been developed
in Siberia.

LIMITING FACTORS

Distances in Pacific Siberia are phenomenal.
From the east to the west of the region the Trans-
Siberian railway traverses over 3,300 miles. Along
its route the railway connects the far-flung industrial nodes centered around Krasnoyarsk, Irkutsk,
Khabarovsk, and Vladivostok; otherwise, it passes
only through individual towns and settlements and a
countryside in which the population density rarely
exceeds 65 people per square mile. Thus, although
the railway and its branch lines probably service at
least 75 percent of the entire population of the region, the overall length of railway track available
per 1,000 square miles of territory is less than 1.6
miles in Eastern Siberia and 2.9 miles in the Far
East, compared with the average for the U.S.S.R. of
8.7 miles. Excluding narrow-gauge lines associated
with mining, there are 3,800 miles of railway in Eastern Siberia and 3,500 miles in the Far East under
the jurisdiction of the Ministry of Transportation.
The Far East's well-populated and more industrialized
southern districts are better serviced by railway
lines than are similar regions in the south of Eastern
Siberia, but this reflects the inheritance of a well-
developed railway network from the Japanese in Sakhalin. Moreover, the Far East suffers from the disadvantage of being further away from the main industrial
centers of the U.S.S.R. than Eastern Siberia. R.
Taaffe states that the Far East has the longest average length of rail haul of freight movements in the
U.S.S.R.[5] He gives an average length of haul for the
Far East of 1,254 miles compared with 604 miles for
Eastern Siberia and 558 miles for West Siberia.
Only 6.1 percent of Far Eastern railway terminations
originate in a contiguous region (i.e., Eastern Siberia); in West Siberia the figure is 7.3 percent
(i.e., for freight originating from contiguous West
Siberia and the Far East), but the average for the
U.S.S.R. is almost 22 percent. Conversely, a high
proportion of rail freight terminations in the Far
East and Eastern Siberia originate from noncontiguous
regions, thus explaining the high average length of
haul.[6] About three-quarters of rail freight terminations in Pacific Siberia originate from within the

region; this proportion also is higher than the Soviet
average, and indicates the dependency of the region
on rail transportation for its internal cohesion.

The big limiting effect of distance in relation
to transport is cost. The relative cost of haulage
by railway, river, and road in the Far East is between
42 percent and 47 percent more expensive than the
average for the U.S.S.R.[7] The cost of transportation
depends not only on the great distances involved in
freighting commodities into and out of the region but
also on the volume of freight using a given transport
system. The cost of rail freighting coal from
Raichikhinsk (Amur oblast') to Khabarovsk is 1.69
kopecks per 10-ton/kilometer whereas Donets coal
sent by rail to Moscow costs only 1.36 kopecks.[8]
River transport also depends on limiting factors
such as the length of the navigation season, etc.;
the costs of river transport on the heavily used
Volga-Kama vary between 0.983 and 1.408 kopecks per
10-ton/kilometer, but for rivers in Pacific Siberia
they are 5.738 to 9.246 kopecks, depending on the
commodity.[9]

A good example of the limiting effect of distance
is that of transporting grain from surplus, relatively
low-cost farms in Kazakhstan to deficit, high-cost
agricultural centers in the Far East. The cost of
producing a ton of grain in Kazakhstan is about 60
rubles whereas in the Far East it is over 80 rubles.
But transport costs between the two regions, from
Tselinograd to Khabarovsk, add about 22 rubles to
Kazakhstan costs and so equate c.i.f. costs Khabarovsk
with high local Far Eastern costs.* Under such circumstances the Far Eastern economy has to pay a high
price for grain whether from local or interregional
sources. Sugar beets in the Far East cost about 55
rubles a ton to produce, but they could be freighted
a distance of over 5,500 miles from the Ukraine for
a total c.i.f. cost of less than 50 rubles. The main
factor limiting such freight movements is the conges-

---

*Transport costs calculated at 0.34 kopecks per
ton/kilometer.

tion of traffic on the Trans-Siberian railway in West
Siberia, and it is then a matter of the authorities
determining the smallest possible losses to the regional economy from overstrained transport.

Climate also imposes restrictions on transportation in Pacific Siberia. Extensive permafrost areas
greatly increase the problems of constructing railways and roads. In the permafrost zone roads are
cheaper to build than railways, but annual maintenance
expenditures on hard-surfaced roads are considerably
more expensive. Consequently, roads are used to
supplement river transport or link settlements to
railheads; only the most important highways in Siberia, such as the Aldan and Kolyma, are open to heavy
trucks for the whole year. River transport is restricted by ice, which on the lower Lena, for instance, persists for six months of the year. Coastal
shipping is only ice-free for a comparatively short
five-month period in the summer.

Another problem with the Siberian rivers is
that, except for the Amur, they flow northward to
the Arctic Ocean whereas the main human and economic
"grain" of the region is in an east-west direction.
For a short and hazardous ten-week period, convoys
of a dozen or so freighters can pass from the White
Sea to the Pacific Ocean via the northern sea route,
but there is little prospect for a regular large-
scale movement of freight by this route despite the
use of nuclear-powered icebreakers.

Mountainous ranges between Lake Baikal and the
Amur Valley only have been penetrated by the Trans-
Siberian railway and a few major gravel roads from
Kultuk to Tunka in Mongolia (through the Buryat
autonomous republic), from Ulan-Ude to the Mongolian
frontier at Kyakhta, and from Chita to Choibalsan
via Borzya.

E. Thiel refers to the significance of permafrost
conditions to transportation.[10] When only a shallow
layer of topsoil thaws each summer, the building
and maintenance of such items of fixed capital as
bridges and buildings associated with transportation

are difficult and expensive. The only other inhabited
parts of the world where similar engineering and technical problems have been encountered are in Alaska
and northern Canada. The expansion of the ground
moisture as it freezes creates breaks in the surface
that seriously damage lines of communication. Deep
cracks occur in the roads. Unfrozen water and mud
well up to the surface where they freeze and force
the cracks open wider and so make the roads impassable. With the summer thaw the surface layers sub-
side into a sea of slush and mud. Bridges are lifted
and tilted and then often break down completely when
the ice thaws in the spring. The building of all-
weather roads in the permafrost zone is therefore
slow and costly and annual maintenance expenditures
very high.

     These problems are magnified for the more demand-
ing task of running a railroad. Soil-creep and land-
slides are particular dangers as well as the effects
on the permanent way of ground heave. Solifluction
fills cuttings with mud and disintegrates railway
embankments. Maintenance and inspection of the lines
and bridges must be on a continuous basis so that
adequate precautionary measures can be taken. Thiel
points to the high construction costs in permafrost
conditions of the western section of the Amur railway
(from Kuenga to Kerak) of 158,000 rubles per verst*
compared with only 67,737 rubles, including all preparatory work, for the Trans-Siberian railway as far
as Sretensk in Transbaikalia.[11] He refers to shifting in 50 out of the 80 bridges along the Amur railway. In the past there were special difficulties in
supplying the railways with water in the winter; this
involved leading it through heated pipes for a considerable distance. Now the use of electric and
diesel locomotives has overcome this problem.

     There are also problems associated with the ef-
ficient operation of transportation machinery and

_____

     *One verst = 0.663 miles; under permafrost con-
ditions construction was limited to the warm season
and even then dynamite was used to break up the subsoil.

equipment in the long Siberian winters. For trucks,
in particular, there are additional costs associated
with servicing, overhauls, the heating of sumps, the
provision of special oils, and antifreeze agents;
when the termperature falls below -40° C. (72° F. of
frost), metal parts under stress become brittle and
can crack quite easily. In the remoter areas of the
Far North the sledge pulled by reindeer or dogs is
still the most dependable form of short-haul transport in the winter.

COSTS OF TRANSPORTATION

The additional costs imposed on the regional
economy by the transport sector are quite significant.
Special budgetary allocations have to be earmarked
for expensive Siberian transport projects. Part of
the additional costs of freighting essential commodities to Siberia is passed on in the form of higher
consumer prices but, generally, this is offset by
special regional wage allowances.

There is an irrational element in the State's
approach to costing transportation services. L. V.
Kantorovich points out that on many busy main railway
lines (such as the Trans-Siberian) the existing railway tariff is too low.[12] Consequently, factories do
not use to the best advantage alternative means of
transport, such as trucks over short distances or
waterways for longer hauls. A uniform price is
adopted for many kinds of important commodities--
which simplifies cost calculations but certainly does
not ensure an optimal plan for transport, which a
system of zonal prices would tend to encourage. The
limited carrying capacity of certain sections of the
Trans-Siberian railway line, despite a marked increase
in capacity due to electrification, justifies the
movement of higher-value/lower-weight goods but not
very heavy loads of a low value over long distances.

Trucks, however, cannot be used economically
for long-distance hauls on poor roads because average
speeds and productivity are lowered by 35-45 percent,
fuel consumption rises by 20-40 percent, and the mileage for major repairs and tire life is reduced by

40-50 percent, compared with good surfaced roads.[13]
With waterways costs are certainly low, but they are
a very slow means of transport; and, moreover, the
navigation season is extremely short.

The only practical alternative for Soviet planners was to increase the capacity of the sole transport artery, the Trans-Siberian, through double-tracking, mainly in the 1930s, and electrification in the
postwar period. As well, there was the use of diesel
locomotives, automatic brakes and couplings, and the
introduction of larger-capacity four-axle (50-ton)
freight cars.[14] Productivity has increased tremen-
dously, but now the State must consider the immense
costs of a new North Siberian line and, at the same
time, endeavor to reduce the huge volume of short-
haul rail traffic by providing more truck capacity
for journeys up to 30 miles. Short-haul rail shipments are exceedingly expensive. What is lacking in
the setting of transport rates is an objectively determined economic rent for the use of transport
equipment.

There is an urgent need for good paved highways.
In the permafrost zone, one mile of all-weather
sealed highway can cost up to 800,000 rubles. Even
the simplest kind of earthen surface costs 85,000
rubles in Yakutia, which is about 1.6 to 1.7 times as
much as the average indexes of construction in the
central regions of European Russia.[15] Relatively,
the cost of building a railroad can be cheaper than
constructing a first-class highway. In West Siberia,
for instance, the cost of 114 miles of railway between
Asino and Belyi Yar in Tomsk oblast' was 288,600
rubles per mile.[16] But these are comparisons of
areas with widely different natural conditions. The
highest railway construction costs in the U.S.S.R.
are experienced in the upland regions of Siberia,
where the cost of one mile of railroad can rise to
over 530,000 rubles, whereas the cheapest are in
Kazakhstan and the south of West Siberia.

Table 1 gives some comparative data for transport costs in the permafrost zone of the north of
West Siberia. This area is not in the study region,

TABLE 1

Projected Costs of Transportation in the Northern Ob' Basin
(for average haul of 500 kilometers)[a]

Type of Cost	Annual Volume of Freight (million tons)					
	0.1	0.2	0.5	1.0	2.0	3.0
Capital investment in 1,000 rubles per kilometer						
Autoroad, hard surface	61.5	68.0	120.5	140.5	--	--
Railroad, diesel locomotive	128.0	135.0	147.0	160.0	175.0	180.0
Annual maintenance expenditure in 1,000 rubles per kilometer						
Autoroad, hard surface	7.3	13.5	15.4	41.6	--	--
Railway, diesel locomotive	7.4	7.5	7.9	8.5	10.3	11.1

	Volume of Freight in 1,000 Tons per Kilometer					
	150	300	750	1,500	3,000	4,500
Estimated cost of haulage in kopecks per ton per kilometer[b]						
Autoroad, hard surface	4.9	4.5	2.1	2.8	--	--
Railroad, diesel locomotive	4.9	2.5	1.0	0.6	0.3	0.3

[a]One kilometer = 0.621 miles.

[b]The cost of river transport in the Ob'Irtysh basin in 1970 is estimated at 0.196 to 0.240 kopecks. By comparison, the cost of moving oil by pipeline is 0.09 to 0.12 kopecks.

Source: "Voprosy Promyshlennogo Razvitiya Raionov Severa," Problemy Severa, No. 12, 1967, p. 177.

but the data does provide the basis for cost estimates
in similar climatic and physical environments. The
north of West Siberia is very marshy, and the costs
of building causeways and getting access to building
materials are high; the remoteness and ruggedness of
many parts of Pacific Siberia would impose comparable
cost disabilities. The high costs of railway construction, compared with the capital investment required for a hard-surfaced road (with a capacity of
up to one million tons of freight per year), are apparent from the table. The disadvantage of the road
occurs with annual maintenance expenditures that increase rapidly with the volume of freight carried.
The estimate for cost of haulage per ton/kilometer
shows that the rates for road transport are comparable
only with those for the railway at very low volumes
of freight loading; at medium loadings of 750,000
tons per kilometer, the cost of road haulage is double
that for railroad freight. In the permafrost zone,
high freight costs plus the size of the annual maintenance bill place hard-surfaced roads at an economic
disadvantage in the formulation of policy decisions
about the allocation of scarce budgetary resources.

     Some local authorities manage to bypass the
cost problem by using frozen rivers as roads in the
winter. In Yakutia, for example, there are over
2,500 miles of such roads comprising almost 30 percent
of the total road mileage of the republic.[17] Roads
based on rivers of ice extend along the Lena River
from Osetrovo to Lensk (590 miles), from Batagai to
Nizhne Yansk along the Yana River (465 miles), and
from Khandyga to Ust' Maiya on the Aldan River (245
miles), as well as others on the Vilyui, Markha,
Olenek, Kolyma, and Indigirka rivers. A winter road
is being used to supply the Bilibino nuclear power
station with construction materials. The climatic
conditions here are favorable with little snowfall
and no snow drifts. Road construction is still a
very labor-consuming industry in the U.S.S.R.; and
in the Far North, where labor is in short supply
and relatively costly, the winter ice roads serve a
purpose. Keeping them in good order also provides
useful employment for idle river transport workers
in the winter. In the summer these northward-flowing

rivers are used for normal river freight, but the
shortness of the navigation season and the low volume
of freight traffic lifts the cost of river transport
in Eastern Siberia and Yakutia to 80 percent above
the U.S.S.R. average.

About three-quarters of the bulk cargo in Pacific
Siberia is handled by railway, but a major cost
problem arises from the movement of empty freight
cars westward from Nakhodka to Irkutsk. The real
cost of utilizing empties is very low; the problem
is one of finding suitable export commodities. Other
than fish and timber, little is exported out of this
region by rail, whereas practically all essential
foodstuffs (grain, meat, and fruit), steel products,
machinery, and oil have to be rail freighted in.
This problem is not as great to the west because between Irkutsk and Krasnoyarsk there is a strong westward export traffic in timber and coal.

Some Soviet economists admit that it is not eco-
nomical to transport by rail most of the bulky, low-
value natural resources of Pacific Siberia to European
Russia when there are favorable opportunities for
transporting these same goods by sea to countries in
the Pacific Ocean.[18] The impact of transport costs
on goods produced in Pacific Siberia and freighted
to European Russia is to add 100 percent to 200 percent to the extraction costs of timber, 30 percent
to 40 percent to coal and cement, and up to 5 percent
to the production costs of machine tools. Generally,
for bulk cargo a transport movement of 1,000 miles
to 1,200 miles adds about 50 percent to the f.o.b.
price whereas distances of 2,000 miles to 2,500 miles
usually involve a doubling of prices.

For some products an equalized price is applied;
thus, timber is delivered at the same price from
Irkutsk to Chelyabinsk, Astrakhan, Pavlodar, and
Krasnodar, but the transport costs per ton are, respectively, 9 rubles, 14.4 rubles, 7.2 rubles, and
14.6 rubles. This anomaly is related to the uniform
wholesale price for timber introduced in July, 1967.
The price of a ton of diesel oil when shipped a distance of some 3,650 miles from Omsk to the Far East

would rise three-fold if actual freight costs were
included. Similarly, the price of Magnitogorsk
rolled steel would rise by 40 percent and of grain
from Kazakhstan by 35 percent. Hauling refrigerated
sheep meat from the Ukraine to Khabarovsk adds at
least 33 percent to costs. Altogether, the annual
cost of shipping essential goods into the Far East
alone from other regions of the U.S.S.R. amounts to
at least 6 percent of the gross value of industrial
and agricultural output of the region. A similar
amount would be spent on shipments out of the region.

Although no specific details of freight rates
are available for Pacific Siberia, a general cargo
rate for long-distance rail hauls of 0.340 kopecks
per ton/kilometer can be regarded as a fairly accurate
estimate.[19] Using this figure, we can arrive at,
for instance, the total cost to the Far East of importing bread grains by rail from other regions.
Table 2 sets out the relevant data. The total
freight cost for wheat shipments is estimated at over
20 million rubles and may be compared with the total
rail freight bill for imports into the Far East of
some 200-250 million rubles annually.[20] The total
cost of rail freight into both the Far East and Eastern Siberia probably exceeds 400 million rubles a
year; this is equivalent to about one-half the cost
of building a large hydro-electric station and dam
(such as the Bratsk hydro station) or some four or
five large timber, pulp, and paper kombinats. This
is not meant to imply that there is a choice of al-
ternatives involved here--merely that any savings in
transport costs could be used for high-priority development projects.

TRANSPORT IN PIONEERING
REGIONS

The scope and rate of economic development of
the Far North largely depend on a successful solution
to the transport problem. The absence of a transport
network causes great losses. Whereas the estimated
period of delivery of cargoes from European Russia
to the Irkutsk region is 80 days, it rises to 180

TABLE 2

Estimated Cost of Rail Freighting Bread Grains into
the Far East

Region of Origin	Quantity (metric tons)	Average Rail Freight Distance[a] (kilo- meters)	Cost Per Ton[b] (rubles)	Total Rail Freight Cost[c] ('000 rubles)
Eastern Siberia	675,000	4,458	15.16	10,233.0
West Siberia	460,000	5,222	17.75	8,165.0
Urals	40,000	6,146	20.90	836.0
Volga	45,000	8,532	29.01	1,305.5
Total	1,220,000[d]	--	--	20,539.5

[a]Eastern Siberia from Krasnoyarsk; West Siberia from Novosibirsk; the Urals from Sverdlovsk; and the Volga region from Volgograd; all distances to Khabarovsk in the Far East.
[b]Estimated at the general cargo rate of 0.340 kopecks per ton/kilometer.
[c]Freight cost per ton multiplied by quantity.
[d]Mainly wheat; wheat flour and rye flour figure was about 400,000 tons.

Source: F. V. D'yakonov et al., Dal'nii Vostok, ekonomiko-geograficheskaya kharakteristika (Moscow: AN SSSR, 1966), p. 194.

days for the Magadan region and up to 270 days for the Yakutsk A.S.S.R.[21] Large stocks of goods accumulate in transit and in warehouses, and financial resources are frozen that could be used for more directly productive purposes.

Isolated mining districts are separated from one another by vast, virtually uninhabited areas of

tundra where fishing, reindeer breeding, and fur
trapping are the main economic activities. Only
those natural resources are exploited in which the
U.S.S.R. is deficient or that are of such high quality
as to compensate for the greater cost of production
and transportation compared with more southerly
resources.

Mining and its service industries account for
most of the industrial output of the North, and industry, in turn, makes up 80 percent of the entire output of the regional economy. The pattern of transport routes and the flow of freight are thus dictated
almost wholly by the development of mining. Many
of the mining centers are far from major transport
routes: The diamond-mining town of Mirnyi, for example, is 1,200 miles from the nearest railhead. The
cost of imported goods is very high, and the local
production of requisites such as fuel, timber, building materials, potatoes, vegetables, and fresh milk
needs to be encouraged.

The loose economic ties that exist between separate districts of the North mainly involve shipments
of coal or timber. For instance, the timber industry
of southwest Yakutia supplies the nearby Mirnyi diamond fields and the Yana and Chaun districts. Sangar
coal, mined on the Lena River north of Yakutsk, is
sent to the tin mines at Deputatskii and Ese-Khaya.
Pre-existing supply routes from distant sources tend
to have a restraining effect on local industrial developments, but as freight costs increase this leads
to a more intensive search for local resources. The
high cost of transporting timber to the Ese-Khaya
district has encouraged the use of local timber even
though its low quality does not meet most housing
and industrial requirements.

Mining activities in the remote North are often
interrupted by shortages of machinery parts. In the
days of Dal'stroi (Far Eastern Construction Trust)
in the 1930s cheap corrective labor made it possible
to establish machine-building plants, fuel-equipment
industries, rubber regeneration, auto battery, plas-
tics fabrication, and insulator factories. In this

way the high costs of transportation were circumvented and continuous mining operations were assured. The demise of the labor camps has increased the operating costs of mining.

The Northeast of Pacific Siberia receives 1.8 million tons of freight a year of which about half originates in the southern part of the Far East and Eastern Siberia. Outgoing freight amounts to less than 100,000 tons but is generally of high value, such as gold, diamonds, and tin concentrates. In the 1920s many of the gold fields, such as those at Aldan, began operation before adequate roads were built, which caused serious problems with the supply of even basic foodstuffs. For the biggest gold-mining region in the U.S.S.R., the Kolyma, corrective labor was used to build a truck road from Magadan in 1932, three years after the initial mine development.

In the postwar period, however, the mistake of not providing adequate transport links at an early stage has been repeated at Mirnyi (diamonds) and Bilibino (tin). "Gateway" supply bases, such as Lensk for Mirnyi, have not been equipped with proper transfer facilities; this has inhibited the development of the mining enterprise.

The economic effect of the construction of a new railroad in a pioneering region is illustrated by Yegorova's study of the Lena railway.[22] Compared with previous routes, this railroad saved almost 13 million rubles. The old route from Taishet to Ust'- Kut by rail, water, and truck was 922 miles, or more than twice the distance of the new railroad. The average cost per ton of freight was 66.7 rubles, whereas by the new route it fell to 19.0 rubles. The 435-mile line was planned before the war as part of the ambitious Baikal-Amur railway (BAM), which was to extend 2,700 miles from Taishet to Komsomol'sk and Sovetskaya Gavan'; only the Lena railroad (1951) and the section between the last two named cities was ever completed. Regular operation of the Lena line began in December, 1958, through to the Lena River and the port of Osetrovo. This railway now services the Bratsk hydro station and freights timber,

paper and board, aluminum metal, and iron ore out of
the region. In 1971 double-tracking was commenced
because of the volume of freight being carried, and
a branch line from Khrebtovaya to the Ust'-Ilim hydro
site was opened. Access to the Bodaibo gold fields
has also been greatly improved by this line, and it
is now only 640 miles to a railhead at Osetrovo.
Gold dredges and industrial equipment from Irkutsk
now can be transported to these fields more easily.

FREIGHT MOVEMENTS AND THE
TRANSPORT NETWORK

In the late 1920s, when the Soviets began to
develop Siberia, transport facilities were basically
comprised of a one-track railway and a run-down river
fleet. Transportation still can be defined in terms
of the Trans-Siberian railway, which now is double-
tracked and, from Moscow through to Lake Baikal,
electrified. In the intervening stretch to Khabarovsk
the capacity of the line has been increased by the
use of diesel trains of heavier weights operating at
greater speeds. For the future, however, there will
be a need for a third track or the construction of a
Northern Siberian railway; the latter is included in
long-term Soviet perspective planning and would open
isolated areas to development, but it would take ten
or more years to complete. Construction of a spur
line to the BAM will start in November, 1972, with
the laying of a 150-kilometer stretch of track from
near Skovorodino north toward the Chul'man coal deposits; this will intersect the BAM but it is not
known when the work will start on the eastward extension of the BAM from Ust'-Kut.

In the meantime, shorter links, such as the one
from Taishet to Abakan--the capital of the Khakass
Autonomous Oblast' (A.O.)--was completed in 1965,
but criticisms have arisen because of the lack of
industrial development along its route.[23] The same
problems seem likely to arise with the recently completed Reshoty-to-Boguchany track of 135 miles and
the branch line from Skovorodino to Chul'man.

As the U.S.S.R.'s road transport industry becomes more highly developed it might be expected that
more sealed highways will supplement long- or medium-
distance rail transport in Pacific Siberia, where
most of the roads are dirt. A Moscow-to-Vladivostok
trans-Siberian trunk road is planned, and sealing of
gravel sections is proceeding slowly; between Sretensk
and Svobodnyi, however, there is no road link for
over 600 miles. At present, only 3.4 percent of the
freight in Eastern Siberia and 4.7 percent of that
in the Far East travels by road; indeed, in the former territory, pipelines (for oil from West Siberia)
carry a slightly greater proportion of the overall
freight traffic. River transport accounts for a substantial part of intraregional freight movements;
the Yenisei alone carries over 14 million tons of
cargo each summer season.

In the Far East sea transport is of very great
importance, carrying some 15 percent of local freight.
The Far East merchant marine has a fleet of 200 ships
totaling 1.1 million tons dead weight. The main sea
freight movements are from Vladivostok, Nakhodka, and
Vanino in the south northeastward to the island of
Sakhalin, the Kamchatka Peninsula, and the sparsely
populated coast of the Sea of Okhotsk. Exports of
timber and fish to Japan are handled by the Far Eastern Shipping Corporation, formed in 1964 to incorpor-
ate the fleets of the Far Eastern, Skahalin, and
Kamchatka directorates. A major problem exists with
long delays, caused by the acute labor shortage, in
which cargo stands idle on the dock sides for several
months.

Table 3 gives a detailed breakdown of freight
movements in the Far East and Eastern Siberia by mode
of haulage and by type of movement for 1965 (later
data are not available). The combined volume of interregional exports and imports by rail, sea, and
river was 61.6 million tons for Eastern Siberia of
which 97 percent was accounted for by rail; comparable
figures for the Far East were 24.3 million tons and
94 percent. Unfortunately, the data do not include
overseas shipments.

TABLE 3

Freight Transport Balance in Pacific Siberia,
(in million tons)

Region and Transport Used[a]	Dis-patched	Re-ceived	Intra-regional Shipments	Inter-regional Exports	Inter-regional Imports	Surplus of Exports (+) or of Imports (−)
			All Freight			
Eastern Siberia	121.96	96.75	78.58	43.38	18.17	+25.21
Rail[b]	99.11	74.84	57.12	41.99	17.72	+24.27
Sea	0.10	0.35	0.05	0.05	0.30	−0.25
River	22.75	21.56	21.41	1.34	0.15	+1.19
Far East	78.27	88.14	71.04	7.23	17.10	−9.87
Rail[c]	57.99	66.72	50.91	7.08	15.81	−8.73
Sea	10.35	10.37	10.35	--	0.02	−0.02
River	9.93	11.05	9.78	0.15	1.27	−1.12
			Coal			
Eastern Siberia	34.71	29.43	28.81	5.90	0.62	+5.28
Rail	34.17	28.83	28.29	5.88	0.54	+5.34
Sea	0.04	0.05	0.04	0.00	0.01	−0.01
River	0.50	0.55	0.48	0.02	0.07	−0.05
Far East	26.74	28.53	26.00	0.74	2.53	−1.79
Rail	23.29	25.07	22.62	0.67	2.45	−1.78
Sea	1.71	1.77	1.71	--	0.06	−0.06
River	1.74	1.69	1.67	0.07	0.02	+0.05
			Oil and Oil Products			
Eastern Siberia	7.12	6.51	2.24	4.88	4.27	+0.61
Rail	6.15	6.00	1.77	4.38	4.23	+0.15
Sea	--	0.03	--	--	0.03	−0.03
River	0.97	0.48	0.47	0.50	0.01	+0.49
Far East	5.81	11.23	5.34	0.47	5.89	−5.42
Rail	2.53	7.62	2.22	0.31	5.40	−5.09
Sea	1.91	1.75	1.75	0.16	--	+0.16
River	1.37	1.86	1.37	--	0.49	−0.49

Region and Transport Used[a]	Dispatched	Received	Intra-regional Shipments	Inter-regional Exports	Inter-regional Imports	Surplus of Exports (+) or of Imports (−)
			Ores			
Eastern Siberia	3.14	0.20	0.08	3.06	0.12	+2.94
Rail	3.10	0.15	0.04	3.06	0.11	+2.95
Sea	--	0.00	--	--	0.00	-0.00
River	0.04	0.05	0.04	--	0.01	-0.01
Far East	0.41	0.15	0.14	0.27	0.01	+0.26
Rail	0.25	0.13	0.12	0.13	0.01	+0.12
Sea	0.15	0.02	0.02	0.13	--	+0.13
River	0.01	0.00	0.00	0.01	--	+0.01
			Lumber (including firewood)			
Eastern Siberia	38.63	16.94	16.61	22.02	0.33	+21.69
Rail	26.85	5.28	4.99	21.86	0.29	+21.57
Sea	0.01	0.02	0.00	0.01	0.02	-0.01
River	11.77	11.64	11.62	0.15	0.02	+0.13
Far East	11.09		9.94	1.15	0.47	+0.68
Rail	7.52	6.66	6.39	1.13	0.27	+0.86
Sea	1.48	1.60	1.48	--	0.12	-0.12
River	2.09	2.15	2.07	0.02	0.08	-0.06
			Cement			
Eastern Siberia	1.86	2.67	1.71	0.15	0.96	-0.81
Rail	1.65	2.59	1.63	0.02	0.96	-0.94
Sea	--	0.00	--	--	0.00	-0.00
River	0.21	0.08	0.08	0.13	--	+0.13
Far East	2.20	2.51	2.14	0.06	0.37	-0.31
Rail	1.77	1.96	1.71	0.06	0.25	-0.19
Sea	0.37	0.37	0.37	0.00	0.00	-0.00
River	0.06	0.18	0.06	--	0.12	-0.12

[a]Freight data excludes truck transport, air freight, and pipelines.
[b]In 1969 the amount dispatched was 120.2 million tons; received, 87.7 million tons.
[c]In 1969 the amount dispatched was 67.4 million tons, received, 84.5 million tons.

Source: Transport i Svyaz' SSSR--Statisticheskii Sbornik (Moscow: Ts.S.U., 1967), pp. 74-91.

Overall, Eastern Siberia is a net interregional exporter of some 25 million tons of goods annually—mainly lumber, which amounts to a net 22 million tons of round logs, sawn timber, and railway sleepers.* The major markets were West Siberia, Kazakhstan, Central Asia, the Urals, and European Russia. Only 200,000 tons were exported down the Yenisei to the timber port of Igarka and thence via the northern sea route to Western Europe. This heavy westerly flow of timber, particularly of bulky round logs of low value, poses a major handling problem on the Trans-Siberian railway, where near Tomsk it provides 50 percent of all freight. Only about 15 percent of the timber produced in Eastern Siberia remains there for local consumption.

Other major cargoes freighted out of Eastern Siberia are coal (almost six million tons) and various mineral ores (about three million tons), mainly iron ore, molybdenum, tin, and fluorspar. The main market for Eastern Siberian coal is the Kuzbass of West Siberia. About one-third of the coal mined in the Cheremkhovo district of Eastern Siberia is exported. Oil is imported into Eastern Siberia by a pipeline with a capacity of about one million tons a year, as well as by rail; about two million tons of steel are also imported, together with large amounts of foodstuffs, machinery, and consumer durables.

The Far East, by contrast, is a net interregional importer of almost ten million tons of freight annually.** Over one-half these imports comprise oil and oil products, which arrive in the Far East by rail from the pipeline terminal at Angarsk in Eastern Siberia. The oil comes from the oil fields at Tyumen' as well as the southern Urals. Other impor-

---

*In 1966 net interregional exports were 26.6 million tons, compared with 21.3 million tons in 1963; thus, the export surplus position is tending to widen.

**In 1966 net interregional imports were 11.9 million tons, compared with 8.3 million tons in 1963; thus, the import deficit position is worsening.

tant imports are black coal, from Cheremkhovo and
Chita, and cement (which Eastern Siberia also imports
in large quantities) from as far away as the Urals.
Foodstuffs are also imported from Siberia, Kazakhstan,
the Urals, Volga, Central Chernozem, and the Ukraine
to the extent of about 1.7 million tons a year; purchases of steel from West Siberia amount to perhaps
a million tons or so. Another item not shown in
Table 3, which is a very significant export commodity
from the Far East to practically all parts of the
Soviet Union, is fish: Upward of 600,000 tons of
fish, in net weight edible form, is railed out of
the Far East each year. Overall, one-fifth of the
Far East's imports and exports by volume are associated with European Russia; the Eastern regions
(the Urals, West and Eastern Siberia, Central Asia,
and Kazakhstan) provide markets for, or are the suppliers of, almost four-fifths of the trade, especially
in bulky products.

In the past, external transport links, particularly Russian-built railways, between the Far East
and Manchuria were exceedingly important for the development of trade. Since the emergence of the Sino-
Soviet conflict, trade across the border, both by
rail and by the Amur and Ussuri rivers, has practically disappeared, and there are no immediate prospects for any major renewal.

NOTES

1. V. A. Krotov, Izvestiya Akademii Nauk SSSR,
seriya geograficheskaya, No. 4, 1964, trans. in
Soviet Geography, No. 9, November, 1964, p. 53.

2. H. Hunter, Soviet Transport Experience: Its
Lessons for Other Countries (Washington, D.C.:
Brookings Institute, 1968), p. 46.

3. V. Conolly, Beyond the Urals (London: Oxford University Press, 1967), p. 281; the annual traffic over one kilometer of Siberian railway is 15 million tons.

4.   Derived from Ya. G. Feigin et al., Zakonomer-nosti i Faktory Razvitiya Ekonomicheskikh Raionov SSSR (Moscow: AN SSSR, 1965), p. 237.

5.   R. Taaffe, Rail Transportation and the Economic Development of Soviet Central Asia (Chicago, 1960), pp. 134-35.

6.   Ibid.; freight originating in noncontiguous regions is 15.7 percent for the Far East, 16.3 percent for Eastern Siberia, but only 10.3 percent for the Soviet average; it is 6.7 percent in West Siberia, which has a high proportion of rail freight (25 percent) originating in contiguous regions, i.e., Kazakhstan, the Urals, and, also, Eastern Siberia.

7.   Ya G. Feigin, ed., Problemy Ekonomicheskoi Effektivnosti Razmeshcheniya Sotsialisticheskogo Proizvodstva v SSSR (Moscow: AN SSSR, 1968), pp. 237-38.

8.   Transportno-Ekonomicheskie Sviazi v Narodnom Khozyaistve SSSR (Moscow: Ekonomizdat, 1963), p. 27.

9.   Ibid.

10.   E. Thiel, The Soviet Far East (London: Methuen, 1957).

11.   Ibid., p. 68.

12.   L. V. Kantorovich, The Best Use of Economic Resources (Oxford: Pergamon Press, 1965), p. 113.

13.   Hunter, op. cit., p. 96.

14.   Ibid., p. 63; electric and diesel-electric locomotives can be built to pull heavy and fast trains without the need for heavy track structure and bridges that steam locomotives of equivalent power require.

15.   Feigin, Problemy Ekonomicheskoi, p. 248.

16.   Ekonomicheskaya Gazeta, No. 12, March, 1967.

17.   V. N. Gerasimov, "Transportnye Reservy
Aziatskogo Severa SSSR," Problemy Severa, No. 12,
1967, p. 14.

18.   G. Rubinstein advocates the creation of a
powerful export base in the Far East and a large reduction in the extra-long-distance rail haulage of
goods from that region to European Russia. Voprosy
Ekonomiki, No. 9, 1966.

19.   E. G. Meerson and F. V. D'yakonov, "Dal'nii
Vostok," in Geograficheskie Problemy Razvitiya
Krupnykh Ekonomicheskikh Raionov SSSR, ed. V. V.
Pokshishevskii (Moscow: AN SSSR, 1964), p. 410.

20.   A. B. Margolin, Problemy Narodnogo Khozyaistva
Dal'nego Vostoka (Moscow: AN SSSR, 1963), p. 11.

21.   G. I. Chiryayev, First Secretary of the
Yakutsk Regional Committee of the CPSU, Ekonomicheskaya
Gazeta, No. 12, 1971.

22.   V. V. Yegorova, Voprosy Geografii Sibiri,
No. 61, 1963, pp. 122-32.

23.   Pravda, April 5, 1966.

PART

II

**THE
SUPPLY
ECONOMY**

3

ECONOMIC
STRUCTURE

The structure of the Pacific Siberian economy
is characterized by a heavy dependence on extractive
industries such as mining, forestry, and fishing.
Although secondary industries are poorly developed,
building construction work and transport and communications are relatively large employers of labor. The
agricultural sector is fairly important in terms of
the employment opportunities it offers, but an adverse
climate over most of the region impedes its real contribution to the economy. In the Far East there is
a relatively large disposition of military, air force,
and naval personnel in addition to normal civilian
employment.

The gross value of output per worker in Pacific
Siberia as a whole is only about 80 percent of the
Soviet average; this is due to the large share of
labor-consuming branches of industry, such as fishing, forestry, and mining.

The reliance on extractive industries makes this
a simply based economy. Yet, the difficulties of extraction, the costs of transportation, and the problems created by a weak infrastructure (especially
railways, roads, houses, and public utilities) all
tend to demand large amounts of capital investment
per head of population.

There is still a very marked regional irregu-
larity in the development of this economy. The
southern areas of the Krasnoyarsk, Khabarovsk, and
Primor'ye krais and Irkutsk oblast' are relatively
well industrialized; on the other hand, the Tuva
A.S.S.R., Magadan, and Kamchatka oblast's have hardly
any industries at all. And there are vast areas in
the hinterlands of the Yenisei, Lena, Indigirka,
Kolyma, and other northern rivers where population
and economic activity is sparse and not much developed
beyond reindeer breeding, fur trapping, fishing, and
hunting.

THE EMPLOYMENT PATTERN

Some idea of the general economic structure of
Pacific Siberia can be gained from the data in Table
4, which shows work force employment by broad industry groups. Most of the work force is located in the
south of the region, with only about 500,000 workers
employed in the Far North in mines, ports, and administration. It is estimated that the total work force
in 1971 may have reached 4.7 million or more (based
on population censuses), but the employment structure
is not likely to have changed significantly from that
shown in the table.

Compared with 20 years earlier, the employment
pattern for industry does not seem to have altered
greatly. Although agricultural employment has declined relatively, the main change has occurred in
the greater importance of the building and construction industry. The service industries, except transport, have also grown in significance as the economy
has developed.

It is instructive to compare the structure of
employment in Pacific Siberia with that in neighboring West Siberia. In West Siberia industry is relatively more important (36 percent of employment)
because of the Kuzbass heavy industrial and coal-
mining district; agriculture, which is highly developed in the Altai krai, accounts for 16 percent of
the work force (about the same as for the Far East);

TABLE 4

Pacific Siberia: Work Force Employment

	Eastern Siberia[a]		Far East		Total	
	Million Workers	Percent	Million Workers	Percent	Million Workers	Percent
Industry[b]	0.70	27	0.50	31	1.20	29
Agriculture	0.68	26	0.24	15	0.92	22
Transport[c]	0.25	10	0.24	15	0.49	12
Building	0.29	11	0.11	7	0.40	9
Others[d]	0.68	26	0.51	32	1.19	28
Total	2.60	100	1.60	100	4.20	100

[a]Includes Yakutsk A.S.S.R.
[b]Includes mining, forestry, and fishing.
[c]Includes communications.
[d]Includes services, catering, and trade.

Sources: F. V. D'yakonov et al., Dal'nii Vostok, ekonomico-geograficheskaya kharakteristika (Moscow: AN SSSR, 1966), p. 108; V. A. Krotov et al.,
Vostochnaya Sibir'--ekonomiko-geograficheskaya kharakteristika (Moscow: AN SSSR, 1963), p. 163.

transport and communications employment, at 10 percent
of the work force, is identical to that in Eastern
Siberia; and building construction employment (10
percent) is slightly less. The category "other" employment in West Siberia (28 percent), compared with
32 percent in the Far East, is divided into retail
and wholesale trade, housing and government administrative services (about 11 percent), and education,
health, science, and culture (17 percent), approximately.[1] The proportion of the population in the
work force in Pacific Siberia is slightly higher than
in West Siberia. This may reflect the faster rate

of economic growth and associated employment opportunities now occurring in the east.

The Soviets include mining, forestry, and fishing under "industry," which explains the relatively high industrial employment in the Far East compared with Eastern Siberia. The Pacific fishing industry in the Far East accounts for about 22 percent of the region's industry--especially in Kamchatka where three-quarters of industrial employment is associated with fishing. Another 21 percent is employed in timber felling and processing and fuel extraction (particularly coal and oil on Sakhalin); a further 14 percent works in foodstuffs processing and canning. The real secondary industry sector of the Far East is quite small and is based on engineering (machinery and metalworking) in Khabarovsk krai. In Eastern Siberia the share of extractive industries in the industrial employment structure is 62 percent; these industries are defined as metal ores, fuels, nonmetallic minerals (e.g., gypsum), natural chemicals (e.g., sulfur, salt, phosphorite), timber, and fish. Timber, coal, and iron ore are particularly important in Eastern Siberia, but it is expected that their relative importance will decline as the large hydro projects and associated industries at Bratsk, Irkutsk, Ust'-Ilim, Krasnoyarsk, and Sayan-Shushenskoe produce electricity, nonferrous metals, and timber-derived products.

Agriculture is a larger employer of labor in Eastern Siberia than in the Far East because the climate and land resources there are more suitable to large-scale grain cultivation and livestock breeding. In some provinces agriculture still employs more than one-half the population. Collective farm workers in Eastern Siberia number about half a million, but this figure includes many workers who spend a great deal of the year on their private plots. The Amur region contains almost 40 percent of the Far East's State and collective farm workers. A significant part of the Siberian agricultural work force is surplus to requirements, except at harvest time, and probably has a marginal productivity of labor approaching zero. Thus, substantial resources could be withdrawn from

the rural work force with no marked loss of output.
Many farm workers are employed on a seasonal basis
in the fish-processing and timber-felling industries.

Construction and building work is also relatively
more important to the economy of Eastern Siberia than
to the Far East. This reflects the large number of
capital works projects currently being undertaken in
areas such as Irkutsk oblast', where construction
workers comprise over 16 percent of the work force.

Transport and communications are an especially
large employer of labor in the Far East because of
its large fishing fleet, Amur River traffic, Trans-
Siberian railway terminal, and extensive servicing
facilities. The Far East has a larger proportion
of its work force in transportation than any other
region in the U.S.S.R. In Eastern Siberia this sector of employment is not as highly developed, although
in Chita oblast' there are fairly extensive locomotive
repair yards to service the Trans-Siberian railway
line and its branch lines.

In the service industries, employment is lower
than in the European parts of the U.S.S.R., especially
for schoolteachers, doctors, scientific workers, and
technicians. This situation reflects the inadequacy
of local education establishments as well as the
problems of attracting and retaining skilled personnel in such an isolated part of the U.S.S.R.

VALUE OF OUTPUT

During the Seven Year Plan for 1959-65, it was
directed that the pace of industrial development in
Siberia would be faster than the all-Union average.
The average annual increase in the value of gross
industrial output, including mining, forestry, and
fishing, was planned to reach 14 percent, compared
with 8.6 percent for the U.S.S.R. as a whole. The
annual rates actually attained were 11.1 percent for
West Siberia, 14.1 percent for Eastern Siberia, and
12.7 percent for the Far East; the claimed rate for
the U.S.S.R. was 12.0 percent.[2] Thus, there was

little difference in the realized rates of growth between Siberia and the U.S.S.R.; consequently, the
European parts of the country maintained their dominant economic position. Similarly, in 1969 industrial
output in Pacific Siberia was only a little better,
compared with 1965, than most of the U.S.S.R. Industrial development in Siberia in recent years had been
behind that of the Union as a whole for several reasons, including inadequate capacities in the construction and assembly industries and a shortage of raw
materials. In addition, of course, there are many
huge developmental projects in the process of construction in Siberia and the Far East in which large
amounts of capital are tied up and from which returns
will be slow to emerge. In the 1966-70 plan period
the index of gross industrial output was about 8 percent greater than the Soviet average in Eastern Siberia, where industrialization associated with large
hydro schemes is occurring.

The mining and timber industries of Eastern
Siberia account for almost one-half its gross value
of industrial output; and food processing, another
fifth. In the Far East the fishing, timber, and mining industries produce over one-half the gross value
of output; and food processing, another sixth. In
both regions the engineering industries account for
less than one-fifth of the gross value of output and
have been severely criticized for their lack of progress.

The value of output in the chemical industry
(for which some limited data on growth rates are
available) grew five-fold in Eastern Siberia during
1958-65 (the largest increase of any region in the
R.S.F.S.R.), compared with less than two-fold for the
Far East. Most of the Eastern Siberian increase was
in Krasnoyarsk where a large wood-chemical kombinat
(including cellulose, paper, rubber, resin, and man-
made fibers) has been in production since 1961.
Preparations have started at Achinsk, near Krasnoyarsk,
for the construction of an oil refinery producing raw
materials for aromatic hydrocarbons in the chemical
industry.[3]

In terms of its contribution to the Soviet gross
value of industrial output, Pacific Siberia is relatively important in some industries. It produces
(with 5.5 percent of the U.S.S.R.'s population) over
11 percent of the Soviet gross value of output of
hydro and thermal electricity; four-fifths of this
is from the Bratsk, Krasnoyarsk, and Irkutsk hydro
stations, together with the thermal stations at
Cheremkhovo, Achinsk, Chita, and Noril'sk.[4] In fuel,
however, Pacific Siberia accounts for only 6 percent
of the Soviet value of output, whereas West Siberia,
with its large coal fields in the Kuzbass, produces
almost 11 percent. The relative weakness of the
Pacific Siberian economy is most vividly demonstrated
by its 0.8 percent and 2.1 percent share in the Soviet
output of heavy and light industries, respectively.[5]

Pacific Siberia produces 7.5 percent of the Soviet value of output in building and construction
materials. Prefabricated concrete structures and
parts are an increasingly important building material,
especially for flats, and production in Pacific Siberia increased four times between 1958 and 1965.
There are, however, two important building materials
in which Pacific Siberia suffers a shortage. The output of cement (over 6 million tons) cannot satisfy
demand from the large construction sites, and, according to a report in Komsomolskaya Pravda in February, 1967, the Far East receives bricks from China.
The production of bricks in Pacific Siberia has not
increased in recent years and is the cause of major
delays in the building industry.

CAPITAL INVESTMENT

State capital investments in Pacific Siberia
during the Seven Year Plan for 1959-65 was 23,751
million rubles, or almost 10 percent of total State
investments (see Table 5).* Per capita investment

---

*The State sector accounts for 86 percent of all
investment activity; the balance comes mainly from
kolkhozy.

in Pacific Siberia over the term of the Plan was
1,962.1 rubles, or 880.8 rubles more than the average
for the U.S.S.R. In the four years 1966-69, investments in the region rose to 19,701 million rubles,
almost half as much again as for West Siberia; per
head of population, Pacific Siberia currently receives
about 408 rubles a year, whereas West Siberia only
gets 304 rubles. Recently, investment in the Far
East has been rising almost twice as fast as investments in Eastern Siberia, which may be partly because
of Soviet concern over relations with China.

Building construction work accounts for 64 percent of total capital investments in Eastern Siberia
but only for 58 percent in the Far East. This difference may be largely explained by several large
capital works projects in Eastern Siberia. The most
expensive of these were the 4.1 million-kilowatt
Bratsk hydro plant, the Irkutsk aluminum factory,
the Angaro-Usol'sk chemical and petrochemical complex, and the Taishet-Abakan railway line (435 miles);
part of the oil pipeline from Tuimazy (in West Siberia) to Angarsk (in Eastern Siberia) must also be
included.[6] The cost of constructing the Bratsk Dam
alone was 730 million rubles. The cost of a housing
program for the 2.3 million people living in Irkutsk
oblast' (where Bratsk is located) was claimed to be
700 million rubles in 1967, rising to 1,000 million
by 1970.

The lack of synchronization among some interdependent capital works projects is serious. For instance, after the Krasnoyarsk synthetic fiber plant
began operation, for a long time it had to get its
cellulose supplies from factories 2,800 miles away
until a paper cellulose plant less than two miles
away was completed.[7] The Krasnoyarsk aluminum plant
started trial runs in 1964, but at that time the
nearby Achinsk alumina plant was only one-fifth completed, and Krasnoyarsk had to pay additional transport costs of nine rubles per ton to get alumina from
more distant suppliers. The delay in completing the
Achinsk alumina plant also had consequential effects
on the Achinsk cement plant, which was put into operation three years before the scheduled completion of

TABLE 5

Capital Investment in State and Cooperative Enterprises and Organizations, Excluding Kolkhozy
(at comparable prices, in million rubles)

	Far East		Eastern Siberia		West Siberia	
Period	Million Rubles	As percent of U.S.S.R.	Million Rubles	As percent of U.S.S.R.	Million Rubles	As percent of U.S.S.R.
1918-28[a]	106	6.3	75	4.5	66	3.9
First Five Year Plan, 1929-32[b]	325	4.8	282	4.2	298	4.4
Second Five Year Plan, 1933-37	872	5.7	531	3.5	610	4.0
Third Five Year Plan, 1938-41[c]	1,146	7.6	570	3.8	558	3.7
1941-46[d]	1,133	7.8	598	4.1	886	6.1
Fourth Five Year Plan, 1946-50	1,566	4.5	1,432	4.1	1,527	4.4
Fifth Five Year Plan, 1951-55	3,209	4.8	3,197	4.8	3,816	5.7
1956-58[e]	2,656	4.1	3,350	5.1	4,068	6.2
Seven Year Plan, 1959-65	10,506	4.4	13,245	5.5	15,570	6.5
1966-69[f]	9,519	4.7	10,182	5.0	13,404	6.6

[a]Excludes the fourth quarter of 1928.
[b]Includes the fourth quarter of 1928.
[c]Planned as 1938 to 1942 but terminated in June, 1941.
[d]July 1, 1941, to January 1, 1946.
[e]The Sixth Five Year Plan (1956-60) was abandoned late in 1957.
[f]Full Data for the Eighth Five Year Plan (1966-70) not yet available.

Note: State capital investments do not include: expenditures on geological field surveys, town planning, and building designs; silviculture and planting of protective forest belts; purchasing and building up breeding herds; purchase of equipment for running schools, hospitals, kindergartens, and nurseries.

Sources: Narodnoe Khozyaistvo SSSR, 1961, 1965, and 1967; Narodnoe Khozyaistvo RSFSR v 1969 god.

the alumina plant but was planned to use alumina
wastes that would increase kiln productivity by 40-45
percent and reduce fuel consumption by 30 percent.
There were similar problems with the Bratsk hydro
plant, which was criticized because initially there
were no electricity-consuming industries and for a
long time it operated at only 25-30 percent of its
capacity. Even after the commissioning of the trunk
transmission line to Krasnoyarsk in 1963, it only
rose to 50-60 percent.[8] Returns on the large investment in the Taishet-Abakan railway may take some
considerable time owing to the lack of planning for
industrial development along its route.[9]

A survey of more than 100 new industrial projects
in Siberia and the results of constructing about 600
new factories, plants, and mines showed that completion took about ten years on average. Even after
commissioning, some plants may take from five to ten
years to achieve planned production levels. Added
to this are wages costs, which are about 20 percent
higher in the East Siberian construction industry
than in Moscow's and, for the Far East, about 40 percent higher.[10] This adds to the unattractiveness of
the region from a Moscow budgetary viewpoint.

Other additional investment imposts involve the
cost of constructing walls that, in order to retain
a normal room temperature, have to be 20 percent
thicker in Irkutsk than in Moscow and 72 percent
thicker in Yakutsk. Accordingly, the cost of one
square meter (10.8 square feet) of brick wall in
Irkutsk is 55 percent more than in Moscow; in Yakutsk
it is 138 percent greater.[11]

Nevertheless, there have been huge amounts of
investment in Pacific Siberia in recent times. Table
5 indicates that investment in the region in the Seven
Year Plan exceeded those of the preceding 40 years.
As a proportion of total investment in the U.S.S.R.,
Pacific Siberia has in the past received relatively
more funds from Moscow. Such were the years after
the Allied intervention when it received almost 11
percent of Soviet capital investments. In the late
1930s Japanese occupation of Manchuria threatened

Soviet borderlands, and the share of Soviet investments rose to 11.4 percent; this was followed by
World War II when investments in the region were almost 12 percent of the Soviet total. At present
Pacific Siberia gets less than 10 percent of all
State investments; this proportion is not expected
to increase over the 1971-75 plan period unless there
is a sudden change in the leadership's regional planning priorities or their perception of the strategic
threat from China.

The Five Year Plan for 1966-70 made special
mention of provisions for "large scale economic construction . . . to be started in the eastern areas
of the country." The economic potential of the Far
East in particular was to be built up considerably,
specific references being made to large investments
in hydro-electric and timber-processing plants, port
facilities, and a wide range of industries using
local cheap supplies of fuel, electric power, and
minerals, especially bauxite, copper, and cobalt.
Housing was to be erected "at rates higher than those
obtaining on the average for the country." Industrial development in the Far East was to be stepped
up including the further exploitation of precious
and nonferrous metals and diamonds and the development, on an industrial scale, of the Ust' Vilyui gas
deposits; the fishing, power generation, and timber-
using industries were all to be expanded. Overall,
the accelerated development of productive forces
(i.e., capital investments) in Siberia and the Far
East was to be regarded as an important economic task.
The Far East alone was allocated investment monies
of 9,000 million rubles, or 40 percent more than in
the previous five years. In fact, by 1969 the Far
East had received 9,500 million rubles, indicating
that planned investment projects were running ahead
of schedule.[12]

There is also a special economic development
program for the Far East region and Chita oblast'
for 1967-75.[13] It includes comprehensive measures
for industrial and agricultural growth and integrated
regional development in relation to local demand.
The program was reinforced by a decree of the

Presidium of the Supreme Soviet providing for sizable
increases in wages for workers in thё Far North and
equivalent remote regions, as of January 1, 1968.[14]
These moves pointed to a greater provision of investment funds, but, at the Twenty-Fourth Congress of
the CPSU in 1971, the Soviet Far East and Siberia
received less attention than at the previous congress
five years earlier. Further wage increases were
granted to workers in the Far North, but relatively
little was said about new Siberian development projects. It may be that the leadership wants the eastern regions to digest current projects before em-
barking on any large new ones. On the other hand,
it may be disenchanted with the high capital/labor
ratios required to develop the area,* and, in view
of the slight improvement in relations with China
recently, it may have decided that investment is not
needed quite so urgently.

                            NOTES

      1. N. P. Kalinovskii and L. A. Shishkina,
"Ispol'zovanie trudovykh resursov i povyshenie urovnya
zhizni," in Zapadno-Sibirskii Ekonomicheskii Raion,
ed. A. B. Margolin (Moscow: Gosplan SSSR, 1967),
p. 178.

      2. Narodnoe Khozyaistvo SSSR v 1965 god, p. 128.

      3. BBC Summary of World Broadcasts, Part I,
U.S.S.R., October 15, 1971.

      4. V. V. Kistanow, Kompleksnoe Razvitie i
Spetsializatsiya Ekonomicheskikh Raionov SSSR, Gosplan SSSR (Moscow: AN SSSR, 1968), p. 94.

      5. Ibid.

_____

*Capital/labor ratios (i.e., the amount of capi-
tal required to increase employment by one additional
worker) in the Far East are about 50 percent higher
than those in West Siberia, where the economic infrastructure is much more highly developed.

    6.   Ekonomicheskaya Gazeta, No. 22, June, 1967,
p. 6.

    7.   Voprosy Ekonomiki, No. 5, 1965.

    8.   Voprosy Ekonomiki, No. 8, 1966.

    9.   Pravda, April 5, 1966, quoting A. A. Kokarev,
First Secretary, Krasnoyarsk Krai Party Committee.

    10.   D. I. Valentei, et al., eds., Narodonaselenie
i Ekonomika (Moscow, 1967), p. 149.

    11.   Razvitie Proizvoditel'nykh Sil Vostochnoi
Sibiri Stroitel'naya Industriya i Promyshlennost'
Stroitel' nykh Materialov (Moscow: AN SSSR, 1960),
p. 32.

    12.   Narodnoe Khozyaistvo RSFSR v 1969 god; in
1971-75 the State plans to invest 5,500 million rubles in the Primor'ye krai alone.

    13.   Izvestiya, July 30, 1967.

    14.   Ekonomicheskaya Gazeta, No. 39, September,
1967.

CHAPTER

4

**PROBLEMS
OF
INDUSTRIAL
GROWTH**

Manufacturing industries as such are heavily
concentrated in the south of the region, especially
along the Trans-Siberian railway. The production of
consumer goods (particularly textiles and footwear),
chemicals, and engineering products lags far behind
local demand. Accordingly, many products of a highly
fabricated nature have to be imported into the region
from other parts of the U.S.S.R. This involves
transportation over distances as great as 6,000 miles
and, because of the uneven distribution of highly
specialized manufacturing plants, costly cross-hauls.

In both the Far East and Eastern Siberia the
engineering industries account for 15-20 percent of
gross industrial output and have been criticized for
their lack of progress and high production costs.
Costs of production in the Krasnoyarsk steel works,
for example, are more than double those of the neighboring Kuzbass; almost all rolled steel requirements
have to be imported. No bulldozers or excavators
and comparatively few heavy turbines and boilers are
manufactured in the region. But a considerable
quantity of various types of machinery is produced
for which there is a relatively small local demand;
these products are exported to European Russia, Eastern Europe, and some developing countries (e.g.,
foundry equipment from the Amurlitmash works at
Komsomol'sk-na-Amure). Equipment for the very important electricity-generating industry is imported from

61

European Russia or from overseas. Only about one-
quarter of requirements for engineering and metalworking products are produced locally. The construction of a vehicle assembly plant at Chita in 1964 was
abandoned when investment funds were cut off by the
Economic Council.[1] The project was not recommenced
until 1971. Production costs in engineering and
metalworking industries are one-fifth more than in
European Russia.[2] The projected Taishet steel works
is still in the planning stages, after more than
13 years of preparatory works and an incompletely
resolved low-grade iron ore base supply far to the
west, at Altai-Sayan.

In several basic industries output has fallen
well below planned levels and there are considerable
delays in meeting demand. The building industry has
been especially affected by inadequate productive
capacity. In Irkutsk oblast', for instance, the
production of bricks and prefabricated concrete fell
short of the Seven Year Plan targets by 30 percent
and 38 percent, respectively; as a result the quotas
set for housing construction were greatly underfulfilled.[3] There have also been serious shortcomings
in the footwear and clothing industries; and, despite
plenty of wood, coal, and cheap electricity, the
chemical industry continues to lag far behind that
of West Siberia.

In short, secondary industry in Pacific Siberia
is poorly developed; the industries that do exist are
relatively small in scale and high in cost structure.

OUTPUT OF SECONDARY INDUSTRY

Significant areas of secondary industry production in Pacific Siberia are not covered by recent
Soviet statistical sources. (See Table 6.) The most
serious gaps are for the steel, chemicals, and
machine-building/engineering industries.

The Steel Industry

The steel industry is not large and is based on
small plants, with a combined capacity of 1.7 million

TABLE 6

The Growth in Secondary Industry, 1960-69

Product	1960	1965	1966	1967	1968	1969
Cement ('000 tons)						
Eastern Siberia	2,088	2,808	3,412	3,608	3,834	3,952
Far East	1,569	1,827	1,940	2,099	2,162	2,054
Bricks (million units)						
Eastern Siberia	921.6	988.1	929.9	946.6	973.0	973.7
Far East	640.7	713.0	721.7	755.1	769.3	793.0
Window glass ('000 square meters)						
Eastern Siberia	6,901	12,943	15,552	14,774	17,480	17,136
Far East	3,327	5,457	5,965	5,921	6,341	5,819
Cotton cloth (million meters)						
Eastern Siberia	81.1	85.1	87.8	86.5	89.9	85.2
Far East	6.9	11.9	12.5	13.6	14.1	13.2
Woolen cloth (million meters)						
Eastern Siberia	1.40	1.42	1.45	1.43	1.30	1.40
Far East	--	--	--	--	--	--
Silk cloth (million meters)						
Eastern Siberia	22.8	38.7	39.2	40.4	42.4	43.7
Far East	--	--	--	--	--	--
Leather footwear (million pair)						
Eastern Siberia	6.59	8.36	8.94	9.61	9.83	10.61
Far East	1.13	1.13	1.42	2.33	2.82	3.47
Knitted underwear ('000 pieces)						
Eastern Siberia	4,669	9,004	9,873	9,429	8,058	9,563
Far East	824	3,326	3,312	3,390	4,581	7,957
Knitted outerwear ('000 pieces)						
Eastern Siberia	1,319	3,442	5,171	7,461	10,430	13,048
Far East	235	803	972	1,053	1,682	2,319

Note: Excludes food-processing and timber-processing industries.

Source: Narodnoe Khozyaistvo RSFSR, 1967 and 1969.

tons, at Krasnoyarsk (special Bessemer steels),
Petrovsk-Zabaikal'sk (very small), and Komsomol'sk
(Amurstal' steel works). The unit at Petrovsk-
Zabaikal'sk produces rolled products from pig iron
imported from the Urals, Kuzbass, China, and North
Korea. The Krasnoyarsk plant was erected in 1951 and
has small electric furnaces. It imports pig iron
from the neighboring Kuzbass. The Amurstal' steel
works at Komsomol'sk was built in 1942 and has open
hearth furnaces and mills for rolling thin and medium
sheet steel. It formerly depended upon local scrap
and pig iron from China but has been enlarged by the
completion of the first Far East blast furnace and
continuous steel casting facilities and electric
furnaces for high-alloy steels.

Until 1965 pig iron production was only 200,000
tons annually. During 1971-75 additional production
of electric steel furnaces are to be built, as well
as shops for producing electrically welded pipes.
By 1975 the annual output of steel from Amurstal'
will be one million tons.

Steel output will remain small in Pacific Siberia until the long-projected Taishet plant comes
into operation. Taishet will be part of the Third
Metallurgical Base; it will use iron ore from Rudnogorsk about 68 miles away and will specialize in
producing pipes.

Production of rolled ferrous metals is only
around 400,000 tons a year, and sheet metal-using
industries have to import most of their requirements
from the Kuzbass and the Urals. This involves high
freight costs and a high proportion of waste due to
the problem of supplying exact cut-to-size sheets.

Chemicals

The chemical industry uses local resources of
timber, salt, coal, and oil. Oil refineries with
up-to-date cracking installations at Komsomol'sk and
Khabarovsk--producing gasoline, kerosene, oil, and
domestic gas--process oil piped over the Tartar
Strait from Okha and Katangli in the north of Sakhalin

Island.   Khabarovsk also processes crude oil from
West Siberia.

Present oil production from Sakhalin is 2.5 million tons a year (1 percent of U.S.S.R. output) plus
1,000 million cubic meters of natural gas.[4] Sakhalin
oil is of high quality and is suitable for refining
into a wide range of petrochemical by-products; some
is exported to Japan. The kerosene content is relatively low and the proportion of sulfur is less than
2 percent, but extraction costs are the highest in
the U.S.S.R. at 8.43 rubles per ton of oil compared
with the cheapest at 1.55 rubles for Tartar (Volga)
oil. The cost of natural gas is also the highest in
the U.S.S.R. at 4.83 rubles for 1,000 cubic meters
compared with the cheapest cost of 0.14 rubles at
Stavropol' (North Caucasus).[5] Nevertheless, the
Sakhalin oil deposits, and the associated refineries
on the mainland, have had considerable strategic
significance for the U.S.S.R. for over 40 years,
despite the costs involved. No mention was made in
the plan directives for 1971-75 of the exploitation
of oil reserves in Yakutia or at Markovo in the
upper Lena; consequently, Sakhalin will remain the
only local source of oil.

In Eastern Siberia there is an oil refinery at
Angarsk (near Irkutsk); the oil stock comes by pipeline from Bashkiria in the Urals and from the Tyumen'
field in West Siberia. The refinery complex includes
petrochemicals, fuel oils and lubricants, bitumen,
and urea manufacture. In 1971 preparations were
started for the construction of new refineries near
Achinsk (gasoline, diesel fuel, and kerosene) and at
Nakhodka (gasoline, diesel fuel, kerosene, and liquid
gas). The Achinsk refinery will be the largest in
the U.S.S.R. and will receive West Siberian crude
oil by pipeline.

A chemical industry based on sodium chloride,
first mined in the region almost 260 years ago, is
located a little way downstream the Angara from
Angarsk, at Usol'e Sibirskoe. With it are associated
coke-chemical works using Cheremkhovo coal and gypsum-
using industries utilizing the nearby Tyret-Balagansk

deposits. The main items produced at Usol'e are
chlorine, caustic soda, polyvinyl chloride, chlorine
methyl, calcium carbide, synthetic rubber, and lac-
quers; mineral fertilizers will also be manufactured.
Carbamid tar is produced here at about two-thirds
the cost of Kuzbass tar; but polyvinyl chloride,
which costs 520 rubles a ton to make, has to be
shipped to Vladimir near Moscow for processing and
is then sold back to Siberia as plastic at 900-1,000
rubles a ton.[6]

In Krasnoyarsk factories are producing synthetic
fibers (including artificial silk and synthetic cord
fabrics), calcium carbide, synthetic rubber from al-
cohols, and tires (this plant was opened in July,
1960). Caustic soda and chlorine can be made in the
Krasnoyarsk region 25-40 percent cheaper than in the
Donbass or Volga; acetylene is also relatively cheap
to produce, and this should lower the local costs of
production for polyvinyl resins and acetate rayon.

The most rapidly expanding sector of the chemical industry in Pacific Siberia is undoubtedly in
cellulose, wood alcohol, viscose, yeast, resin, and
other timber-derived chemicals. This industry is
considered in more detail in the following chapter.
Mineral fertilizers are produced only in Eastern
Siberia (since 1960); output exceeds 600,000 tons or
two-thirds of West Siberian production. In the fats
and oils industry large amounts of edible (animal)
fats, rather than acid by-products from the petroleum
industry, are used to manufacture soaps. Soap and
detergent output is about one-third of production
levels in West Siberia, but in 1972 the second stage
of the Khabarovsk detergent works will be producing
30,000 tons of powdered and liquid detergents an-
nually--enough, it is claimed, to satisfy the needs
of the entire population of the Far East and Eastern
Siberia.

The greatest problem is the high degree of
specialization in the chemical industry in relation
to the local market; this means that because of inadequate local demand a large proportion of output
has to be shipped elsewhere in the Soviet Union and,

conversely, despite the availability of basic raw
materials, large amounts of salt, sulfuric acid,
alcohol spirit, and chlorine have to be freighted in.

Machine-Building and
Engineering

The machine-building and engineering industries
are widely spread across the southern parts of the
region, but there are major gaps. In the Far East a
Soviet analysis of 20 engineering works showed production costs to be 20 percent higher than in European
Russia, and, for many types of machines, 30-35 percent higher.[7] The high cost of importing sheet and
fabricating steels, the shortage of skilled labor
and high labor turnover, and high wages and plant
construction costs all help to explain this disparity.
The main factories in the Far East are at Khabarovsk;
Vladivostok-Ussuriisk, Komsomol'sk, Blagoveshchensk
(shipbuilding), Svobodnyi (agricultural machinery),
Raichikhinsk (coal-mining equipment), Yuzhno Sakha-
linsk, Petropavlovsk, and Magadan-Orotukan; the main
centers in Eastern Siberia are Krasnoyarsk (agricultural machinery), Irkutsk, Chita (truck assembly,
commencing in 1972), and Ulan-Ude (railway engineering). A large railway wagon works at Abakan (eventual capacity, 40,000 freight cars per year) will
start production in the 1971-75 plan period; a
300,000-ton capacity foundry, sawmills, and concrete
works will be included as ancillary facilities, as
well as worsted cloth, knitwear, shoe, and artificial
leather factories.

Khabarovsk's Energomash works is the U.S.S.R.'s
only producer of medium-size centrifugal compressors,
turboblowers, turbine pumps, and 3,000-kilowatt gas
turbines; a works in Komsomol'sk specializes in
cranes for export. This fits in well with the Soviet
concept of specialization in which a particular plant
supplies a large part of total Soviet requirements of
any one machine, irrespective of local demands. On
the other hand, three-quarters of the region's requirements of machines and engineering products have
to be imported.[8] Locally required products such as
bulldozers, excavators, cranes, and tractors are not

produced at all. Electrical engineering machinery
to service the important electric power generation
industry is inadequately provided by three small factories.

Railway engineering works are located at Ulan-
Ude (including a large repair workshop and the manufacture of some wagons and coaches), Chita, Khabarovsk
(which also has a railway engineering academy), and
near Vladivostok. Krasnoyarsk will have Siberia's
first continuous line for the overhaul of electric
locomotive engines and a works being built there for
the production of 100,000 truck trailers a year, for
the Kama truck factory near Moscow, will be the
largest factory of its kind in the eastern part of
the U.S.S.R. Agricultural machinery is made at
Khabarovsk and Krasnoyarsk (Sibiryak combine harves-
ters). Sovetskaya Gavan' makes seagoing tugs, barges,
and lighters for local use.

Textiles

Statistical data on the textile industry is
much more comprehensive (see Table 6). The woolen
fabric industry is very poorly developed despite regional production of about 20,000 tons of greasy
wool a year. Less than 1,500 tons of scoured wool
is produced, and woolen cloth production, at 1.4 million meters, comes from one factory at Ulan-Ude.
This factory has not increased its output since 1960
and accounts for less than 0.4 percent of Soviet output. Finished woolen fabrics have to be imported in
large quantities from European Russia. East Siberian
consumption of woolen cloth is at least 20 million
meters--indicating a production deficit of around 18
million meters. A new worsted mill with a capacity
of 13.5 million meters was to be completed by the
end of 1971 at Chernogorsk; it will use local wools.[9]
The Far East produces very little wool (the climate
is too damp), and it has no local wool textile industry; it imports an estimated 10 million meters of
woolen cloth per year.

The Far East is also a small producer of cotton
cloth. There is a plant at Birobidzhan in the Jewish

A.O. Far Eastern production almost doubled in the
Seven Year Plan for 1959-65 to 12 million meters; it
has since risen slightly to about 13-14 million
meters. A new cotton-spinning factory at Blagoveshchensk will produce 5,400 tons of cotton yarn annually; it will be associated with a garment factory
recently built at nearby Svobodnyi. In Eastern Siberia the industry is much larger, with an output of
85 million meters in 1969, but it has not expanded
since 1957 when it produced 86.2 million meters.
The main factory at Kansk commenced manufacture in
1945. Over three-quarters of the cotton fabric consumed in Pacific Siberia is imported from other parts
of the U.S.S.R., primarily from European Russia; the
volume of such imports is probably about 260-280 million meters annually.

    Silk fabric (synthetic) is made only at the
Krasnoyarsk Silk Weaving Kombinat; in 1969 it produced 44 million meters of cloth, or about 4 percent
of the entire Soviet output. It is associated with
a large wood-chemical complex.

    Hosiery was not made in the Far East until the
Birobidzhan plant came into operation in 1968; it is
expected to make 30 million pairs of hose per year.[10]
A new hosiery factory was opened in Eastern Siberia
at Cheremkhovo (Irkutsk oblast') in 1967 with a
capacity of 10 million pairs; by March of 1968 output
was reported to be 12 million pairs. The Krasnoyarsk
factory apparently closed down in 1965; in the previous year it had produced only 224,000 pairs. Estimated imports into the whole region on a Soviet
average per capita consumption basis are put at over
70 million pairs.

    The main centers of the knitwear industry are
at Khabarovsk and Irkutsk. Production falls far
short of local demand, but new factories have been
opened at Abakan (capacity, 6 million garments) and
Chita; a knitwear works with a capacity of 4 million
garments annually was opened in Khabarovsk krai in
April, 1971, and another similar works is under construction. In the Seven Year Plan, production of
knitted underwear in Pacific Siberia increased almost

three-fold to 12.3 million pieces and that of outer-
wear by the same amount to 4.3 million pieces. Combined output of knitwear is now about 33 million
garments per year, but supplies per head of population
are less than 20 percent of the Soviet average. The
most rapid expansion is occurring in the Krasnoyarsk
and Khabarovsk regions.

Footwear

The footwear industry is also poorly represented.
The climate dictates a fairly widespread use of felt
and rubber footwear and overshoes in the long winter
months. About 500,000 pairs of felt boots are made
each year in Eastern Siberian factories at Irkutsk
and Krasnoyarsk. Leather footwear accounts for 65
percent of all footwear sales (the average for the
U.S.S.R. is 75 percent), but only about one-third of
demand is met by a local production of 14 million
pairs. The balance, perhaps 18 million pairs, is
imported into Pacific Siberia from factories in
European Russia, particularly Moscow and Leningrad.
As living standards have risen, the demand for such
simple consumer goods as shoes has grown rapidly.
A shortage of leather has resulted in the use of inferior grades.[11] Labor productivity is low, and less
than one-third of the machinery used is modern.
There is also a shortage of chemical materials, such
as polyvinyl-chloride resins. The percentage of
footwear rejects returned from wholesale and retail
outlets is very high, and the problem of quality control is acute. Some factories, such as the one at
Chita, produce a very poor-quality shoe that is heavy
and without gloss. Others are working well below
capacity because of a shortage of leather. Thus,
the new leather footwear kombinat at Ussuriisk produced only 567,000 pairs of shoes in the first six
months of 1968, whereas its rated capacity is 3.5
million pairs per year.[12]

There are plans to build leather footwear factories at Ulan-Ude and Irkutsk, with a combined
capacity of 8 million pairs. In December, 1971, a
plant that can produce 4.2 million pairs per year
started manufacturing in Birobidzhan. The factories

at Krasnoyarsk, Minusinsk, Achinsk, Kansk, Irkutsk,
and Chita use locally produced leathers from the livestock regions to the south (Kyzyl, Kyakhta, and
Sretensk), but in the Far East there has been a
noticeable fall-off in output from the major shoe-
producing regions since the early 1960s because of a
leather shortage. Some factories, such as the one
in Kamchatka, have gone out of production altogether.

Consumer Durables

Consumer durables such as domestic washing machines and radio sets have been manufactured in significant quantities in Pacific Siberia only for about
13 years. Some products, such as domestic refriger-
ators--for which the demand is in any case less than
in the warmer parts of the U.S.S.R.--have been manufactured only since 1965 at Krasnoyarsk (a half million units in 1968). Washing machines are made at
Krasnoyarsk (which also manufactures television sets),
Irkutsk, Khabarovsk, and Ussuriisk; but the biggest
factory is at Ulan-Ude. Total output for Pacific
Siberia is about one machine for every 30 persons,
compared with the U.S.S.R. average of one machine for
60 people. This data suggests a much greater availability of washing machines per head of population
in Pacific Siberia than in the U.S.S.R. as a whole,
but no information is available to indicate whether
all the regional production is consumed locally or
whether a proportion of it is exported to deficit
areas such as West Siberia, where output is only one
machine for every 90 people.

It is not known where in Pacific Siberia the
domestic radio sets are made; production in the Far
East is extremely small and that in Eastern Siberia
is probably centered in Krasnoyarsk. Total output
for the region is probably less than 500,000 units.
Television sets are also manufactured at the Krasnoyarsk factory: Production may now approach 250,000
sets per year.

Furniture

Before the Revolution the furniture industry in
Siberia was poorly developed despite the area's vast

timber resources. Now there is a sizable industry
accounting for about 5 percent of the U.S.S.R.'s
value of output of furniture (122 million rubles in
1967 wholesale prices). There is still a sizable
shortage in meeting local demands. In the past some
Chinese furniture was imported from Heilungkiang
Province to offset local shortages.

The main centers of the furniture-making industry
are in the Krasnoyarsk, Primor'ye, Irkutsk, and Khabarovsk regions; at Khabarovsk, for instance, there
is the Zaria Furniture Kombinat, which makes ward-
robes and cupboards of a reasonable quality, using
local timbers and hardboard (there are sawmills just
to the south of the city at Khor).

Building Materials

The building materials industry has grown rapidly
in response to the high rate of economic development
in Pacific Siberia and the large number of huge construction works being built there. The region produces almost 6 million tons of cement, or about 7
percent of Soviet output; in Eastern Siberia production is increasing at almost 10 percent per year.
About one million tons of cement per year are railed
into the region from West Siberia and the Urals.
Such shipments are sent along the Trans-Siberian
railway at a cost of about 4 rubles per ton per
1,000 kilometers. For the future, expansion is
planned to take place using the Borzya lime deposits
and large quantities of alumina waste (belite slurry)
from Achinsk; the latter will not be suitable for
dam building because of its high alkaline content.
Output of cement from the Novospasskiy works will be
2.3 million tons per year when it is completed.[13]

Pacific Siberia makes asbestos cement tiles (especially in the Buryat region) and pipes, using Ural
asbestos, as well as significant quantities of prefabricated ferro-concrete buildings. (Many apartment
buildings in the region are constructed from prefabricated panels.) There are large factories at
Khor, south of Khabarovsk, for instance. Capital
investment in the building construction industry in

Khabarovsk krai in 1971-75 will be double that of
1966-70; new prefabricated house-building works are
being built at Khabarovsk, Nakhodka, and Komsomol'sk,
each with an annual capacity of about 100,000 square
meters of panels.*

The output of bricks in 1969, at 1,767 million
units, was only 4 percent greater than in 1965. The
shortage of bricks has caused very serious delays in
building programs. Window glass manufacture is over
23 million square meters a year. There is a large
factory at Ulan-Ude (14 million square meters), and
the Tulun works (3 million square meters), which uses
local quartz sand deposits, was opened in 1963. In
the Far East all window glass is made at Raichikhinsk
(6 million square meters). The small factory near
Magadan may have closed down. It is likely that the
region is now self-sufficient in this product, but
some shipments of plate glass shop windows have been
delivered to Nakhodka from Japan.

SOME PROBLEMS OF
MANUFACTURING

Pacific Siberian industries have all the usual
problems of manufacturing enterprises located in a
large sparsely peopled region. Transport costs are
high and the local market is relatively small, which
leads to high unit costs of production. In the long
winter period there are delays in delivering goods to
their correct destinations, and factories suffer
from seasonal variations in production. Wages are
higher in this part of the Soviet Union, thus adding
to manufacturing costs, particularly in labor-intensive industries such as textiles. There is also the
problem of excessive regional specialization, especially in the engineering industry, which gives rise
to the costly cross-hauls previously mentioned. The
alternative--manufacturing only for local needs--is
likely to result in even higher unit costs of production due to the small regional market available.

---

*One square meter = 10.764 square feet.

There is also a grave shortage of productive capacity in some basic industries, such as building materials. This has had an effect on the rate of construction of factory buildings and has offset one of the intended purposes of greater capital investments in the region, i.e., to reduce the number of partly completed construction projects. Table 7 illustrates the problems of regional supply and demand of prefabricated concrete; as a result, building projects frequently remain in a partly finished state for over five years.

There is also a serious problem with the synchronization of interdependent capital works projects; some examples from the Krasnoyarsk-Achinsk region were given in Chapter 3. There are inordinate delays, too, in mastering production techniques once a factory is built. Frequently the project drafting stage is 2-3 years, the time needed for construction varies from 4-5 years up to 7-8 years, and the time required to master production techniques in order to fulfill the planned level of output might take 2-4 years.[14]

TABLE 7

Eastern Siberia--Demand and Supply of Prefabricated
Concrete
('000 cubic meters)

Region	Demand	Supply	Surplus (+) or Deficit (-)
Achinsk	85.3	58.0	-27.3
Abakan-Chernogorsk	86.8	31.0	-55.8
Yeniseisk-Maklakovo	23.2	10.0	-13.2
Kansk	24.8	38.0	+13.2
Tuva	36.7	12.0	-24.7
Krasnoyarsk	374.0	413.0	+39.0
Total	630.8	562.0	-68.8

Source: Voprosy Ekonomiki, No. 5, 1965.

In all, the time lag involved often exceeds 11 years.
This situation is compounded both by a shortage of
skilled labor and by a high labor turnover.

The location of some manufacturing plants has
been irrational. The Eastern Siberian cement manufacturing industry has been criticized because the
processing units are often located far away from
suitable raw materials.[15] For example, the Angarsk
plant uses marble mined in the mountains 106 miles
away; marble is a poor cement material because of
its high magnesium content and the difficulties of
grinding it. Another irrational feature is the use
of long-haul pyrite cinders to ensure a proper iron
oxide-silica mixture. Because Eastern Siberia has
no chemical industry that can supply this product, it
must be railed all the way from Perm' in the Urals.
Granulated blast-furnace slag used in the local manufacture of Portland cement has to be sent to Eastern
Siberia from Novokuznetsk, Chelyabinsk, and Nizhniy
Tagil. Blast-furnace slag cement is more expensive
to manufacture than ordinary Portland cement of the
same type; moreover, it has no particular market in
Eastern Siberia and large amounts have to be back-
hauled to West Siberia.

High production costs as well as transport costs
are typical of the Siberian cement industry. Average
costs of production are 15 rubles per ton, compared
with a European Russian figure of about 9 rubles.
It is expected that the use of alumina waste materials
will reduce costs to 6 rubles; at that price the
East Siberian industry will be able to supply some
cement to the Far East, where manufacturing costs
are even higher--at over 18 rubles per ton.

The cement industry happens to be a well-docu-
mented but not isolated case study of a Siberian manufacturing industry. Another is the Krasnoyarsk
refrigerator plant, which produces 500,000 refrigerators per year, using sheet metal from far-off Chere-
povets, north of Moscow; if cut-to-size sheet metal
was supplied, waste materials would be reduced by
20-25 percent, i.e., equivalent to an additional
100,000 refrigerators.[16]

As a result of delays in the manufacture of
building materials, considerable funds allotted to
capital works are unused; the building of the chemical complex at Usol'e Sibirskoe has been slowed down
for several years because of this factor. Lack of
coordination between the planning agencies responsible for manufacturing industry and housing also means
that a shortage of houses has hindered the recruitment of adequate numbers of workers to operate plants
at full capacity. In addition, in the past some
workers in light industry did not get all of the
special regional wage incentives other workers
received.

THE FIVE YEAR PLANS

The Five Year Plan for 1966-70 recognized that
light and other manufacturing industries were insuf-
ficiently developed in Pacific Siberia. Still, most
of the planned development for Siberia centered
around the use of natural resources such as minerals,
timber, and hydro-electric power. For manufacturing
industries development will proceed slowly, although
processes associated with the simpler forms of manufacturing, such as aluminum extrusions (Krasnoyarsk)
and cardboard (Amursk), will develop. Chemicals and
electrochemicals should expand rapidly at Angarsk,
Usol'e Sibirskoe, and Krasnoyarsk, together with textiles at Chita. Typical small plants being put into
commission include a fertilizer plant and a paint
and lacquer factory at Zima; a knitted underwear
kombinat at Nizhneudinsk; steel frames and engineering works at Cheremkhovo; concrete wall panels at
Taishet; felt boots, brickworks, and building materials at Tulun; light aluminum and plastic construc-
tions at Shelekhov; and a porcelain works at Vladivo-
stok--with a capacity of 8 million articles in 1971,
rising to 24 million at full capacity.

The broad aim of the last Five Year Plan was to
make East Siberia and the Far East self-sufficient
in products such as footwear, clothing, and other
consumer goods. At the present time the output of
these commodities is two to three times less per

capita than the average for the U.S.S.R. Annual incomes per head increased by about 60 percent in gross terms between 1965 and 1970, compared with real per capita increases for the work force of the U.S.S.R. as a whole of 33 percent. However, a great deal of the apparent benefits of higher gross wages in Pacific Siberia are eroded by the higher price of both local and imported goods and services.

In the new Five Year Plan for 1971-75 the economies of Siberia and the Far East are planned to grow by 50 percent, compared with an expected increase in the national income of the U.S.S.R. as a whole of 37-40 percent.[17] About 80 percent of the growth of the Soviet eastern regions is planned to be achieved through higher productivity. Industrial output in the Primor'ye and Khabarovsk krais will grow by 70 percent and 60 percent, respectively, in 1971-75, compared with 47 percent for the U.S.S.R. as a whole; consumer goods, chemicals, and machine building will be the main growth sectors.[18] More capital-intensive industrial complexes will be established at such locations as Sayan in Eastern Siberia (near the Sayan-Shushenskoe hydro plant), where an aluminum works, electrical engineering factory, steel foundry, railway carriage works, and food industry enterprises are planned to begin production during the five-year period. Automation and computer control systems are expected to reduce the demand for labor at such new industrial complexes. A Minsk 32 computer is in operation at the Krasnoyarsk aluminum works, and computer centers equipped with Minsk 22 computers have begun work at the Krasnoyarsk krai statistical directorate and Glavkrasnoyarskstroi (Krasnoyarsk Chief Construction Department). The wide use of computers in the krai's industry will probably serve as a pilot project for the rest of Pacific Siberia.

NOTES

1. Voprosy Ekonomiki, No. 8, 1966.

2. Voprosy Ekonomiki, No. 10, 1965.

3. P. P. Silinskii, Planirovanie Narodnogo
Khozyaistva v Oblasti (Moscow, 1967).

4. M. M. Brenner, Ekonomika Neftyanoi i Gazovoi
Promyshlennosti SSSR (Moscow, 1968), pp. 33-36; BBC
Summary of World Broadcasts, Part I, U.S.S.R., Sep-
tember 24, 1971.

5. Ya G. Feigin, ed., Problemy Ekonomicheskoi
Effektivnosti Razmeshcheniya Sotsialisticheskogo
Proizvodstva v SSSR (Moscow: AN SSSR, 1968), p. 218;
and M. M. Brenner, op. cit., pp. 178 and 180.

6. Voprosy Ekonomiki, No. 8, 1966.

7. Voprosy Ekonomiki, No. 10, 1965.

8. Voprosy Ekonomiki, No. 8, 1966.

9. BBC Summary of World Broadcasts, September
13, 1971.

10. Ibid., January 22, 1968.

11. Ekonomicheskaya Gazeta, No. 12, March, 1967,
p. 17.

12. Pravda, October 5, 1968 (quoting N. Tarasov,
Minister for Light Industry).

13. BBC Summary of World Broadcasts, October 12,
1971.

14. Problemy Ekonomicheskogo Stimulirovaniya
Nauchno-Tekhnicheskogo Progressa (Moscow: AN SSSR,
1967), pp. 102-19.

15. V. P. Gukov, Doklady Instituta Geografiy
Sibiri i Dal'nego Vostoka, No. 4, 1963, pp. 49-55.

16. Pravda, January 5, 1968.

17. BBC Summary of World Broadcasts, September
24, 1971.

18.   Ibid., January 7 and 14, 1972; industrial output in Magadan oblast' is to increase by 54 percent, but in the Amur oblast' (42 percent) and Sakhalin oblast' (35 percent) it will be below the Soviet average.

CHAPTER

5

**PRESENT
STRENGTHS:
FISH
AND TIMBER**

The timber and fish industries are especially
important to the Pacific Siberian economy not only
because of their employment of labor but also because
of the large surpluses of products they generate for
export both to other regions of the U.S.S.R. and
overseas. In this latter aspect they are different
from other industries in the region (except furs,
gold, diamonds, and--increasingly--minerals). Pacific Siberia's exports of timber and fish help to
pay for imports of essential foodstuffs and manufactured goods in the regional balance of trade. The
U.S.S.R. has resources of timber and fish in Pacific
Siberia on a world scale, and, given reasonable care,
they should last indefinitely. Both commodities
should find a ready and continuing market (subject to
quality) both in the U.S.S.R. and in the Pacific region generally--especially Japan.

The fishing industry of the Far East produces
about one-third of the Soviet catch, or some 2.5 million tons. In terms of the regional economy, about
one-quarter of gross industrial output is derived
directly from fishing. The industry is located almost exclusively in Kamchatka (35 percent), Primor'ye
(33 percent), and Sakhalin (22 percent).[1] The main
fishing grounds are the coastal waters of the Japan
Sea, the Sea of Okhotsk, and the Bering Sea, although
fishing vessels based in the Far East make catches
in the South Pacific, Indian Ocean, and Antarctic

waters. By 1975 the volume of fish marketed from
the Far East is planned to be 50 percent more than
in 1970, but there are several factors that may cause
this target to be underfulfilled. The proportion of
inedible fish caught is rising as fishermen endeavor
to attain planned quotas set too high and without
much regard to quality differentials. Another disadvantage is the limited assortment of fish landed
(mainly herring, flounder, and cod) and the resulting
marketing problems. Repair and unloading facilities
are also inadequate for the trawler fleet; improvements to the major ports of the Far East are planned,
but fish landings are expected to be much larger.
Other problems in this industry relate to the severe
seasonal shortage of process workers and the high
transport cost on fish carried to European Russia
by the Trans-Siberian railway.

The timber industry is also important to the
Pacific Siberian economy, particularly to that of
Eastern Siberia. In the Far East timber and woodworking account for only 13 percent of the value of
industrial output, but in Eastern Siberia the proportion is over 18 percent and it occupies 31 percent
of the industrial work force.[2] Siberia and the Far
East contain most of the unexploited timber reserves
of the U.S.S.R.: Eastern Siberia alone has over 50
percent of the Soviet total, and the Far East has
another 17 percent. Access to the Siberian taiga
(dense forest), however, is difficult, and the distances involved in getting the felled timber to European Russian markets are great. Consequently, the
rate of forest exploitation is low; in Eastern Siberia, which has the richest timber reserves in the
U.S.S.R., the annual cut is only some 13 percent of
the estimated possible utilization. Also, sawmill
capacity is inadequate, which means that over one-
half of the timber sent out of the region has to be
shipped in the form of unprocessed round logs. The
resultant costs of haulage have been estimated at
about one and one-half times more than production
costs.[3] Some of the timber is sent overseas; the
region ships around one-fifth of Soviet timber exports.

The wood-using industries, including pulp, paper, cardboard, plywood, and wood-derived chemicals, are not very highly developed at present. Almost one-half of the paper and cardboard produced still comes from the southern part of Sakhalin Island, where the industry was started by the Japanese before World War II. The wood-chemical industry, after many years of neglect, is developing quickly in new industrial complexes at Bratsk, Krasnoyarsk, and Amursk.

THE FISHING INDUSTRY

In 1913 the Far East fisheries caught only 107,200 tons of fish--little more than 10 percent of the Russian commercial catch; the Caspian Sea accounted for 61 percent. Fifty years later the position had changed entirely with the Caspian producing less than 8 percent of the catch and the Far East, 35 percent. This radical geographical change was marked by a switch in the Soviet era to ocean fishing. As the Caspian, Aral, and Azov seas continue to present difficulties with silting and salinity it can be expected that the Far East fishing grounds will become more and more important. The relatively high volume of capital investment needed in this industry is a restraining factor, but in the long run the fish resources of the Far East and the north Pacific may well be developed as export industries to meet some Asian, as well as Soviet and Japanese, needs. Soviet technology is already being used to advance the fishing industries of many developing countries; Asia has a great need for protein and fertilizer.

Regionally, the west coast of Kamchatka, the estuary of the Amur, and the Okhotsk coastline and southern parts of Sakhalin are especially dependent upon this industry. In Kamchatka the fishing industry provides almost three-quarters of gross industrial output and employs directly and indirectly 70 percent of the work force.[4] The benefits to Kamchatka of this extreme specialization are its exports of 420,000 tons of fish--mainly herring, flounder, salmon, and

crab (local consumption is only 4,400 tons). The
fish exported helps to pay for imports of oil (300,000
tons), coal (421,000 tons), timber (180,000 cubic
meters), cement (52,000 tons), salt (65,000 tons),
meat (10,000 tons), vegetables (16,400 tons), and
grains (38,200 tons). These interregional trade
flows illustrate the importance of the fishing industry to the economy of certain parts of Pacific Siberia. Along the coastline fishing generally con-
stitutes the only source of livelihood and the only
reason for habitation other than fur hunting and
reindeer farming.

Development

The initial progress of the industry was slow.
Before the Revolution and until the late 1920s development was largely in the hands of the Japanese.
Under the terms of the Russo-Japanese Fishing Convention of 1906, Japanese fishermen had the same rights
as Russians to fish in the Sea of Okhotsk. During
the Allied intervention the Japanese took advantage
of the confused situation to put all the fisheries
of the lower Amur, Sakhalin, and associated islands
under their control. Later they seized the Kamchatka
fisheries. After the withdrawal by Japan from northern Sakhalin in 1925 the Soviets found that they
still needed help from Japanese seasonal workers for
the canneries. (In 1928, 53 percent of the seasonal
workers in the Far Eastern fishing industry were
Japanese.) But in 1933 the U.S.S.R. announced that
it required no more Japanese assistance.

In the Second Five Year Plan (1933-37) extensive
provision was made for port facilities, cold storage
plants, canneries, and vessels. As a result of this
determined effort, and the creation of a large State-
owned trawler fleet, the Far East fish catch rose
from 162,000 tons in 1928 to 347,000 tons in 1932
and 405,000 tons in 1937; the number of canneries
increased from 2 in 1913 to 42 in 1938. After World
War II the Japanese lost the rich fishing grounds
off the Kurile Islands and southern Sakhalin as well
as the concessions to fish for salmon in the Kamchatka rivers; the Russians also imposed a 12-mile

limit that restricted foreign fishing activities even
further.

In 1956 a ten-year Soviet-Japanese Fishing Agreement was signed, fixing quotas for Japanese catches
in North-West Pacific waters and declaring the waters
of the Sea of Okhotsk a restricted area.[5] The quotas
for salmon have declined steadily since 1957, and
there have been frequent arrests of Japanese fishermen for infringing upon the 12-mile limit. Annual
conferences on fish quotas still take place; in 1969
Japan suspended catches of flatfish off Kamchatka
owing to strong Russian pressure and a desire to
protect valuable salmon fishing rights off Soviet
territory. In 1971 the U.S.S.R. declared that fishing
for crab on the continental shelf--over which it
claims sovereign rights--would be further restricted
and that fishing for herring in the Sea of Okhotsk
was banned.

Output

Detailed data on the Far East fish catch by
quantity, type, and location is difficult to obtain
through Soviet sources. The fact that a large part
of the catch is inedible has given rise to attempts
to cover up the facts. In 1966 Dal'ryba (Far Eastern Fishing Department) caught 2,056,600 metric tons
live weight of fish but only a little over one-half
(1,098,100 tons) was actually used for fish products;
of this amount 711,400 tons were processed for foodstuffs. The balance of 386,700 tons was inedible
(see Table 8). Compared with 1964 the edible portion
fell from 42 percent to 35 percent of the gross
catch, the inedible portion rising from 13 percent
to 19 percent (U.S.S.R. average is about 16 percent).
Most of the inedible fish is manufactured into fertilizer or animal meal and fodder for local agriculture
as well as into feed for the fur-farming industry.

In the Seven Year Plan the Far East fish catch
grew by 134 percent, compared with the average for
the U.S.S.R. of 97 percent; taking into account,
however, the net output of foodstuffs only, the rate
of growth was 60 percent for the U.S.S.R. and 56

percent for the Far East. It is not surprising, then,
that a special conference was held in 1968 at Vladivostok to discuss the problems of the Far Eastern fishing industry.[6] As a result of the conference a new
method of incentive payment was introduced in which
fishermen's earnings depend on the catch of first-
grade fish for foodstuffs; wages were expected to
rise by at least one-quarter over the old quota system. The planned gross fish catch for 1970 was almost 3 million tons (an increase of 50 percent over
1965), but--probably because of the new quota system--
the actual catch was only 2.5 million tons (an increase of 25 percent). In future the catch is not
likely to increase by much more than 200,000 tons a
year. Thus, by 1975 output is likely to be around
3.3 million tons, or still about one-third of the
planned total for the U.S.S.R. of 10 million tons.
The original target for 1975 was 3.7 million tons.

The importance of particular departments of
Dal'ryba as producers of fish is shown in Table 9.
During the ten years for which data is available,
Kamchatka's share of the catch has fallen markedly
from 35 percent to 21 percent; and Sakhalin's also
fell slightly from 20 percent to under 19 percent.
The most important change was the rapid expansion of
the Primor'ye fisheries from 36 percent of the catch
in 1955 to almost 52 percent in 1965. Considering
the concentration of the oceangoing fleet in Vladivostok and Nakhodka, this trend has probably continued. These two ports are better equipped with
handling and unloading facilities and ship repair
yards (Vladivostok also builds trawlers) than any
other ports in the Far East. They have railway links
for quick movement of fish to European Russia. In
Kamchatka and Sakhalin, on the other hand, there is
not only a shortage of port and repair facilities
but the fish unloaded there has to be back-hauled,
after processing, and reloaded onto mainland railway
terminals for marketing. The oceangoing nature of
the Primor'ye fleet enables it to range well into
the Pacific, Indian, and Antarctic oceans in the
northern hemisphere winters, as well as being active
in the northern Pacific waters in the summer. The
running expenses, including repairs and crew accommo-

TABLE 8

Far East Fish Catch by End Uses
(thousand metric tons)

End Use	1964	Percent	1965	Percent	1966	Percent
Live weight catch	1,785.1	100.0	1,981.6	100.0	2,056.6	100.0
Fish products output	968.2	54.3	1,049.7	53.0	1,098.1	53.4
Foodstuffs	743.7	41.7	719.9	36.3	711.4	34.6
Nonfoodstuffs	224.5	12.6	329.8	16.7	386.7	18.8
Fishmeal	63.1	3.5	80.6	4.1	88.5	4.3
Technical[a]	134.8	7.6	228.1	11.5	276.8	13.5
Not specified	26.6	1.5	21.1	1.1	21.4	1.0

[a]Fertilizer and animal feedstuffs.

Source: I. P. Mal'tsev, Ekonomicheskoe Stimulirovanie v Rybnoi Promyshlennosti v Novykh Usloviyakh Planirovaniya (Moscow, 1968), p. 10.

dation, of a large refrigerated trawler based at
Vladivostok or Nakhodka are 500,000 rubles less per
year than for such a ship based on Kamchatka.[7]

Most of the fish caught by the Magadan and
Khabarovsk departments is coastal or river (salmon
and some herring). In Sakhalin and Kamchatka the
share of locally caught fish is as low as 20-25 percent because of the increasing emphasis on deep-sea
fishing, especially in the Bering Sea. Much of the
coastal fishing is organized by collective fisheries
with small boats; they are particularly active during
the main fishing season (second and third quarters of
the year) and, at other times, engage in forestry
(Sakhalin), agriculture (Amur), or trapping (Kamchatka)
to supplement their incomes.

Species and Fishing Grounds

The species of fish caught in the Far East are
mainly herring (32 percent of the catch), flounder
(29 percent), and Pacific cod (15 percent), including
large quantities of Alaskan pollack. Pacific salmon
comprises less than 10 percent of the catch. The
balance of some 14 percent is mainly whales, crab,
sardine, redfish, and Pacific saury (mullet). Generally, not more than 20 species of fish are caught in
Far Eastern waters, whereas Japanese fishermen in
the same waters use more than 100 species for food.
Sea products such as octopus, cuttlefish, and oysters
are not popular in the U.S.S.R., and so far the
catches of tuna, sea perch, bream, mackerel, sardine,
and anchovy are small. In Kamchatka and the adjoining mainland the rivers are visited every year by
large shoals of red, silver, and king salmon. King
crabs have moved south since the early 1960s from
the west coast of Kamchatka, where Bol'sheretsk was
the most famous center, to the southern Kuriles
(Kunashir and Shikotan islands). Marine mammals
such as seal, walrus, and whale are hunted in the
Bering Sea.

Before the Revolution, in 1913, salmon comprised
89 percent of all fish caught. But by 1957 this had

TABLE 9

Far East Fish Catch by Departments of Dal'ryba
(thousand metric tons)

Department	1955		1960		1965	
	Quantity	Percent	Quantity	Percent	Quantity	Percent
Khabarovsk	33.0	5.2	53.9	6.2	107.9	5.4
Kamchatka	222.9	35.1	253.8	29.5	418.1	21.1
Sakhalin	129.1	20.3	168.4	19.6	370.2	18.7
Primorye	228.3	36.0	364.1	42.3	1,023.7	51.7
Magadan Trust	21.5	3.4	20.8	2.4	61.7	3.1
Far East	634.8[a]	100.0	861.0	100.0	1,981.6	100.0
Far East as percent of U.S.S.R.		23.2		24.3		34.3

[a]Other sources put this figure at 647.4 (24.6 percent of U.S.S.R.).

Sources: N. P. Susoev, Razmeshchenie Rybnoi Promyshlennosti (Moscow, 1967), p. 62; Narodnoe Khozyaistvo SSSR v 1965 god.

89

fallen to less than 19 percent, and in subsequent
years it has fallen even further under the quota re-
straints agreed to with the Japanese; in 1963 and
1964 the proportion was as low as 9 percent and 6
percent, respectively. Herring is now the dominant
species caught (about one-third of the catch); the
main fishing grounds are the Olyutor Bay in northeast
Kamchatka and off the Okhotsk-Magadan coast (see
Table 10). Some is caught in the winter in the
Bristol and Alaska bays because formerly rich herring
grounds, such as the Babushkin Bay off Magadan Province, have been overfished. Pacific cod is rapidly
increasing in importance, especially Alaskan pollack
caught in the Primor'ye seas and off the Chukotka
coast in Anadyr Bay. The Bering Sea is the main
fishing ground for flounder, redfish, and mackerel.
Mullet is caught off the South Kuriles, where there
is also halibut in commercial quantities. The east
coast of Sakhalin is important for herring, cod, and
mackerel. Whales comprise some 10 percent or so of
total landings, but seal hunting and shrimp fishing
are done only on a small scale as yet.

       Of the edible fish varieties landed in the Far
East, over one-half is frozen for marketing. There
are 116 coastal cooling stores in the Far East; the
largest stores are at Nakhodka, Vladivostok, and
Petropavlovsk-Kamchatskii. Their total daily freezing capacity is about 2,000 tons, or 34 percent of
Soviet total capacity. Utilization of cooling stores
capacities is 99.5 percent (U.S.S.R. average is only
78 percent), indicating a high degree of pressure on
available resources. By 1975 the output of frozen
fish is planned to increase by 44 percent, compared
with 50 percent for chilled and lightly salted fish.
Salted herrings and other salted fish are still very
important products in the Soviet diet, although they
have declined relatively from over one-half the catch
ten years ago to about 30 percent.

                        Canneries

       Canning was greatly stimulated by the increased
output of salmon and crabs, which were in demand before World War II not only in Central Russia but also

TABLE 10

Far East Fish Catch by Fishing Grounds
(thousand tons)

Fish Species	Bering Sea	Olyutor Bay[a]	North Kuriles-West Kamchatka	Okhotsk-Magadan	Pri-mor'ye	Sa-khalin	East Kam-chatka	Amur	South Kuriles	Total
Herring	24.5	164.0	2.9	117.2	0.9	11.0	--	--	--	320.5
Mullet	--	--	--	--	--	--	--	--	44.8	44.8
Large chastik[b]	61.9	--	--	--	6.6	--	--	5.5	0.1	74.1
Redfish	61.7	--	--	--	1.0	--	--	--	--	62.7
Pacific cod	--	--	2.7	--	0.6	0.8	5.3	--	--	9.4
Wachna cod[c]	--	--	15.7	0.4	1.4	3.8	4.7	0.1	--	26.1
Alaskan pollack[c]	--	--	--	--	79.4	14.6	3.2	--	--	97.2
Small chastik[b]	--	--	3.5	0.1	7.4	9.9	1.7	4.9	--	27.5
Flounder	142.8	0.1	48.8	--	5.6	7.4	14.3	--	--	219.0
Paltus	1.0	0.1	0.2	--	--	--	0.6	--	--	1.9
Others	10.7	--	13.0	14.5	2.1	7.7	14.5	12.8	--	75.3
Shrimp	0.25	--	--	--	--	--	--	0.02	--	0.27

[a]Northeast Kamchatka.
[b]Large and small chastik are species of redfish and mackerel.
[c]Wachna cod and Alaskan pollack are species of Pacific cod.

Source: A. N. Ivanis, Rybnaya Promyshlennost' Dal'nego Vostoka (Vladivostok, 1963), pp. 47-48; data exclude salmon, crab, seals, and whales.

on export markets. Canneries were established along
the coast, especially in Kamchatka and later in Sakhalin. By 1955 there were about 600, mostly small,
processing plants along the whole coastline. Many
small enterprises were closed down or amalgamated in
the following years to obtain economies of scale.

Between 1960 and 1965 canned fish production
rose from 146.7 million cans to 243.9 million cans
when it accounted for almost 26 percent of total
Soviet output. Only the Western, Atlantic-based canneries were slightly more important. Up to 1965 the
Far East was the only Soviet territorial fishing
ground where floating canneries were operating. The
most important of these are the crab catching and
processing fleet. Floating canneries for salmon (in
the open seas) and, more recently, for Pacific mullet
are also very active. About one-half of the Far
East's canned fish output comes from floating canneries. Because of the seasonal nature of fishing and
the problem of coping with spells of bad weather it
is usual to have some unused shore-based canning capacity; in the Far East there are few alternative
products, such as vegetables or fruit, to can, and
the floating canneries enable a higher utilization
of capacity to be attained. Total output of canned
fish in 1969 was probably about 330 million cans--
up about 35 percent over 1965. By 1975 shore enterprises in the Primor'ye will be producing another 8
million cans, and Nakhodka will have the largest
fish cannery in the U.S.S.R. (construction started
in 1971).

Fishing Fleet

Dal'ryba's headquarters in Vladivostok controls
the entire Far Eastern fishing fleet, including fish-
catching, processing, cool stores, whaling, and fishing expeditions. Four whaling fleets operate from
Far Eastern waters: "Aleut" (1933), "Vladivostok"
(1963), "Sovetskaya Rossiya" (1961), and "Dal'nii
Vostok" (1964). The first two whale in the waters
of the Kurile, Commander, and Aleutian islands. The
latter two operate there only in the summer (processing fish); in the winter they are whaling in Antarctic

TABLE 11

Fishing Vessels Used by Dal'ryba

BMRT   Large refrigerated trawler; engine capac-
              ity, 2,000 HP (10 percent).

SRTR   Medium-sized trawler with cooling hold;
              engines, 400-540 HP (25 percent).

SRT   Medium-sized trawler; length 30-35 meters;
              engines, 300-400 HP (40 percent).

SO, RS   RS = fishing seiner. SO = oceangoing
              seiner. Both same length and power as SRT
              (20 percent).

Other vessels are small coastal boats, mainly MRS-80
type.

Source: F. V. D'yakonov et al., Dal'nii Vostok, ekonomiko-geograficheskaya kharakteristika
(Moscow: AN SSSR, 1966), p. 132.

waters. Excluding whalers, medium-sized trawlers
are the most important component of the fleet, but
the emphasis now is on commissioning large refrigerated vessels and floating factory ships.

The emphasis in commissioning new vessels is
mainly on the large BMRT type (see Table 11), which
are most efficient in their operations. The growing
oceangoing component of the fleet is explained by
the need to exploit more distant fish resources.
The Sea of Japan is already heavily fished; as
trawling extends to the Alaska and Bristol bays,
Queen Charlotte Islands, and the south Pacific and
Indian oceans, the need for larger oceangoing vessels
increases.

Larger vessels also can be more closely geared
to the large shore-based rybokombinats (fish-processing factories), which are capable of processing
20,000-30,000 tons of fish per year and frequently
contain cool stores, a cannery, oil and fish meal
manufacturing, and sometimes salting and vitamin-
producing facilities. There are 35 such units in the
Far East.

The Far Eastern fishing fleet in 1966 numbered
5,320 vessels (3,200 self-propelled); Dal'ryba's
capital investment in it was 4,444 million rubles.
The Deep-Sea Long Range Department alone had 22
BMRTs, 15 SRT/SRTRs, four tuna catchers (for the
Indian Ocean), two tuna mother ships, and three
floating factories. In the 1966-70 plan period, over
500 additional fish-catching, processing, and transport vessels were acquired by the Far East fleet at
a capital cost of 630 million rubles; this represented
70 percent of its total capital investments. The Far
Eastern fleet is being provided with the most modern
equipment. Another 500 vessels will be purchased
in 1971-75, including 17 large factory ships; some
of the vessels will be built in Poland and East Germany as well as locally at Nikolaev.

Collectives

The organization of fisheries in the Far East
is divided between State-owned units and collective
fisheries. Collective fisheries account for about
25-30 percent of the catch. Gradually their share
is declining--mainly because most of them cannot afford large seagoing vessels and, also, because of
the declining productivity of the coastal fishing
grounds. The number of marine fishing kolkhozy has
fallen from a peak of about 300 in the early 1950s
to 148 in 1960 and 82 in 1965. Over one-half the
fishing kolkhozy in the Far East are in Khabarovsk
krai, particularly along the lower Amur, north of
Komsomol'sk, for seasonal salmon fishing. Collectives
in Magadan provide slightly less than one-half the
oblast's catch, mainly herring and salmon.

The Far East collective fisheries are the most
productive in the U.S.S.R.; in 1970 their gross

income exceeded 155 million rubles. In the past the
collective fisheries have delivered most of their
catch to the State rybokombinats for processing, but,
recently, some collectives have undertaken their own
processing, due to the shortage of imported seasonal
labor to operate the rybokombinats. Collective processing saves the State monies normally spent on
transportation of seasonal labor and housing. Some
collectives are renting fishing vessels from State
enterprises, although many still own sail- or rowboats;
in Kamchatka such small boats operate within the 20-
mile coastal zone.* In the next few years the collectives will acquire about 130 new vessels, enabling
them to bring their fish catch to perhaps 800,000 tons
by 1975, or still about 23 percent of the total Far
Eastern catch.

Costs and Prices

For a long time the fishing industry was not
profitable. In 1955 Dal'ryba had a loss of 118 million rubles.[8] For the four years ended 1967 it made
a profit of 333 million rubles. This change was due
partly to greater productivity through the introduction of BMRTs, especially since 1963, and partly to
a more realistic pricing policy introduced under the
new economic reforms. Nevertheless, serious anoma-
lies still exist. Complaints have been raised about
the inflexibility of prices in relation to changing
market conditions. The fish species for which there
is now a high market demand sometimes make a loss;
the production cost of one ton of frozen cod is 390
rubles, but its selling price is only 270 rubles.[9]
On the other hand, frozen Pacific herring, for which
there is diminishing demand in the U.S.S.R., costs
190 rubles a ton to produce but sells for 580 rubles.
Almost all of the chilled fish delivered at sea by

---

*In Kamchatka the collectives provide 47 percent
of the catch and act as suppliers to the rybokombinats; some of them are buying BMRTs (e.g., the Lenin
collective, which has 2,000 members, catches 80,000
tons of fish and owns 30 large ships, including five
BMRTs).

Kamchatka's SRT fishing vessels to the refrigerator
ships of Vostokrybkholodflot (the Far Eastern Refrigerated Trawler Fleet, a branch of Dal'ryba) is sold
at a loss.[10] The alternative is to freeze and double-
load the fish caught in Kamchatka, transport it to a
Primor'ye port, and then reload it onto railway cars
for transport to markets in European Russia. Vostokrybkholodflot caught and processed over two million
tons of fish in the last Five Year Plan (1966-70)
and, not surprisingly, made a profit of 68.5 million
rubles.

Sakhalinrybprom (the Sakhalin Fishing Industry)
is sustaining a loss of about four-five million rubles a year, mainly because the price obtained from
Dal'ryba for Alaskan pollack (40 percent of the catch)
does not cover costs.[11] Dal'ryba has fixed low purchasing prices for fish delivered to it (about 60
rubles per ton) but after processing obtains 120
rubles of profit for each ton of frozen pollack. In
addition, because of delays by Dal'ryba in paying for
the fish delivered to it, the Sakhalin fisheries incurred extra interest charges for overdue credit
from the Gosbank (State Bank) of 450,000 rubles in
1967.

Profitability can be increased for some fish
species by shifting to a higher-quality end-product.
Pacific strong-salted herring incurs a loss of 240
rubles a ton, whereas medium- and mild-salted products
bring in a profit of 300-440 rubles. Losses are incurred when a large part of the catch has to be manufactured into fishmeal because of poor quality or
spoiling; the price received for this fish is less
than one-third of the edible price.

Costs of production have tended to increase
quite sharply with mounting delays incurred in unloading fish either at the ports or onto processing
ships. In the first three-quarters of 1968 the fishing boats of Sakhalin lost 1,633 ship days as a result of this. Running costs of a BMRT are about
4,500 rubles a day and delays are costly. The fleet's
efficiency also drops because of delays in Nakhodka
and Vladivostok, which are not able to provide suffi-

ciently rapid unloading and servicing. Studies are
being made of the possibility of transshipping fish
direct from the fishing grounds to European Russian
ports.

Labor Force and Marketing Problems

There are some 160,000 fishermen in the Far
East. These are supplemented each year by about
20,000 imported seasonal workers who work mainly in
the coastal canneries.* They arrive for work in the
second and third quarters of the year when most of
the fish is caught. The working time lost by each
seasonal worker traveling to and from the Far East
fisheries is about one month on the average. If,
instead, they were gainfully employed in manufacturing
enterprises at home, they could produce an additional
40-50 million rubles worth of commodities. The labor
efficiency of temporary seasonal workers is, as a
rule, about 30 percent below the level attained by
permanent workers. The labor shortage is such that
crews load and unload their own fishing vessels.
Labor-intensive operations, such as filleting, are
not carried out, which means the Far East has to
forego potential income.

The retail outlets in the U.S.S.R. have problems
in selling the type of fish supplied by the Far East.
In the first quarter of the year, for instance, 80
percent of the fish from the Far East is flounder.
Fish still are being caught, irrespective of the
level of market demand, just to fulfill some arbitrary
quota set by Gosplan. Potentially valuable earners
of foreign exchange, such as Alaskan pollack or hake,
are virtually ignored, whereas others in strong domestic demand, such as herring or salmon roe, are
processed in an inferior way and lose quality. In
the retail shops so-called fresh frozen fish is often
presented on display in unappetizing 20-kilogram
cartons containing a great variety of hardly distin-

---

*It costs the State 300-400 rubles a head in
transport for seasonal workers.

guishable species.[12] Herring is delivered in 200-
kilogram barrels, and, in a typical village shop, a
large part of it will go rotten. More urban processing kombinats are required in order to present the
fish in an attractive way to Soviet consumers. Fish-
catching facilities in the Far East have outstripped
the capabilities of the Soviet work force and marketing system to deal with them.

THE TIMBER INDUSTRY

Before the Revolution the timber industry in
Siberia was poorly developed. The difficult terrain,
lack of transport facilities, and long distances from
major Russian markets favored timber production in
the north and northwest of European Russia. Transportation still is a serious problem for low-cost
timber exploitation in Siberia. The only alternative
to the Trans-Siberian railway is the short ice-free
season for river transport.

Until about the mid-1950s the corrective labor
camps in Siberia were very largely concerned with
lumbering, but productivity was relatively low because of the lack of experience and poor condition
of many of the laborers.[13] With the withdrawal of
forced labor after Stalin's death in 1953 the production of timber in such labor camp areas as Magadan
oblast', for instance, fell by almost 75 percent.

Resources

There is a large discrepancy between the vast
resources of timber in Pacific Siberia, especially
in Eastern Siberia, and the scale of current output.
Utilization rates in accessible forests are low,
and output is largely restricted to unprocessed
round logs because of the lack of sawmills and processing plants. Eastern Siberia's timber resources
(including Yakutia) amount to 50 percent of the Soviet
total, or 38,700 million cubic meters.* The estimated

---

*Seven cubic meters = 35.3 cubic feet or 423.8
super feet solid volume.

amount of timber available for cutting annually is
about 750 million cubic meters. The estimated possible annual cutting from accessible reserves is 384
million cubic meters, but actual removals in 1969
were only 17 percent of that amount--and of this
only 50 million cubic meters was commercial timber.

     In the Far East timber removals are a higher
proportion of the possible cut (20 percent in 1969).
Total resources are estimated at 11,700 million cubic
meters, and the possible annual cutting is around 121
million cubic meters. Removals were some 24 million
cubic meters in 1969 of which four-fifths was classified as commercial. The annual growth alone in the
exploited forests of Pacific Siberia is between 1.0
and 1.1 cubic meters per hectare (14 cubic feet per
acre), and this in itself provides 462 million cubic
meters of new exploitable timber every year--361 million for Eastern Siberia and 101 million for the Far
East. There is some doubt about the definition of
"exploitable" in both the physical and economic
sense, and the Soviets seem optimistic in this regard. Very substantial timber resources do exist,
however, in Krasnoyarsk (where there is perhaps four
billion cubic meters of high-quality easily accessible timber), Irkutsk, and Khabarovsk territories;
between them, these three regions have two-fifths of
the U.S.S.R.'s resources of mature timber. Nevertheless, the forests in the south of Irkutsk oblast'
are nearly exhausted because of high deliveries to
the State.

     Intensive felling in the southern parts of the
Far East has also depleted reserves and will lead
to a move to exploit timber in more remote river
valleys tributary to the Ussuri and Amur, such as
the Zeya, Bureya, Khor, and Iman. The milder climate
of the Far East makes the exploitation of more distant resources easier than in Eastern Siberia. And
the flow of many streams into the eastward-flowing
Amur is considerably more favorable for transportation than is the northward flow of the East Siberian
rivers. The clearance of huge hydro sites in Eastern
Siberia will upset this prediction in the short run
(e.g., when the Bratsk reservoir was being prepared

for flooding, over 38 million cubic meters of timber
was felled for use at the Bratsk timber kombinat).

Species

   In Eastern Siberia the forests consist mainly
of larch and pine as well as substantial quantities
of Siberian kedr, fir, and spruce. Overall timber
resources, including Yakutia, are about 22 billion
cubic meters of larch (57 percent), 7.6 billion
cubic meters of pine (20 percent), 3.3 billion cubic
meters of kedr (8.5 percent), 3.0 billion cubic meters of fir (8.0 percent), 0.6 billion cubic meters
of spruce (1.5 percent), and about 2.1 billion cubic
meters of deciduous species (5.0 percent), mostly
birch and some aspen. Although larch is the predominant species, especially in Yakutia, it is not utilized very much because it is difficult to transport
(owing to the fact that it sinks in water) and, also,
because the stands are frequently of poor quality.
Larch is often left standing when other species are
being cut. Pine, including kedr, is regarded as
being more valuable and is generally preferred to
larch.

   Some of the best timber stands occur in Krasnoyarsk, but more than one-half of them are inaccessi-
ble in the wild interior of the Tunguska valleys.
The present exploitation of timber there is confined
to about 10 percent of the total forested area. Particularly valuable commercial stands are located in
the upper and middle reaches of the Yenisei and
along the Angara and upper Lena; the Taishet-Ust'-Kut
railway passes through extensive accessible reserves.

   The main timber produced in Eastern Siberia is
pine. In regions where selective felling is not
practiced--such as at Bratsk, Ust'-Ilim, and Krasnoyarsk hydro reservoir sites--fir, spruce, and larch
are also cut. The deciduous species, such as birch,
are used to a limited extent by furniture factories
in the south, and aspen goes to the match plant at
Usol'e Sibirskoe. Some broad-leaved timbers, amounting to 10 percent of local consumption, are imported
from the Far East. The upper Angara pine forests

have mature stands with reserves of 206 to 216 cubic
meters per hectare and an annual growth of 1.8 to
2.2 cubic meters per hectare, whereas those around
Yeniseisk (to the northwest) deteriorate to 173 cubic
meters per hectare with a growth of 1.3 cubic meters.
To the north again, along the middle course of the
Yenisei, there are extensive stands of spruce in
the Turukhansk forestry farm, but reserves and growth
fall to 146 and 1.0 cubic meters per hectare, respectively.* The least valuable woods are the poor larch
forests of Yakutia: At Verkhoyansk, north of the
Arctic circle, sparse stands of 62 cubic meters per
hectare yield a growth of 0.4 cubic meters per year.

A belt of birch forests extends from Lake Baikal
to the middle Yenisei, embracing reserves of more
than 1.4 billion cubic meters, but, like larch, it
is used mainly for firewood or local mining needs.

In the Far East the forests are characterized
by a greater variety of species. The proportion of
deciduous trees is three times greater than in Eastern Siberia. Almost all of the Primor'ye and the
southern part of Khabarovsk territory contain mixed
coniferous-deciduous forests, including the valuable
kedr and Amur cork oak. The Far East exports deciduous hardwood, especially ash, to most other regions
in the U.S.S.R. In Sakhalin, on the lower Amur,
along the coast of the Tartar Straits, and on the
upper slopes of the Sikhote Alin mountains, there are
large resources of Ayan spruce and fir, providing a
good raw material base for the pulp, paper, and cellulose industry. To the north, in Amur and Magadan
oblasts', along the Sea of Okhotsk coast, as well as
in the basins of the Bureya and Amgun, the Dahurian
larch predominates, but, as in Eastern Siberia, it
is little utilized. In Kamchatka the birch is of
considerable economic importance because in many districts it is the only available wood for the needs
of the fishing industry and, also, for fuel.

----

*This is the largest forestry farm in the U.S.S.R.
and covers 216.4 million acres.

About 15 percent of the R.S.F.S.R.'s conifers
and 60 percent of its broad-leaved hardwoods are in
the Far East (see Table 12). Overall, there are resources of 5.8 billion cubic meters of larch, 2.8
billion of spruce and fir, 1.0 billion of Siberian
pine, 0.6 billion of Kamennaya birch, and 0.2 billion
of oak. In the Ussuri Valley, the Bureya slopes,
and the western side of the Sikhote Alin, the Siberian
pine gives 180 to 265 cubic meters per hectare with
a growth of 1.3 to 1.5 cubic meters, which is slightly
lower than the best forests in Eastern Siberia.

Production

Total removals of timber in Pacific Siberia
were 88.9 million cubic meters in 1969, an increase
of only 10 percent in five years. It must be re-
membered, however, that significant quantities of
timber are felled only for firewood, and the real
increase in commercial timber extraction was over
16 percent. In Yakutia alone about two million cubic
meters of larch provide the main fuel for heating,
and in the whole of Pacific Siberia almost 18 million
cubic meters of timber are cut for noncommercial uses.
The highest yields of commercial timber in relation
to total removals are in long worked regions such as
Sakhalin, Khabarovsk, and Irkutsk, where the remain-
ing timber is too valuable to be used as firewood.

During World War II Eastern Siberia and the Far
East produced about the same amount of timber; but
after 1950, and especially after 1955, the much
greater resources of Eastern Siberia were exploited
at a faster rate so that by 1969 it was producing
over 30 million cubic meters more than the Far East.
In the Seven Year Plan for 1959-65 the increase in
commercial timber production in the Far East was double the Soviet average, but that for Eastern Siberia,
at 27.5 percent, was three times greater. The total
share of Pacific Siberia in Soviet commercial timber
production has risen from 17 percent to over 22 percent in the last ten years or so, although the Far
East's contribution has increased very little in
that period. (In 1969, however, Khabarovsk krai recorded a 16 percent increase in roundwood timber

TABLE 12

Timber Resources by Species in the Far East
(in million cubic meters)[a]

Oblast' or Krai	Total Timber Resources	Coniferous					Broad-Leaved Hardwoods			Broad-Leaved Soft-woods	Mature Re-sources	Annual Growth
		Larch	Spruce and Fir	kedr[b]	Pine	Total	Oak	Birch[c]	Total			
Khabarovsk	5,412	2,727	1,800	376	14	4,917	63	42	130	230	4,107	45.9
Amur	2,303	1,990	37	1	52	2,081	16	--	16	181	1,814	24.8
Primor'ye	1,722	135	579	598	--	1,312	138	8	286	123	1,421	15.3
Kamchatka	1,052	134	34	--	--	168	--	514	514	70	1,041	5.4
Magadan	921	585	--	--	--	585	--	--	--	26	775	4.8
Sakhalin	675	185	376	--	--	561	0.1	59	60	46	503	6.5
Far East	12,085[d]	5,756	2,826	975	66	9,624	217	623	1,006	676	9,661[e]	102.7
As percent of R.S.F.S.R.	16	20	20	16	0.5	15	37	95	61	8	17	13

[a]One cubic meter = 35.3 cubic feet solid volume.
[b]Siberian pine.
[c]Kemennaya species only.
[d]Forest resources nonexploitable by law comprise 1,293 million cubic meters.
[e]Of which 80 percent were conifers.

Source: F. V. D'yakonov et al., Dal'nii Vostok, ekonomiki-geograficheskaya kharakteristika (Moscow: AN SSSR, 1966), p. 149; excludes Yakutia.

output--probably as a result of exports to Japan.)
Eastern Siberia is a more important timber producer
than the Urals and ranks second only to the European
northwest, which is the traditional supplier of commercial timber to urban Russia.

West of Lake Baikal, the main timber-producing
regions are at Angaro-Yeniseisk, Achinsk-Abalakovo
along the railway line, Verkhne-Yeniseisk, Kansk-
Reshetino east of Krasnoyarsk, and new fellings in
the middle Angara at Bratsk-Chuna. The old cutting
area at the foothills of the Sayan mountain range and
the adjacent upper valleys of the Angara-Biriusa,
Uda, Oka, Iya, Kita, Belaya, and Irkut rivers serves
mostly the needs of the Irkutsk sawmills and other
mills located at the junction of these rivers (which
are used for floating the logs) and the Trans-Siberian
railway. The Pribaikal region has good prospects
for commercial timber development.[14] This region
covers the eastern side of Baikal and the valleys of
rivers flowing into it, such as the Barguzin and
Turka; at present, timber is floated by rafts across
the lake to sawmills and wood-processing enterprises
on the southern shores (Baikal'sk, Vydrino, and
Babushkin).

Timber is produced mainly for local needs in
Chita, Tuva, Yakutia, and Magadan, especially for
the building and mining industries; and requirements
have to be supplemented by imports--in Magadan's case
from as far away as Primor'ye.

About four-fifths of the timber shipped out of
Eastern Siberia to other districts is in the form of
round logs. Most of this goes by railway, but some
high-quality export-grade sawn timber is shipped
down the Yenisei through Igarka and then by the
northern sea route to Europe. Only 800,000 cubic
meters of timber is transported down the Lena each
summer, compared with 3 million cubic meters down
the Angara and Yenisei from Boguchanles bound for
Igarka. In 1965 some 27.3 million cubic meters of
timber was freighted out of Eastern Siberia by railway to other regions (mainly to wood deficit areas
in West Siberia, Kazakhstan, and Central Asia); this
was double the volume of movements in 1957.[15]

The reason for the large-scale movement of unprocessed logs is the inadequate sawmilling capacity
in the region. Pacific Siberia produces only about
18 percent of the U.S.S.R.'s sawn timber, whereas,
according to its share of commercial timber output,
it should be producing over 22 percent. This discrepancy represents well over 4 million cubic meters.
The lack of sawmill capacity has caused a fall in
the output of sawn timber in the five years ended
1969. In Eastern Siberia the decline was over 1
million cubic meters and occurred mainly in the
Irkutsk and Krasnoyarsk regions, which are the most
important exporters. There is a general shortage of
sawmill facilities throughout the Soviet Union.
Sawn timber production in the Seven Year Plan grew
very slowly and has remained static since then;
growth rates attained in the Plan period were 18.2
percent for the U.S.S.R. (Plan, 36 percent) and 48.5
percent for Eastern Siberia (Plan, 115 percent).
The installation of many of the 170 or so frame saws
planned for Siberia did not eventuate, and this situation also affected the performance of the timber industry in the 1966-70 plan--which was particularly
erratic in Eastern Siberia.

Nevertheless, in the last few years the production of sawn timber in both the Irkutsk and Krasnoyarsk territories has become about as important as
that of the entire Far East (see Table 13). The main
sawn timber "export" areas in the Far East are along
the Ussuri Valley (e.g., Khor, Iman, Lesozavodsk)
where the Trans-Siberian railway crosses tributary
streams and along the Amur River.

For Pacific Siberia as a whole, the output of
sawn timber is probably at least double local requirements. Exports out of the region may be around 10
million cubic meters, even after extensive local
consumption of sawn lumber for housing, construction
works, railways, and boat building.

Wood Products

In contrast to the surpluses of sawn lumber and
round logs, there is a shortage in Pacific Siberia
of wood products such as plywood, fiber and particle

boards, paper and cardboard, and wood-chemical de-
rivatives. The latter industry has been almost completely neglected until recently.

The acquisition of south Sakhalin from Japan
greatly enhanced the Far Eastern timber-processing
industry. Before World War II there were on the island 68 sawmills and 11 large cellulose and paper
factories that exported to Japan. The timber and
paper industries in Sakhalin still account for almost
one-quarter of the island's industrial output by
value. On the mainland, however, development has
been comparatively slow despite the superior quality
of Siberian timbers for both chemical and mechanical
processing.

With plywood manufacture a great deal of waste
occurs because of inferior processing.[16] Although
this industry has expanded since 1960, when it was
producing around 48,300 cubic meters, by 1969 output
was still only 78,700 cubic meters and its share of
total Soviet production had fallen. In Eastern Siberia there is a factory at Usol'e Sibirskoe and in
the Far East a small plant at Birobidzhan in the
Jewish A.O., but most plywood is produced at larger
factories in Vladivostok and Iman. The output of
plywood in Siberia and the Far East is to increase
by 130 percent in 1971-75, whereas chipboard and
fiberboard production is planned to grow by more
than 300 percent and 780 percent, respectively, from
new timber-processing enterprises in Krasnoyarsk,
Irkutsk, and Khabarovsk territories.[17]

No cardboard was produced in Pacific Siberia before World War II; in 1940, 200 tons of paper was
made at the Birakan factory in the Jewish autonomous
region. After the annexation of the southern part
of Sakhalin several important Japanese plants were
obtained at Poronaisk and Kholmsk, and Sakhalin still
provides almost one-half of Pacific Siberia's paper
and cardboard production. The pulp mills take 70
percent of the island's total roundwood output. It
was not until 1960 that a new mainland factory, at
Krasnoyarsk, started to manufacture paper and cardboard in association with cellulose for the artificial

TABLE 13

Sawn Timber Production in Pacific Siberia, 1959-69
(thousand cubic meters)[a]

Region	1959	1960	1961	1962	1963	1964	1965	Percentage Increase SYP[b]	1966	1967	1968	1969
Eastern Siberia	11,143	11,585	12,411	12,914	13,566	14,684	14,964	48.5	13,919	14,667	14,667	13,941
Krasnoyarsk	4,420	4,750	5,152	5,365	5,678	6,179	6,016	42.1	5,589	5,790	5,678	5,596
Irkutsk	4,984	5,010	5,385	5,476	5,694	6,126	6,569	54.9	5,999	6,414	6,582	6,073
Chita	660	731	739	778	828	907	934	47.8	881	963	929	868
Buryat	940	935	994	1,149	1,207	1,319	1,289	46.5	1,300	1,351	1,320	1,242
Tuva	139	159	141	146	159	153	156	67.7	150	149	158	162
Far East	4,828	5,089	5,111	5,130	5,912	5,554	5,485	20.9	5,755	5,934	6,075	6,289
Primor'ye	1,358	1,394	1,392	1,253	1,722	1,422	1,487	16.0	1,385	1,474	1,479	1,554
Khabarovsk	1,543	1,634	1,682	1,706	2,075	2,030	2,027	35.1	2,102	2,189	2,301	2,318
Amur	577	585	594	676	593	622	676	30.8	715	758	753	795
Magadan	152	187	151	178	157	151	163	22.6	162	152	199	218
Kamchatka	164	153	169	186	200	169	191	41.5	214	224	208	193
Sakhalin	691	693	655	618	675	670	647[c]	-3.0	716	683	672	673
Yakutia	343	443	468	513	490	490	294	-2.3	461	454	463	538
Pacific Siberia	15,971	16,674	17,522	18,044	19,478	20,238	20,449	39.9	19,674	20,601	20,742	20,230
As percent of U.S.S.R.	15.3	15.8	16.8	17.4	18.4	18.2	18.4	--	18.5	18.9	18.8	18.0

aOne cubic meter = 35.3 cubic feet.
bSeven Year Plan for 1959-65, base year 1958.
cIn later sources this figure is given as 457.

Source: Narodnoe Khozyaistvo RSFSR, Promyshlennost' RSFSR, for several years.

fiber plant there; its capacity is 265,000 tons.*
The Bratsk timber <u>kombinat</u> came into operation in
1967; eventually its cost will be 800 million rubles,
and already it is claimed to be one of the largest
timber complexes in the world. It uses over 4 million
cubic meters of timber a year (rising to 7 million
cubic meters by 1975) to produce 200,000 tons of viscose cellulose, 280,000 tons of kraft paper and cardboard, and 90,000 tons of fodder yeast a year. Some
of the cardboard is sent to East Germany and some of
the cellulose is exported to Japan, Czechoslovakia,
Bulgaria, and Rumania.[18] Over 8,000 men are employed
in timber extraction at Bratsk; about three-quarters
of the logs are felled around the Bratsk Sea and the
rest are brought in by rail or road from Ust'-Kut and
Osetrovo on the Lena River. The pulp, paper, and
cardboard section of the factory is highly automated
(including a computer for sorting logs by size, quality, and type); it uses machinery almost wholly of
foreign manufacture--from Finland, Sweden, West Germany, and the United States. By 1975 Bratsk will be
the U.S.S.R.'s largest pulp and paper enterprise.
Its cellulose output will rise to 950,000 tons per
year (both viscose and sulphate), and 200,000 cubic
meters of plywood will be made as well as 440 tons
per day of fiber building board (using Polish machinery). There has been "serious negligence," however, in the construction of the complex.[19]

The Krasnoyarsk mill is also expanding fairly
rapidly; in November, 1967, a new cardboard section
came into production with a capacity of 265,000 tons.
Since 1965 a mill has also been in operation at
Baikal'sk (on the southern shore of the lake) with a
capacity of 250,000 tons of pulp (200,000 tons of
viscose cellulose, 10,000 tons of paper). Despite
some controversy about the possible pollution of Lake
Baikal waters by this mill, another mill, with a
capacity of 140,000 tons of cardboard, will be in
operation by 1972 at Selenga to add its pollution
to the raw sewage entering Lake Baikal from Ulan-Ude.

---

*Chemical pulp at Krasnoyarsk is based on the
waste from sulfate cellulose production.

Total production of paper and cardboard in Pacific
Siberia is now almost 600,000 tons--an increase of
55 percent in five years.

   Wood-derived chemicals had an even slower start,
possibly because of the very considerable capital
outlays required. For a long time Krasnoyarsk was
the only important manufacturer of turpentine. Fodder yeast has been made for a while at Kansk and
Khakass in Eastern Siberia as well as at Krasnoyarsk.
In the Far East there is a turpentine-resin plant at
Svobodnyi, ethyl alcohol is made at Khor near Khabarovsk, and there are several hydrolysis units in
southern Sakhalin attached to the cellulose-paper
factories there. But the major developments in this
industry occurred under the last Five Year Plan
(1966-70) with the construction of large factories
at Krasnoyarsk, Bratsk, and Amursk (near Komsomol'sk)
to produce cellulose, tire cord, man-made fibers,
and synthetic rubber. Stage 1 of the Amursk cellu-
lose-cardboard plant began operation in January,
1968; it produces viscose, fodder yeast, ethylene
spirit, artificial protein, and fiberboard. A large
sawmill provides offcuts for chemical pulp manufacture. A plant making cellulose, resins, and fodder
yeast (as well as wrapping papers and 5 million
square meters of fiberboard) is to be set up at Chuna
to the west of Bratsk, as well as a hydrolysis factory at Tulun and a large timber-processing factory
near the Ust'-Ilim hydro-electric power station. A
major timber industrial complex is also being built
at Poronaisk (Sakhalin), and a processing complex
is to be set up in Oktyabrskiy Settlement on the
Tartar Strait coast.[20]

Developmental Problems

   The biggest problems facing the Pacific Siberian
timber industry are inadequate sawmill capacity and
equipment, poor quality control, the shortage of
labor, the high costs of transportation, the lack of
electric power in some remote regions, inadequate
port facilities, and the varying costs of timber extraction in different areas. The lack of proper
utilization of timber waste for wood products--such

as pulp and paper, plywood and chemicals--is also a
serious deficiency.

The cost of extracting timber in Eastern Siberia
is the lowest in the Soviet Union (about 22 percent
below the Soviet average).[21] This is primarily because of the higher yield of forest stands in some
parts of the region, especially in Irkutsk and Krasnoyarsk. In the Far East, however, costs are about
50 percent above the average for the Soviet Union,
although in the better-yielding Khabarovsk territory
they are only around 25 percent more. A great deal
of the cost difference between the Far East and Eastern Siberia is due to the fact that wages and increments (which make up about 40 percent of extraction
costs) in the Far East are much higher; in Khabarovsk,
for instance, they are about one-third more than
those in Krasnoyarsk. Wages in the timber industry
are differentiated by a regional coefficient varying
between 1.15 and 1.3 above European Russian norms;
and in remote localities such as Kamchatka and Sakhalin it rises to 1.7 or 1.8 above the basic rate.
This regional increment is limited to a maximum of
300 rubles per month over and above the basic day
rate for felling and rafting of three rubles per
day.[22] As a result of these incentives, the highest
timber output per worker is in Pacific Siberia, where
productivity was planned to equal that of the United
States and Canada in 1970.

In the timber-felling region of northwest Russia
the cost of production for a cubic meter of timber
is 6.64 to 7.60 rubles, whereas in Krasnoyarsk krai
it is 6.18 rubles and in Irkutsk, 5.39. In some
areas, of course, such as Verkhoyansk, costs are much
higher; in others, such as Kirensk, they are substantially lower.* The main factor reducing Pacific
Siberia's comparative advantage in timber felling is
the high costs of transportation out of the region.
Thus, the costs of transporting by rail one cubic
meter of timber from the Far East to Alma-Ata (in

_____

*Verkhoyansk, 8.72 rubles per cubic meter;
Kirensk, 3.76 rubles.

Soviet Central Asia) is 17.2 rubles; although the
cost from Irkutsk oblast' or Krasnoyarsk krai is only
6.1 rubles and 4.7 rubles, respectively, these costs
are still about the same as the cost of felling.
Even within the region the cost of moving timber from
surplus to deficit areas is very high, especially
away from the Trans-Siberian railway. In other areas,
such as Krasnoyarsk, there is a shortage of suitable
railway cars and large stockpiles of timber accumulate in the railway yards.[23]

There are also very serious problems in getting
timber out of the region by river and by sea because
of the short ice-free season of less than five months
and because of poor port facilities. Igarka on the
Yenisei River (560 miles from its mouth) is normally
open to shipping from mid-July to the beginning of
October. Its piers can take five to seven freighters
of up to 24 feet draft, and a further seven or eight
vessels can be berthed in the river.[24] There are
three sawmills in the town. Vessels leaving the
Yenisei River after October 1 are liable to increased
insurance premiums because of the greater ice hazard.
About 70,000-80,000 tons of Soviet timber shipping
uses this port every year to take timber to markets
in East Germany, Britain, France, and the U.A.R.[25]
Igarka will be developed further as an export facility
because of its suitable deep-water stream and absence
of tides. Novyi Port, in the shallow Ob' estuary,
has no deep-water quays for seagoing vessels and is
not suitable for timber shipments. The small port
of Tiksi near the delta of the Lena has started to
ship timber to Japan using the northern sea route.[26]

Nakhodka exports over 1.5 million cubic meters
of timber per year; six deep-water quays for the
direct loading of timber from trains to ship have
been put into service since 1967 to alleviate the
problem of ships queueing in the Nakhodka roadsteads
waiting to be loaded.[27] Work has begun on constructing wharves for timber carriers at Vanino, and there
have been some trial voyages by Amur River vessels,
of 2,000 tons cargo capacity, to Niigata on the west
coast of Japan.

There is also a shortage of special timber-carrying vessels, too few forklift trucks and cranes, inadequate kiln drying and barking equipment for the sawmills, and poor marking techniques and grading for export.

The supply of skilled timber workers is so critical that in an agreement signed on June 30, 1957, between the U.S.S.R. and North Korea it was stipulated that 1.5 million cubic meters of coniferous timber would be cut in Khabarovsk krai between 1957 and 1962 by Korean labor. Recently the emphasis has been on supplying the Far East with modern Japanese logging equipment in exchange for timber; this will lift productivity and so help to offset the shortage of labor.[28]

Of more immediate concern is the provision of adequate sawmilling facilities. The policy is not to increase sawmilling capacity by establishing small new mills but, rather, to construct large and expensive integrated processing centers such as the one at Novomaklakovsk (near Yeniseisk). This new lesokombinat (timber-processing combine) has a first-stage capacity of 75,000 cubic meters of sawn timber per annum rising to an eventual capacity of 625,000 cubic meters of sawn timber and 20 million square meters of fiberboards, as well as producing furniture worth three million rubles per year.[29] It will become one of the main sawmill centers in Eastern Siberia, consuming 1.1 million cubic meters of lumber annually. In the long run the area around this mill and neighboring Maklakovo and Yeniseisk could be using up to 12 million cubic meters of lumber.

The Outlook

In Eastern Siberia development will be rapid and centralized under the large state leskhoz (forest economy) enterprises, which already control 70 percent of production. The main limiting factor will be labor supply and the shortage of railway freight wagons and sawing equipment. In the Ussuri and Amur basins exploitation will be stepped up. The area between the Ussuri and the timber-loading port of

Ol'ga has large, unexploited resources, and a sawmill complex has been built at Novo-Mikhailovka. Large reserves also in the vicinity of the Iman and Bikin rivers need improved access for timber haulage.

The Amur basin has 76.7 million acres of unexploited forest. The Bureya basin and the lower Amur between Khabarovsk and Nikolaevsk contain good commercial stands of timber; the latter region supplies the new timber complex at Amursk. Logging on a large scale is developing on the shores of lakes Innokentoevka, Khummi, and Kizi, which are linked by waterways to the lower Amur. A pulp and paper mill is planned at Nizhnii Amur on Lake Kizi. Exports of timber from the Far East to Japan exceed 1.3 million cubic meters per year at present and are likely to rise. Most of the felling for export is from the Amur Valley region but the Sikhote Alin area, on the Tartar Strait coast, may provide export timber after 1975 when the processing complex at Oktyabrskiy Settlement will be handling nearly 1 million cubic meters of lumber and wood chips. A great deal, however, will depend on the development of port-handling facilities at Nakhodka and elsewhere.

NOTES

1. F. V. D'yakonov et al., Dal'nii Vostok, ekonomiko-geograficheskaya kharakteristika (Moscow: AN SSSR, 1966), p. 126.

2. V. A. Krotov et al., Vostochnaya Sibir'-- ekonomiko-geograficheskaya kharakteristika (Moscow: AN SSSR, 1963), p. 237.

3. Voprosy Ekonomiki, No. 8, 1966.

4. F. V. K'yakonov, "Ekonomiko-Geograficheskie Osobennosti i Problemy Kamchatskoi Oblasti," Sibirskii Geograficheskii Sbornik, No. 5 (Leningrad: AN SSSR, 1967), p. 13.

5. V. Conolly, Beyond the Urals (London: Oxford University Press, 1967), p. 309

6. _Ekonomicheskaya Gazeta_, No. 8, 1968; 450 officials attended the conference, including the Minister for Fisheries (A. A. Ishkov) and representatives of _Dal'ryba_, the ports, the fishing fleets, and regional authorities.

7. O. Krivoruchko, _Planovoe Khozyaistvo_, No. 8, 1967.

8. _Ekonomicheskaya Gazeta_, No. 50, December, 1967 (A. A. Ishkov, Minister for Fisheries).

9. I. P. Mal'tsev, _Ekonomicheskoe Stimulirovanie v Rybnoi Promyshlennosti v Novykh Usloviyakh Planirovaniya_ (Moscow, 1968), p. 61.

10. _Ekonomicheskaya Gazeta_, No. 2, 1968.

11. _Ekonomicheskaya Gazeta_, No. 7, 1969.

12. _Ekonomicheskaya Gazeta_, No. 50, 1967.

13. S. Swianiewicz, _Forced Labour and Economic Development: An Enquiry into the Experience of Soviet Industrialization_ (London: Oxford University Press, 1965), p. 202; D. J. Dallin and B. I. Nicolaevsky, _Forced Labour in Russia_ (New Haven: Yale University Press, 1947), p. 215.

14. V. A. Krotov _et al._, _op. cit._, p. 280.

15. _Ibid_.

16. A. B. Margolin, _Problemy Narodnogo Khozyaistva Dal'nego Vostoka_ (Moscow: AN SSSR, 1963), pp. 107 ff.

17. _BBC Summary of World Broadcasts_, Part I, U.S.S.R., October 18, 1971

18. Interview with T. Polyanskaya, chief engineer of the wood _kombinat_, September 27, 1968.

19. _BBC Summary of World Broadcasts_, October 15, 1971.

20. Ibid.

21. Problemy Ekonomicheskoi Effektivnosti Razmeshcheniya Sotsialisticheskogo Proizvodstva v SSSR (Moscow: AN SSSR, 1968), p. 122.

22. R. V. Iurkin et al., Ekonomika Organizatsiya
i Planirovanie Predpriyatii Lesnoi Promyshlennosti
(Moscow, 1967), pp. 86-88.

23. Pravda, December 6, 1968.

24. W. Pfeifer, "Soviet Timber Shipping," Bulletin No. 3 (Munich), March, 1967.

25. BBC Summary of World Broadcasts, November
22, 1967.

26. Ibid., October 31, 1966.

27. Ibid., October 8, 1971.

28. Nihon Keizai Shimbun, August 6, 1968.

29. Pravda, January 24, 1968.

6

**POWER
AND MINERALS:
FUTURE
PROMISE**

The future economic strength of Pacific Siberia
lies with the exploitation of its hydro-electric
power and coal resources and its mineral wealth.
Cheap electricity will be used to produce large quantities of primary metals. There already has been
some development in the aluminum industry. The electricity-generating industry has expanded quickly
under the impetus of new hydro stations at Irkutsk,
Bratsk, and Krasnoyarsk, but much of the electricity
has been exported out of the region because of the
lack of suitable local industry.

The geographical axis of this development is in
Eastern Siberia along the Angara and Yenisei rivers.
The cheapest hydro-electric power in the U.S.S.R. is
generated at locations along these two rivers. By
1975 other large plants will be in production.
Large thermal stations also have been built on the
Kansk-Achinsk lignite field, and, in the more distant
future, the black coal resources of the Tunguska
basin in the north may be used for power. In the
Far East prospects are less clear. Plans for using
the Amur River as a source of hydro-electric power
have been thwarted by the deterioration in relationships between China and the U.S.S.R. Instead, hydro
schemes are to be developed on the Zeya and Bureya
rivers--tributaries of the Amur--and the thermal power
resources of the Suchan basin are to be further
exploited.

Gold was the first source of economic strength, but now industrial minerals--iron ore, copper, nickel, wolfram, tin--hold much greater promise. Some of the more recently discovered nonferrous minerals, such as the huge Udokan copper deposit in the far north of Chita oblast', present great difficulties for exploitation because of the complete absence of transport facilities. Most nonferrous minerals have a low content of metal in relation to their parent ore-bodies and must be processed close to the location where the raw material is extracted. This gives rise to problems of establishing industries in extremely sparsely populated and remote areas. For metals such as aluminum, the manufacturing location must be near to cheap and plentiful sources of energy, which often means freighting in the raw mineral (alumina or bauxite) over considerable distances.

The Twenty-Third Congress of the CPSU stressed that in the Five Year Plan for 1966-70, there would be an accelerated development of cheap fuel, power, and nonferrous mineral resources east of the Urals. The Krasnoyarsk hydro station, the Irkutsk, Bratsk, and Krasnoyarsk aluminum factories, and the Achinsk alumina plant were singled out for special mention, together with a cobalt plant in Tuva, extensions for the Noril'sk nickel and copper mines, and the need to start work on the Udokan copper ore deposit. Several of these projects, however, have run into difficulties either of a technical nature (the Achinsk alumina plant) or because sufficient investment funds have not been made available (Udokan). The new Five Year Plan for 1971-75 does not appear to give quite so much attention to minerals in the eastern regions --possibly because so many of the projects mentioned in the previous plan still have to be completed. Nevertheless, more large hydro-electric power stations and dams will be completed before 1975 (e.g., at Ust'-Ilim), and this will ensure that the momentum of development is not entirely lost.

There have been conflicting arguments, both in the U.S.S.R. and in the West, about the Siberian power-generating industry. Some have said that large thermal stations using open-cut techniques are

a more economic proposition than giant-size hydro
stations with large capital investment requirements.
Others have criticized the lack of phased development
of electricity-consuming industries and the consequent
underutilization of generating capacities.[1] Some of
the arguments seem to forget that the policy decision
to develop Siberian industries must also have contained defense and settlement factors (cf. Australia,
Canada, and Alaska).

ENERGY RESOURCES

The development of Pacific Siberia's resources
of energy has been slow. In the early part of the
twentieth century electricity was used by enterprising
industrialists in the gold, coal, and salt industries,
but it was not until after the Revolution that significant improvements occurred in municipal power generation. The Soviet Government did not order work to
begin on developing the hydro resources of the large
Siberian rivers until after World War II.

In the interwar years the power-generating net-
works of the cities and towns of Siberia operated in
isolation from each other, owing to the absence of
trunk transmission lines or even elementary trans-
former stations. Small, uneconomic generating plants
were installed in every town; frequently, factories
and farms had their own generators. Fuel consumption
was high, the cost of current was expensive, and
breakdowns were frequent.

Power stations were commonly located either
along the Trans-Siberian railway, at mines, or in
the larger towns such as Ulan-Ude or Chita. Farms
and fishing enterprises in the Far East were provided
with their own generating equipment in the 1940s and
early 1950s--some of which were operated by gasoline
or wood waste. In general, electricity stations were
built wherever power was needed with little regard
to the supply of fuel and transportation costs.

There has been a fundamental change in this
pattern in the last decade or so toward large, low-

cost, integrated units. The Irkutsk, Bratsk, Krasnoyarsk, Vilyui, and Mamakan hydro stations have added
over 11 million kilowatts of new generating capacity.
Large new thermal plants at places such as Nazarovo
(1.4 million kilowatts rising eventually to 2.5 million), Chita (320,000 kilowatts rising to 650,000),
and Raichikhinsk (800,000 kilowatts) have also been
put into operation using cheap open-cut coal. Remote
parts of Yakutia and Magadan are being serviced by
the Chul'man and Arkagala thermal stations.

During the Seven Year Plan for 1959-65 the output of electricity in Pacific Siberia increased more
than 350 percent from 14,298 to 52,448 million kilowatt-hours; nearly all of this increase occurred in
Eastern Siberia where major generation schemes were
commissioned.[2] In 1962 output of electric energy
outstripped that of the neighboring heavily industrialized economic region of West Siberia. The pace
of development was so rapid that by 1965 Pacific
Siberian production was one-half as much again as
that of West Siberia, and by 1969 Pacific Siberia
accounted for 11.2 percent (77,413 million kilowatt-
hours) of Soviet electricity generation, compared
with 7.3 percent in 1960. This reflects a major
shift in energey resource allocation in the U.S.S.R.
In terms of output per capita, Pacific Siberia produces more than double the Soviet average.

Much of the surplus energy so generated is fed
into the Central Siberian grid system, which operates
between Novosibirsk (Barabinsk) and Ulan-Ude. High-
voltage lines (500,000 volts) already connect the
Bratsk and Krasnoyarsk hydro stations, and another
unified grid for the southern Far East is to be based
on a thermal power station called Primorskaya.
Bratsk and Krasnoyarsk have a combined capacity of
10 million kilowatts (making them the two largest
hydro stations in the world), and within the next
few years, together with the Ust'-Ilim and Sayan
schemes, they should lift regional output to 140,000
million kilowatt-hours, or almost double the 1969
level. By 1975 new stations will be generating electricity at Zeya, Kolyma, and Boguchany in relatively
remote areas. Table 16 shows the projected capacities

of all hydro plants in Pacific Liberia for the foreseeable future. Beside feeding the grid systems,
the major use of hydro power will be for smelting
aluminum. The production of primary aluminum metal
requires 15 to 20 times more energy than the manufacture of a similar quantity of iron. Some 18,000-
22,000 kilowatt-hours of electrical energy are needed
to reduce two tons of alumina to a ton of aluminum.
This means that the dominant consideration in the
location of an aluminum smelter is the availability
of large quantities of cheap power. The first such
aluminum smelter has been in operation since 1964 at
Shelekhov, near the Irkutsk hydro, and since then
the Krasnoyarsk aluminum plant has been producing
metal first from Bratsk and now from Krasnoyarsk
hydro power. The Bratsk hydro itself will support
one of the biggest aluminum factories in the U.S.S.R.

There have been problems with excess capacity
and inadequate transmission lines because the generating units (e.g., Bratsk) are located in sparsely
populated regions away from established industries.
Similar "short-run" problems may occur with the commissioning of Ust'-Ilim and Sayan-Shushenskoe hydro
stations (4.3 million and 6.4 million kilowatts, respectively) unless uses are found for the surpluses
of electricity in the Far East or in European Russia.[3]

Plans for building large thermal stations on the
Kansk-Achinsk lignite field appear to have been suspended. This is not surprising in view of the fact
that the Bratsk hydro alone is capable of producing
as much electrical energy in a year as a thermal
station using 20 million tons of brown coal. In
Irkutsk oblast' almost 70 percent of the energy produced now comes from hydro-power, despite the relatively low costs of obtaining coal from the Cheremkhovo coal field. But in areas of poor water
resources, such as Sakhalin, the development of large
thermal stations will proceed; in territories with
excess water, such as the Zeya and Bureya plains,
new hydro stations will be built to control flooding.
The Zeya hydro, near Zeya township, will have a
capacity of 1.5 million kilowatts by 1975 (the generators are to be built by Sibelektrotyazhmash at

Novosibirsk), and much good agricultural land will
be drained and saved from spring flooding; that on
the Bureya probably will be smaller, at about 600,000
kilowatts. Plans for taming the mighty Amur River,
which has an estimated power potential of about 20
million kilowatts, or the same as the Yenisei, have
been shelved since the worsening of the Sino-Soviet
dispute in the 1960s. Prior to this a joint Sino-
Soviet development project had envisaged five stations
on the upper reaches of the river with an aggregate
capacity of 5-6 million kilowatts.

    In opportunity cost terms, given the similar
operating efficiency of modern large hydro and thermal
plants, it seems likely that if a policy decision
had been taken to exploit the Kansk-Achinsk open-cut
brown coal deposits rather than the Angara-Yenisei
cascade, such a decision would have been wrong. A
large hydro plant, such as the Bratsk, is capable of
producing some 22,600 million kilowatt-hours of electricity in a year of average water flow. At current
Bratsk operating costs of 0.054 kopecks per kilowatt-
hour (the lowest in the U.S.S.R.),* the annual production costs are 12.2 million rubles. For a large
thermal plant with a similar output, the extraction
costs alone of 20 million tons of Kansk-Achinsk open-
cut brown coal (also the cheapest in the U.S.S.R.),
at 1.06 rubles per ton,[4] would be 21.2 million rubles.
This does not take into account, of course, any differences in capital outlay in favor of thermal stations
or the possibilities of utilizing black coal, which
is thermally much more efficient but which in Eastern
Siberia is relatively more expensive to mine than
brown coal. It is claimed that in the long run
brown coal costs will fall to between 0.4 and 0.7
rubles per ton, with an output of 600 million tons
from reconstructed Nazarovo and Irsha-Borodino open-
cut fields. This would lower coal extraction costs
to perhaps 10 million rubles and so be competitive
with hydro generation. It was expected, however,
that Krasnoyarsk hydro costs would be only 0.04

----

*The planned cost of power from Nurek hydro
(Tadzhikistan) is one-half that of the Bratsk.

kopecks per kilowatt-hour, or less than 9 million
rubles annually when full capacity of 6 million kilowatts was reached at the end of 1971. Present plans
for erecting large hydro stations along the Angara
and Yenisei are more than sufficient for foreseeable
regional energy demands; this will delay indefinitely
the construction of large thermal plants such as the
projected 3 million-kilowatt Irsha-Borodino, which
would be the biggest coal-fired station in the
U.S.S.R.

   In total energy resource potential, Pacific Siberia has about 73 percent of all Soviet resources;
it contains 79 percent of the assessed reserves of
coal in the U.S.S.R. and 56 percent of the hydro potential, as well as over 20 percent of the natural
gas (see Table 14). The figure for hydro potential
in the Far East has probably deliberately underesti-
mated the resources of the Amur in view of the poor
prospects for joint cooperative development. Moreover, the combined fuel/energy estimates in the table
only give the hydro resource equivalent at 100 years,
whereas, in fact, its life is indefinite. The data
given for coal resources, on the other hand, are
optimistic and include not only deposits with difficult access, such as those of the Tunguska and Lena
basins, but obviously embrace tentative reserves--
which in the Kansk-Achinsk field are put at two and
one-half times the proven reserves of 99 billion
tons. The possible black coal reserves of the Lena,
Tunguska, Taimyr, and Ust'Yenisei coal fields are
some 5,000 billion tons. These fields reportedly
have the largest coal reserves in the world, but
open-cut mining operations are severely restricted
by the permafrost. Nevertheless, some seams, such
as those near where the Angara and Yenisei meet, are
over 90 meters (295 feet) thick with a light overbur-
den. Deposits of coking coal are found near the
surface in the Aldan basin (a tributary of the Lena),
and this is where the Chul'man mines operate.[5] In
general these vast Siberian coal fields are being
exploited only at isolated outcrops along their margins. Similarly, the natural gas reserves of Irkutsk
and northern Krasnoyarsk (over 4,000 billion cubic
meters) hardly have been developed--although a

160-mile pipeline costing 50 million rubles now supplies Noril'sk.

The upper and middle Yenisei and Angara rivers
are not only nearer than the coal fields to major
consuming centers for electricity but they also provide a great deal of scope for development. The
Angara alone offers more than 13 million kilowatts
of water resources, of which scarcely one-third has
been exploited, and the potential hydro-power from
the basins of the Yenisei and Lena rivers is greater
than all Canada's hydro resources.

The coal fields will be exploited increasingly
not so much for power generation but for the manufacture of chemicals (the Angarsk-Usol'e Sibirskoe complex) and for export out of the region. In 1971
exports of black coal from the Cheremkhovo field exceeded 10 million tons, compared with 5 million tons
in 1965.[6] Most of it went to West Siberia and the
Far East. Total coal production in Eastern Siberia
exceeds 50 million tons (about 70 percent from Cheremkhovo and Kansk-Achinsk basins), and output in the
Far East is another 30 million tons. Coal mining in
the Far East, however, is among the most expensive
in the entire Soviet Union; even the most favorable
projected data for Raichikhinsk (open-cut brown coal)
gives a cost per ton of fuel equivalent of 4.6 rubles,
or more than double the actual extraction costs of
the Kansk-Achinsk basin.[7] Sakhalin coal (about 5
million tons per year) is especially expensive; 75
percent of it is used locally for power generation
and the balance is exported to Magadan and Kamchatka.
Kansk-Achinsk costs are low and productivity is high
(see Table 15), but brown coal cannot be transported
very great distances because of its relatively high
moisture content. With the further development of
Kansk-Achinsk to a projected output of 600 million
tons annually sometime after the year 2000, however,
costs of production could fall very substantially
(as mentioned earlier), and this could tend to offset
transport costs to a greater degree than at present.

Eastern Siberia also has the lowest costs of
hydro-electric power generation. Average costs of

TABLE 14

Potential Energy Resources of Pacific Siberia

Resource Type	Eastern Siberia	(as percent of U.S.S.R.)	Far East	(as percent of U.S.S.R.)
Fuel (billion tons, comparable fuel equivalent)	2,597	42.7	1,864[a]	30.6
Coal (billion tons)	3,561	45.2	2,681[b]	34.0
Natural gas (billion cubic meters)	4,150[c]	6.2[c]	9,600[d]	14.3
Hydro-electric power (billion kilowatt-hours, annual output)	998	26.2	1,139[e]	29.9
Total fuel energy resources (billion tons, comparable fuel)[f]	2,627	42.6	1,898	30.3

[a]Of which Yakutia is 94.3 percent.
[b]Of which Yakutia is 94.1 percent.
[c]In Ya. A. Mazover, Toplivno Energeticheskie Bazy Vostoka SSSR (Moscow: AN SSSR, 1966), these figures are given as 4,880 and 8.1 percent (p. 82).
[d]Of which Yakutia is 82.8 percent (balance Sakhalin).
[e]Of which Yakutia is 64 percent.
[f]Hydro-electric power resources calculated in fuel equivalent terms for a 100-year comparative period.

Source: A. E. Probst, ed., Razvitie Toplivnoi Bazy Raionov SSSR (Moscow, 1968), pp. 36, 175 and 196.

TABLE 15

Production, Productivity, and Costs of Mining Coal
in Eastern Siberia

	Output (thousand tons)		Output per Worker[a] (tons per month)		Production Cost[b] (Rubles per ton)	
Coal Deposit	Total	Open-Cut	Open-Cut	Pit	Open-Cut	Pit
Krasnoyarsk krai	20,297	14,872	410.0	63.6	1.4	7.0
Kansk-Achinsk	13,162	13,125	468.9	45.8	1.0	6.4
Minusinsk	4,338	1,434	226.0	63.6	4.3	7.1
Noril'sk	2,770	313	n.a.	n.a.	n.a.	n.a.
Tuva (Ulukhemsk)	240	96	71.7	66.9	4.6	5.7
Irkutsk basin	18,890	15,059	286.6	66.9	1.8	5.9
Buryat (Gusinoozersk)	945	391	--	72.1	--	6.6
Chita oblast'	4,096	1,528	252.1	57.7	2.6	7.2
Chernovsk	1,731	600	277.8	70.8	3.0	6.5
Kharanor	802	802	353.9	--	1.9	--
Arbagar	255	--	--	37.1	--	9.4
Bukachacha	1,019	--	--	54.2	--	7.6
Eastern Siberia	44,468	31,946	325.6	63.3	1.7	6.8
For comparison						
Kuzbass	93,066	20,265	244.0	53.3	4.2	8.1
Donbass	198,848	--	--	32.7	--	12.0

[a]Total productivity per worker for Eastern Siberia was 158.6
tons per month, compared with 63.6 tons for the Kuzbass and 32.7
tons for the Donbass.
[b]Average production costs for Eastern Siberia were 3.0 rubles
per ton, compared with 7.3 rubles for the Kuzbass and 12.0 rubles
for the Donbass (in terms of comparable fuel equivalent 4.5
rubles, compared with 8.2 rubles and 13.3 rubles, respectively).

Source: Ya. A. Mazover, Toplivno-Energeticheskie Bazy
Vostoka SSSR (Moscow: AN SSSR, 1966), p. 96.

generation for the exploited rivers of Eastern Siberia are about one-half those of the Volga. Most
of the big new hydro stations are planned to have
costs of 0.05 kopecks per kilowatt-hour or less, compared with over 2.5 kopecks per kilowatt-hour at an
isolated high-cost thermal station such as Arkagala
in Magadan. The main problem awaiting a solution
in Siberia is the erection of a comprehensive network
of high-voltage, low power loss transmission lines to
service isolated communities at a reasonable cost.

Industrial users are charged the same price for
electricity in Siberia as in European Russia (0.9
kopecks per kilowatt-hour), despite much lower generating costs.[8] It is little wonder, then, that the
cost of capital construction for the dam at Bratsk
of 730 million rubles was written off between 1961
and 1967 by the sale of electricity to local industries so that when the operation changed hands from
the Bratsk hydro station Stroi (Hydro Electric Construction Authority) to the U.S.S.R. State Electricity
Commission in September of 1967 it had paid its own
way. Similarly, the Krasnoyarsk hydro station (capacity six million kilowatts) recouped its construction costs by 1971. Special low user rates may be
offered in the future to the large aluminum plants
at Shelekhov, Bratsk, and Krasnoyarsk to encourage
greater use of hydro-electric capacity.

The low unit costs of output for electricity
may also be used at some future date for exploiting
the time gap of several hours existing between the
eastern and western parts of the U.S.S.R. so that a
rational balance can be achieved for daily peak consumption periods.[9] This development will have to
await the completion of a super high-tension grid
system.

MINERALS DEVELOPMENT

Minerals, especially gold, have long been a
source of wealth in Siberia; in Yakutia they still
comprise over 40 percent of the value of industrial
output. The use of forced labor to mine these

minerals, both under the Tsars and in Soviet times
until the mid-1950s, did much not only to open up
sparsely settled areas but also to give Siberia its
unsavory reputation.[10]

The Kolyma gold fields were discovered in 1931
and together with Yakutian gold, at Aldan and
Ust'Nera, now produce perhaps three-fifths (about
200 tons) of all Soviet gold. In general, production
is fixed about a specific cost of gold extraction
and no deposits are worked unless their gold content
is high enough to ensure that definition of economic
working. However, extensive breakdowns and stoppages
to machines increase costs considerably--especially
at the placer mines at Susuman and Magadan where working conditions are difficult. To Western standards,
Siberian gold production costs are high, and, with
the gold content of many deposits declining as they
are worked out, costs will escalate. Gold production
in Madagan in 1970 was 24 percent over the 1965 level
but required the washing of 60 percent more gravel
because of the decline in gold content.

Gold is also produced now at the Ichuveyen
River Valley in Chukotka (southwest of Pevek on Chaun
Bay), and a large new deposit was discovered in 1971.[11]
There is some gold mining in Eastern Siberia, at
Bodaibo and Barguzin north of Lake Baikal, where pro-
duction started in the 1870s, and along the Shilka
River near Balei; but the fields are not as important
as those of the Far East and Yakutia and often their
yield per ton of ore is much lower.

Alluvial diamonds were discovered in the Vilyui
basin of Yakutia in 1949; this was followed in 1954
by the first kimberlite pipe of industrial importance
at Mirnyi. The main diamond-bearing region covers
an area of some 115,000 square miles and includes
the basins of the Olenek and Muna. Some of the rivers
yield up to 10 carats per cubic meter of sand. The
Seven Year Plan for 1959-65 envisaged a sixteen-fold
increase in the diamond industry, and it is believed
that further rapid expansion has occurred since then.

Mirnyi is supplied with electricity from the
Vilyui hydro station (320,000 kilowatts). It has a

TABLE 16

Projected Capacities of Pacific Siberian Hydro Plants

Location	Capacity (kilowatts)	River
Constructed or being constructed		
Irkutsk[a] (upstream from city)	660,000	Angara
Sukhovskaya (near Angarsk) and Tel'minsk (Usol'e Sibirskoe)	200,000 to 300,000 each	"
Bratsk[b]	4.5 million	"
Ust'-Ilim[c] (Angara-Ilim)	4.3 million	"
Krasnoyarsk[d] (Divnogorsk)	6 million	Yenisei
Sayan-Shushenskoe (near Minusinsk)	6.4 million	"
Zeya[e] (Zeya township)	1.5 million	Zeya
Bureya (Dzhamudinsk)	600,000	Bureya
Vilyui[f] (near Mirny)	320,000	Vilyui
Mamakan (near Bodaibo)	450,000	Vitim
Boguchansk (Boguchany)	4.0 million	Angara
Kolyma[g]	medium	Kolyma
Khantayka (near Igarka)	500,000	Yenisei
Other possible sites		
Yeniseisk (Angara-Yenisei)	6 to 8 million	Yenisei
Osinovsk (Tunguska-Yenisei)	5 million	"
Nizhnetunguska (Turukhansk) and Igarka	large	"
Minusinsk (downstream Sayan)	small	"
Khaa Kol'sk (Shagonar, Tuva)	medium	"
Irkut	small	Irkut
Khilok (near Ulan-Ude)	less than 600,000	Selenga
Nizhnelena[h] (near Tiksi)	15 to 20 million	Lena
Yakutsk (near Yakutsk)	4 million	"
Olekminsk (near Olekminsk)	medium	"
Mukhtui (near Mukhtuya)	4 million	"
Mokskaya[i]	medium	Vitim

[a]Full capacity 1968.
[b]Current capacity: 4.1 million kilowatts (225,000-kilowatt turbines).
[c]First current planned for early 1970s.
[d]Installed capacity December, 1971: 6.0 million kilowatts (500,000-kilowatt turbines). Now biggest power station in world. Construction started in 1956; first power generated in 1967.
[e]To be completed by 1975.
[f]Built under permafrost conditions.
[g]Construction started in 1972; it will serve Kolyma and Kamchatka areas.
[h]If constructed, this plant would have an annual output of 100,000 million kilowatt-hours, or equivalent to total Soviet electricity production in 1951. It would consist of 20 one-million kilowatt generators (500,000 kilowatt units in pairs); the Lena River at this point is 2.3 kilometers wide and 25 meters deep; a sea of 61,000 square kilometers would be ponded back. Construction is not expected to start until 1980 or 1985 (there is considerable doubt about this huge project).
[i]Other small hydro sites on the Vitim could include Bodaibo, Amalyk, Karalon, and Tsikin; on the Lena, Verkhnelena, Kirensk, and Shorokhov have been suggested for small plants together with Bielimei on the Amga River.

number of diamond-dressing mills, but in the past
they were worked only in the summer because of inadequate attention paid to requirements for normal operating in the severe Yakutian winters. The diamonds
mined at Mirnyi are air-freighted to Moscow and become the responsibility of the Ministry of Finance;
those weighing more than 20 carats are distinguished
by name--the largest so far being the Oktyabrskii,
weighing 69.4 carats.[12] A pipe richer than Mirnyi
is being worked to the north at Aikhal near the
Markha River, another tributary of the Vilyui. Total
output of diamonds from Yakutia may be in the order
of five million carats annually; in addition to
making the U.S.S.R. self-sufficient in industrial
diamonds, some exports are made.

Production and processing of ferrous and nonferrous metals will give Pacific Siberia much more
value-added income than the simple extraction of
gold and diamonds. Although statistical data on the
extraction, processing, and capacities of nonferrous
metal mines and factories are not generally available
in the U.S.S.R. because of its strategic implications,
it is possible to obtain some idea of the distribution
and magnitude of nonferrous metal resources in Siberia.

The Noril'sk nickel mine is the best example of
Soviet industrial development within the Arctic Circle. It is further north than either the Vorkuta coal
mines or the Murmansk apatite deposits. Noril'sk
(population 140,000) is located in the Taimyr tundra;
a railroad of about 55 miles connects it to Dudinka
on the Yenisei and thence to the northern sea route.
Nickel was first produced at Noril'sk in 1940. The
complex polymetallic ores are mined from the spurs
of the Putorana mountains and yield copper, cobalt,
and platinum, as well as nickel. Some of the nickel
ore is sent to Murmansk for smelting. Just to the
south of Noril'sk there are coal mines producing
about three million tons of black coal per year--some
of which is used by the mine for electric smelting
and by a new thermal power station at Talnakh; the
balance goes to Dudinka and Dikson for ships' bunk-
ers.[13]

Noril'sk probably produces about one-half of
the total Soviet nickel production (up to 60,000 tons)
and 120,000 tons of copper--although there is considerable doubt about the accuracy of these figures,
owing to inadequate information about the development
of the adjacent Talnakh copper-nickel deposits discovered in 1959-60. Two-thirds of Talnakh's metal
is produced by the Mayak mine; by 1970 a settlement
of 10,000 people was established at nearby Snezhno-
gorsk.[14] Talnakh probably will become the biggest
nonferrous metals mine in the U.S.S.R., and by 1974
over 14 million tons of ore will be freighted out
of the mine. The Noril'sk nickel mine is already
the largest in the Soviet Union and despite its
remote location, will continue to expand.[15] It produces the cheapest copper in the U.S.S.R., which tends
to offset the costs of its remote location. Talnakh
dressed ores will be conveyed hydraulically by a pipeline to a metal-processing works at Noril'sk, but
there are no plans at present to establish fabricating
stages.

Another example of a remote, rich, and very large
mineral body, promising a future development similar
to that of Noril'sk, is the copper sandstone deposits
at Udokan in the far north of Chita oblast'. The
copper is found near the settlement of Chara on the
headwaters of the river of the same name (itself a
tributary of the Lena). The rugged Udokan mountains
are a part of the Stanovoi range; the Chara River is
contained by these mountains to the south (over
8,000 feet) and by the Kodar mountains to the north
(9,500 feet). The nearest railhead is near Mogocha,
some 225 miles to the south as the crow flies, whereas
the nearest good highway (the Aldan) is at Chul'man,
some 260 miles direct east. This region is very
sparsely populated; the closest large settlement is
a rugged 170 miles to the northwest at the gold-mining
town of Bodaibo.

The announcement in January, 1966, of a decision
to build a 4,350-mile Northern Siberian railway,
Sevsib, from Tyumen' to Tobol'sk and Surgut (by 1970)
and thence via Yeniseisk, Osetrovo, Chara, and

Chegdomyn to Komsomol'sk has obvious long-term implications for the development of mineral resources,
such as the Udokan, along its route.[16] But the likely
construction period for such a large-scale undertaking is from 10 to 25 years or more. In the meantime,
adequate access to Udokan was to have been provided
in the Five Year Plan for 1966-70 and work was to
have begun on the exploitation of the copper ore.
So far, however, there is no evidence of any development. Access could be provided by a line about 340
miles long from Mogocha, or Chichatka, on the Trans-
Siberian across the turbulent Tungir, Olokma, Kalakan,
and Kalar rivers and the rugged Olekminsk-Stanovoi
ranges and the Yablonovoi mountains. So difficult
is this terrain that one writer describes it as "generally unexplored, so much so that even the structure
of the big mountain ranges has not yet been clearly
ascertained."[17]

    The copper belt at Udokan is reported to be one
of the largest and richest in the world, measuring
4.5 miles long, 3.0 miles wide, and some 650 feet
thick. There are good-quality coal deposits to the
east at Chul'man, and a nonferrous metal-processing
complex could develop in this region, based on exports to Japan. The Soviets have sought Japanese
participation in Udokan, so far with no success. An
extraction rate of between 20 million and 40 million
tons of ore is possible, which would give a copper
metal yield of perhaps 400,000 to 800,000 tons.

    The processing of locally mined nephelines (low-
grade aluminum-bearing minerals) is at an early stage
of development and has encountered severe technical
difficulties (the U.S.S.R. is the first country in
the world to pioneer the use of nonbauxite raw materials). The bauxite resources of Siberia are poor,
and, until recently, the Kamensk Ural'skiy and
Krasnaya Shapochka workings in the Urals were the
main suppliers to the Shelekhov aluminum smelters.
The development of the Achinsk alumina plant--it was
finally completed in December, 1971--as one of the
biggest in the U.S.S.R. (over 750,000 tons) will supply only part of the eventual raw material requirements of the Shelekhov, Krasnoyarsk, and Bratsk

smelters for over 2.0 million tons of alumina.
Achinsk is based on the exploitation of local nepheline syenites and bauxitic deposits from the Yenisei
ridge and the Kiya River and produces cement and
sodium carbonate as well as alumina. Some alumina
still will be freighted into Eastern Siberia from
the Urals and also from the Pavlodar alumina plant
in Kazakhstan (which uses bauxites from the Turgai
depression) until the very serious technical problems
and high costs of processing nephelines are overcome.
Better-grade bauxite deposits have been discovered
at Ibdzhibdek and Chadobets north of the Angara and
also at Bokson in the Sayan mountains of Buryatia,
but their extent is not known.

The large aluminum smelters currently coming
into operation, albeit very slowly (the Shelekhov
plant took 11 years to complete), probably have combined capacities in excess of 800,000 tons of metal,
rising to over one million tons. Assuming a median
power consumption of 20,000 kilowatt-hours per ton
of aluminum reduced from alumina and that at least
one-half of the Bratsk electricity output is used
for aluminum smelting, the capacity of the Bratsk
smelters would be about 600,000 tons; a more accurate
assumption would be to take, for example, 60 percent
of Bratsk's electricity, to give over 700,000 tons.
The Shelekhov plant probably has a capacity of 120,000
to 140,000 tons. The Krasnoyarsk smelters may be
producing only 100,000 tons of metal at present, but
it is believed that their ultimate capacity will exceed 300,000 tons. In 1971 a high-capacity refining
section and a new electrolysis section came into
operation at Krasnoyarsk, and extrusion facilities
will be built there.[18] The first trainload of alumina
from Achinsk was delivered to Krasnoyarsk aluminum
works in April, 1970--previously the raw material
was obtained from Pavlodar at four times the transport cost.

Iron ore mining is expanding at a fast rate.
The extraction of iron ore in Eastern Siberia in
1955 was a mere 4,400 tons, but by 1958 it had risen
sharply to 1.11 million tons; in 1961 it exceeded 2
million tons, and by 1965 output had reached 3 million

tons. This quick growth came from the Angara-Pit and
later the Angara-Ilim ore deposits. The latter are
located in the Korshunovo region, astride the railway
line, midway between Bratsk and Ust'-Kut. Iron ore
output (open-cut) from this field started in 1965,
with 776,000 tons;[19] by 1970 it was probably about
12 million tons, and in 1972 ore-processing capacity
was 15 million tons. A concentration plant has been
built at Zheleznogorsk on the railway; this supplies
the Kuzbass steel works. If a steel plant is ever
built at Taishet, Zheleznogorsk will supply it with
iron ore.

The iron ore resources of the Angara-Pit basin
have been put at 4.5-5 billion tons, with 1.4 billion
tons being of 40 percent iron content and requiring
only simple dressing (qualities $A+B+C_1+C_2$).[20] Those
for the Nizhne-Angara field are at least 1.2 billion
tons. The Angara-Pit basin has one of the largest
iron ore deposits in the U.S.S.R.; its cost of production at an annual output of 10 million tons is
about 0.83 rubles a ton falling to 0.65 rubles when
an output of 25 million tons is reached. In comparison the Altai-Sayan (West Siberia) costs are 1.5
rubles. Some of the Angara ores are concentrated to
60 percent iron content and are used at the Sibelek-
trostal' steel works in Krasnoyarsk.

In the Far East there are iron ore reserves of
some 800-1,300 million tons in the Aldan region of
Yakutia with an iron content of 45 percent that can
be raised to 62 percent by concentration. It is estimated that the cost of pig iron produced from
Aldan iron ore and Chul'man black coal (reserves up
to 4,000 million tons) would be 15.3 rubles per ton
and that the only other competitive site for a blast
furnace in the Far East would be at Svobodnyi, using
power from the projected Zeya hydro scheme (see Table
17). The problem of constructing a major steel plant
in the Far East was raised in the 1930s, 1940s, and
1950s, but it is only recently that the discovery of
new iron ore deposits, the construction of the Zeya
hydro, and the development of steel-using industries
has seriously raised the question of locating a sizable iron- and steel-making plant in the Far East.

TABLE 17

Estimated Cost of Pig Iron Production

Plant: Actual or Projected Location	Pig Iron Cost of Production (rubles per ton)	Capital Investment Per Ton of Output (rubles)	Capital Repayment Period (years)
Kuznetsk kombinat	21.4	236.1	10.9
Barnual	21.0	249.4	10.9
Taishet	18.4	207.7	9.8
Svobodnyi	15.3	202.9	7.2
Novolipetsk	23.7	232.3	6.3
Krivoi Rog	26.6	219.2	15.1
Zaporozhstal'	26.6	269.1	8.3
Karaganda kombinat	20.4	237.4	10.5
Aldan	15.3	197.4	7.7

Source: Materialy 1-i Khabarovskoi Kraevoi
Nauchnotekhnicheskoi Konferentsii, Mart 1965 god
(Khabarovsk: Ts.B.T.I., 1966), p. 86.

The expected shortfall in Far Eastern steel output
of some 3.7 million tons per year in 1970 led the
Twenty-Third Congress of the CPSU to direct that
prospecting and planning for a new iron and steel
base in the Far East should be carried out in the
1966-70 Five Year Plan period. No plans have been
announced, however, for the location of a new steel
works.

The annual expenditure on transporting rolled
steel into the Far East is some 35 million rubles,
whereas the capital investment needed to build a
steel plant is 1,500 million rubles. From a transport cost aspect alone such a plant would be repaid
in about 40-45 years. A plant of 6-6.5 million tons

pig iron capacity would supply regional needs for
some time; but Gosplan experts in Moscow consider
that the Garinsk (93 miles northeast of Svobodnyi)
and Kimkansk (5 miles from Izvestkovyi in the Jewish
A.O.) iron ore deposits would be exhausted in less
than 30 years with such a plant. Owing to this the
recommended capacity of the steel works is only 3
million tons.

Surplus electricity from the Zeya hydro could
be used for manufacturing special types of steel.
The average annual output of the Zeya in 1975 is estimated to be 4.7 billion kilowatt-hours at a cost
of 0.1 kopecks per kilowatt-hour. Of this amount of
energy, about 1.3 billion kilowatt-hours will be
used for electric railway haulage between Mogocha
and Svobodnyi, 0.5 billion for the needs of the
Garinsk iron ore mines, 0.6 billion for agriculture
in the fertile Zeya plains, and the balance of 2.3
billion for metallurgy.

Other minerals are mined in Pacific Siberia on
a smaller scale. Mining operations to suit local
needs are too small and too expensive, but exploitation of scarce metals (such as tin) in remote areas
can be justified on an import-saving basis for the
U.S.S.R. economy as a whole. Even then, some rich
deposits, such as the lead-zinc of the Verkhoyan
mountains, are too difficult to mine economically.
The mining of strategic metals, such as uranium at
Sludyanka in association with tantalum and columbium,
can also be defended on noneconomic grounds. The
main advantage of mining the scarcer minerals in the
sparsely peopled parts of Siberia is the employment
and settlement opportunities it provides (e.g., the
large mica mines at Mama near the Bodaibo gold fields).

Tin has been mined in the tundra of Chukotka
(near Pevek and at Iul'tin) and Yakutia (at Deputatskii and Ese-Khaya) since 1937; costs of production
are increased greatly by heavy transport expenses,
both for getting the mineral product out and for
freighting essential supplies into these mines.
Labor turnover is a continuing problem. Yakutia
probably produces almost one-quarter of Soviet tin

output--and the whole of the Far East, perhaps one-
half of the total production. There are lower-cost
mines at Gorniy (Khabarovsk krai, 1963), where a
tin smelter is in operation, and in the Sikhote Alin
ranges of coastal Primor'ye (e.g., Kavalerovo and
Khrustal'niy, where production costs are among the
cheapest in the U.S.S.R.). The dressing capacity of
Khrustal'niy is planned to increase by nearly 40
percent before 1975.

High-quality lead and zinc are found in the
Sikhote Alin at Tetyukhe. These deposits were developed by the Briner Company of Vladivostok between
1911 and 1919; a British concession then worked the
mine and exported ore to Europe from 1924 to the early
1930s when it was taken over by the Soviet Government.
Metal concentrates (which include silver) are transported by narrow-gauge railway to docks at the mouth
of the Tetyukhe River. This mine is being expanded
at Nikolaevsky and by 1975 should be exporting larger
quantities. Large lead deposits have been reported
at Gorevskoe on the Angara (associated with tin),
but no development plans are known.

In the Five Year Plan for 1966-70 a cobalt plant
was provided for in the Tuva A.S.S.R. (at Khovu Aksi),
and by 1971-72 a large tungsten (wolfram) concen-
trating kombinat was to be operating at Armu-Imam in
northern Primor'ye, using power from the new Primorskaya thermal electric station.

CONCLUSIONS

The development of mineral resources in Pacific
Siberia has been hampered severely by completely inadequate railway links with the main Trans-Siberian
artery. Major mineral developments have occurred
along or near that railway (e.g., at Cheremkhovo,
Sludyanka, Kansk, Raichikhinsk, Usol'e Sibirskoe,
Petrovsk-Zabaikal'sk). Transportation is a very serious problem, even for rich mineral deposits such
as the Udokan copper; others, such as the iron ore
at Korshunovo, are being opened up precisely because
of railway and hydro construction activities in the
vicinity of the ore-body.

The advent of cheap hydro-electric power undoubtedly will play a decisive role in the development of mining. The low costs of electricity for power-intensive nonferrous and ferrous metallurgy will assist in offsetting, at least in part, the high cost of transport access to minerals. In the Far North, atomic power stations, such as the 48,000-kilowatt one to be completed at Bilibino by 1973, will lower local electricity costs by some 60-90 percent; this should encourage gold and tin mining. The opening up of natural gas fields in Yakutia (the Lena-Vilyui reserves now are put at up to 12,800 billion cubic meters) and at Messoyakha in Krasnoyarsk krai will provide cheap power for isolated settlements. A large diameter gas pipeline stretching about 125 miles across the Iruchi marsh will be completed by the end of 1973; it will supply all the industrial and household needs of central Yakutia.

NOTES

1. P. P. Silinskii, Planirovanie Narodnogo Khozyaistva v Oblasti (Moscow, 1967); Voprosy Ekonomiki, No. 8, 1966; Ekonomicheskaya Gazeta, No. 20, 1969.

2. Narodnoe Khozyaistvo RSFSR v 1965 god, p. 82.

3. See the Conference on the Economic Problems of Irkutsk Oblast', Ekonomicheskaya Gazeta, No. 20, May, 1969.

4. Ya. A. Mazover, Toplivno-Energeticheskie Bazy Vostoka SSSR (Moscow: AN SSSR, 1966), p. 96.

5. I. P. Bardin, ed., Problemy Razvitiya Chernoi Metallurgii v Raionakh Vostochneye Ozera Baikala (Moscow, 1960).

6. BBC Summary of World Broadcasts, Part I, U.S.S.R., October 15, 1971

7. A. E. Probst, ed., Razvitie Toplivnoi Bazy Raionov SSSR (Moscow, 1968), p. 200.

8.   Silinskii, op. cit.

9.   V. Conolly, "Sibirien Heute und Morgen,"
Osteuropa, July, 1968, p. 539.

10.   R. Conquest in The Great Terror (London,
1968), p. 532, states that the Kolyma camps alone
probably accounted for over two million deaths up to
1950.   But several Western critics have said that his
figures are too high, being based on a wastage rate
of 30 percent.   Conquest claims that even at the end
of 1956 there were still over a million prisoners in
the Far Eastern camps.   There is no doubt that corrective labor was responsible for the development in the
1930s and 1940s of large-scale gold mining in the
Kolyma and Magadan districts, the Noril'sk nickel
mine, and lumbering in the Lena region.

11.   BBC Summary of World Broadcasts, October 22,
1971.

12.   V. Conolly, Beyond the Urals (London: Oxford University Press, 1967), p. 317.

13.   V. A. Krotov et al., Vostochnaya Sibir'--
ekonomiko-geograficheskaya kharakteristika (Moscow:
AN SSSR, 1963), p. 576.

14.   Pravda, September 4, 1970.

15.   By December, 1971, over 4,500 former members
of the Ministry of International Affairs (MVD) internal troops were working on priority construction
projects, sponsored by the Komsomol, at Noril'sk.
Komsomol'skaya Pravda, November 26, 1971.

16.   Izvestiya, January 28, 1966.

17.   E. Thiel, The Soviet Far East (London:
Methuen, 1957), p. 278.

18.   BBC Summary of World Broadcasts, October 29,
1971.

19.   Narodnoe Khozyaistvo Irkutskoi Oblasti
(Irkutsk, 1967), p. 21.

20.   A. I. Zubkov and B. B. Gorizontov, Promyshlennye Uzly Krasnoyarskogo Kraya (Moscow: AN SSSR,
1963), p. 66.

CHAPTER

7

A HIGH-COST
SECTOR:
AGRICULTURE

Agriculture in the Soviet Far East and Eastern Siberia is poorly developed. Costs are high in relation to the rest of the U.S.S.R., yields are low, and for most commodities production does not satisfy local demand. The Far East is the highest-cost producer in the entire Soviet Union for livestock produce. Overall, it is estimated that Pacific Siberia produces only two-fifths of its food needs for over 13 million people.

The climate in this part of the U.S.S.R. does not encourage the development of agriculture. Even in the most favored areas of the south the growing season rarely exceeds 120 days; wheat and barley must be spring sown and even the hardy winter-sown rye and oats yield poorly. Maize does not ripen into grain except in the upper Ussuri Valley where soybeans and rice are also grown. The grains area has not expanded much since the late 1950s, when 10 million acres of virgin and fallow lands were ploughed up in the Krasnoyarsk, Irkutsk, Chita, and Amur regions; only 1 percent of the total territory of Pacific Siberia is classified as arable. The livestock industry is fairly well developed in some of the valleys in Chita oblast' and in the mountainous Tuva A.S.S.R.; but over most of the region the prolonged winter imposes heavy costs through extended stall-feeding periods. Local fodder supplies are inadequate

and expensive. Attempts, much publicized in the Soviet press, to develop commercial agriculture in the
Far North have not been very successful.

PHYSICAL LIMITATIONS

In Eastern Siberia the only area normally free
from permafrost is between Krasnoyarsk and Irkutsk.
The wooded steppe to the east of Krasnoyarsk and
along the Yenisei is particularly well favored by
fertile chernozem soils and is a good area for grain
cultivation--especially spring wheat, which normally
yields as well here as in adjoining West Siberia.
Inadequate moisture in the summer is the main problem
for crops; in Transbaikalia annual rainfall averages
less than 12 inches, and in the valley of Barguzin
the Buryat settlers are forced to use artificial ir-
rigation. Chita oblast' is dry also and suitable
only for beef cattle and wool production. The summers in Eastern Siberia are somewhat drier than in
West Siberia, and the winters are longer--up to seven
months even in the southern regions. In the valleys
of the Buryat and Tuva A.S.S.R.s, however, livestock
can graze in the open during autumn and part of the
winter because there is relatively little snow. Yet,
a few hundred miles to the north, at Yeniseisk, the
snow cover lasts for more than six months, and agriculture is severely restricted; only 107 days are
frost free. Coarse grains (rye and barley) are sown
in May and harvested in July; yields are poor with a
high moisture content.

In the middle Lena, around Yakutsk, natural conditions are closer to those of the wooded steppe
areas far to the south. The deep permafrost helps
to keep the soil moist during the short relatively
hot summer when the rainfall is insufficient to sustain grains. Nevertheless, in the whole of Yakutia
(an area of 1.2 million square miles) there are only
175,000 acres of sown land; the main agricultural
pursuit is the raising of reindeer and cattle. The
rainfall in this central part of Siberia is very low
(8 to 10 inches), and if it was not for the perma-
frost-derived moisture the land would be impossible

to cultivate--even for the very limited agriculture
that now exists.

The Far East presents quite a different set of
physical problems for farming. In the Amur-Ussuri
region in the south, permafrost is not present, winters are shorter than in Eastern Siberia, and the
growing period for crops, of four to five months, is
longer. The major hazard is excessive moisture in
summer from the East Asian monsoon, which gives an
annual rainfall of 24 to 28 inches over much of the
south of the Far East (about double that of Transbaikalia), 70 percent of which falls in summer. Heavy
rainstorms, frequently lasting several days, lead to
widespread floods in the Amur, Zeya, and Bureya basins
and to waterlogging of fields. In the spring, before
flooding occurs, dust storms are prevalent. With the
onset of the monsoon in July, falls of up to 4 inches
in 24 hours can occur, and for two months there is
rarely a day free from rain.[1]

Meadows become bogs, livestock suffer (especially
sheep), and excessive moisture prevents the ripening
of grain, encourages pests, and, in flooded areas,
causes plants to rot. Consequently, the Chinese
method of sowing grain into ridges separated by soak-
age furrows is favored rather than the European flat
type of cultivation. Even so, European varieties of
grain do not do well because of the high humidity
and heat. The shoots are luxurious but yields are
small, because the critical ripening stage is hindered
by the summer monsoon; moreover, because harvesting
also coincides with the rainy season it is often difficult to use machinery successfully. Fungi damage
many grains and the water content of fruits is very
high.

These conditions do, however, tend to favor crops
whose vegetative growth occurs late in the summer,
i.e., soybeans, maize, millet, and rice under irriga-
tion.* The availability of suitable flat land is the

_____

*Rice has been cultivated in Primor'ye since
1917 (by Koreans); the soybean was introduced in 1915
from Manchuria.

limiting factor for these crops, which presently are
restricted to the alluvial areas of the Lake Khanka-
Ussuri region. More than one-third of the arable
land of the Far East is under soybean cultivation;
it is the only agricultural product this region produces in excess of its own requirements. The Far
East produces more than 400,000 tons of soybeans from
an area of almost 2.1 million acres.[2]

North of Amur oblast', climatic conditions become increasingly unfavorable as the growing season
shortens and the need for quick-maturing grain varieties is greater. Here agriculture has been developed
only to serve the needs of the sparse local population. In Magadan oblast', there are only 12 farms
and 17,000 head of cattle in a total area of almost
a half million square miles; in this remote province
there are over twice as many reindeer as there are
people. Most requirements of potatoes, vegetables,
and milk are imported. In Kamchatka the only significant cultivated areas are restricted to the lower
valley of the Kamchatka River where root crops and
vegetables are grown.

A Siberian branch of the U.S.S.R. Academy of
Agricultural Sciences has been established in Novosibirsk. One of its tasks will be to evolve new varieties of plants and strains of livestock adapted to
local Siberian conditions. It will be a long time,
however, before any results are achieved in the
field; it took the Khabarovsk Agricultural Research
Institute many years to develop a strain of spring
wheat (Amurskaya 75) adapted to local conditions.

LOW YIELDS AND HIGH COSTS

The adverse physical conditions for agriculture
not only restrict farming opportunities; they also
depress yields to very low levels. The farming activity that does take place does so at a relatively
high cost. Until recently the emphasis in Soviet
agriculture was on expanding land inputs to increase
production; the need for higher yields was totally
ignored. A further disability is that State farms

(sovkhozy) occupy 60 percent of the farmland in this
part of the Soviet Union, and their labor productivity
is significantly below the U.S.S.R. average. Sovkhozy
are unwieldy units that suffer from diseconomies of
scale; their yields are generally lower and their
costs much higher than for kolkhozy (collective farms).

Even according to Soviet standards yields for
farm produce in the Far East are very low, whereas
those in Eastern Siberia barely approach average
levels. Table 18 shows that average grain yields in
the Far East are about two-thirds of the Soviet average and that yields for all other products except
eggs and milk are well below average; yields for
sugar beet are less than one-half those of the
U.S.S.R. Average yields for crops in the Far East
tend to fluctuate a great deal from year to year.
The best grain yields often come from the Primor'ye
and Khabarovsk krai, but the Amur region is the most
consistent in its yields and also the biggest producer
of grains. For some products, such as vegetables,
Far Eastern yields are the lowest in the entire
U.S.S.R.; for others, such as the wool clip, it ranks
among the poorest.

In Eastern Siberia, yields are generally much
closer to the Soviet average; for spring-sown wheat
they are above it. Wheat yields in Eastern Siberia
are higher than those in neighboring West Siberia and
are considerably more reliable, but there is a lack
of suitable land to cultivate, especially near Lake
Baikal. Sugar beet yields in Eastern Siberia are
the lowest in the U.S.S.R., and milk output per cow
is among the worst. Meat production is much the
poorest anywhere in the Soviet Union, and animal husbandry in Tuva A.S.S.R. is particularly backward.

The most important drawback to the expansion of
agriculture in this part of the Soviet Union from
Moscow's viewpoint is the extremely high costs of
production. A part of this cost problem undoubtedly
derives from extreme climatic conditions and low
average yields; another part is self-inflicted--the
preponderance of high-cost state farms. One of the
reasons for the higher costs on sovkhozy in the past

TABLE 18

Relative Annual Yields in Agriculture

Commodity	Unit of Measure	U.S.S.R.	Eastern Siberia Yield	Eastern Siberia As per cent of U.S.S.R.	Far East Yield	Far East As Per cent of U.S.S.R.
All grains	bushels per acre	15.3	13.4	88	10.6	69
Spring wheat	"	11.7	14.3	122	10.0	85
Winter rye	"	13.8	12.9	93	10.3	75
Grain maize	"	32.6	--	--	22.4	69
Sugar beet	tons per acre	6.8	1.9	28	3.1	46
Potatoes	"	3.8	3.5	92	2.9	76
Vegetables	"	4.6	4.1	89	3.2	70
Milk yield	tons per cow	1.79	1.66	93	1.65	92
Wool clip	lbs. per sheep	5.91	5.86	99	4.32	73
Meat output	tons per 100 acres[a]	0.84[b]	0.50	60	0.68	81
Eggs production	1,000 per 100 acres[c]	8.37[d]	5.82	70	15.72	188

[a] slaughter weight per 100 acres of agricultural land.
[b] R.S.F.S.R. only.
[c] Per 100 acres of sown grain land (excluding milk-wax maize).
[d] R.S.F.S.R. only.

Sources: Narodnoe Khozyaistvo SSSR and Narodnoe Khozyaistvo RSFSR, for several years.

was that <u>sovkhozniki</u> received wages about 25 percent
higher than the net incomes accruing to <u>kolkhozniki</u>.*
This difference is being eroded as guaranteed monthly
remuneration for the <u>kolkhoznik</u> (first introduced in
July of 1966) is established throughout the Union.
Another reason for higher costs on <u>sovkhozy</u> was the
lack of a direct link between incentive payments for
workers and the profitability of the farm--conse-
quently, the peasant had no interest in keeping costs
down. The <u>kolkhoznik</u>, however, as a claimant to net
farm income, is more interested in farm costs (although he does devote a great deal of time to his
private plot, from which 30 percent of family income
is derived). The situation on <u>sovkhozy</u> should improve, in theory, with the introduction of a <u>khozra-
shchot</u> (profit accountability) system of farm accounting and related incentive payments.

Only 34 percent of the state farms in Irkutsk
oblast' make a profit.[3] The net income per acre for
state wheat farms in the Far East in 1965 (the first
year of the new prices introduced by Brezhnev in
March, 1965) was minus 8.5 rubles for deliveries
within the quota and plus 0.1 rubles for over-quota
deliveries. Under these circumstances there can be
little incentive to improve productivity; hence,
farming as a whole has made little headway compared
with most other regions of the U.S.S.R.

The costs of production for farm produce on
<u>sovkhozy</u> and <u>kolkhozy</u> in the Far East and Eastern
Siberia, in relation to the average performance for
the U.S.S.R., are set out in Tables 19 and 20. In
the Far East the costs of producing most agricultural
commodities seem to be about 75 percent above the
norm for the U.S.S.R.; on <u>sovkhozy</u>, which possess 70
percent of the farmland, the costs of producing

----

*Thus, in Eastern Siberia in 1965 the cost of
producing one ton of grain was 57 rubles for <u>sovkhozy</u>
and 54 rubles for <u>kolkhozy</u>; the assumption for the
latter of wages equivalent to norms paid to <u>sovkhozniki</u>
raised the production cost to 55 rubles--but still
below actual <u>sovkhozy</u> costs.

TABLE 19

Pacific Siberia: Cost of Production for Farm Produce on <u>Sovkhozy</u> for 1967

Cost of Production in Rubles per Metric Ton[a]

Economic Region	Grain[b]	Sugar Beet[c]	Pota- toes	Vege- tables	Beef[d]	Pork[d]	Mutton[d]	Milk	Eggs (per '000)	Wool (per kilogram)[e]
Far East	80	60	116	131	1,570	1,648	1,281	253	99	7.11
Eastern Siberia	45	63	69	81	1,028	1,055	678	185	74	3.40
West Siberia	59	31	68	86	929	918	769	152	65	3.88
U.S.S.R.										
Average	55	24	64	71	1,092	1,042	643	166	67	2.98
Most expensive region	188	63	161	131	1,646	1,877	1,487	253	99	7.11
Cheapest region	29	17	45	45	857	744	576	116	46	1.38
Percent of U.S.S.R. average										
Far East	145	250	181	185	144	158	199	152	148	239
Eastern Siberia	82	263	108	114	94	101	105	111	110	114

[a]Excludes rent and interest on capital. Includes wages and social insurance; raw materials such as seed, fertilizer, oil, and grease; maintenance of and repairs to farm machinery; depreciation; other general expenditures.

[b]Excludes maize.

[c]For sugar manufacturing.

[d]Live weight equivalent; approximate slaughter weight conversion factors are 40 percent for sheep, 50 percent for cattle, and 60 percent for pigs.

[e]One kilogram = 2.21 pounds.

Note: Sovkhozy account for 70 percent of the farmland in the Far East and 60 percent of the farmland in Eastern Siberia.

Source: <u>Narodnoe Khozyaistvo SSSR v 1967 god</u>.

TABLE 20

Pacific Siberia: Cost of Production for Farm Produce on <u>Kolkhozy</u> for 1967

Cost of Production in Rubles per Metric Ton[a]

Economic Region	Grain[b]	Sugar Beet[c]	Pota-toes	Vege-tables	Beef[d]	Pork[d]	Mutton[d]	Milk	Eggs (per '000)	Wool (per kilogram)[e]
Far East	68	48	87	130	1,301	1,612	1,438	222	73	7.02
Eastern Siberia	51	55	61	100	1,045	1,311	639	199	75	3.25
West Siberia	56	34	66	160	863	999	738	150	63	3.59
U.S.S.R.										
Average	48	21	49	83	1,089	1,183	718	163	71	3.47
Most expexsive region	169	55	146	194	2,192	2,627	1,438	288	144	7.02
Cheapest region	33	19	41	44	794	893	549	116	59	2.06
Percent of U.S.S.R. average										
Far East	142	229	178	157	119	136	207	136	103	202
Eastern Siberia	106	262	124	120	96	111	89	122	106	94

[a]Estimated labor costs for <u>kolkhozniki</u> by actual payments in money and in kind.
[b]Excludes maize.
[c]For sugar manufacturing.
[d]Live weight equivalent; approximate slaughter weight conversion factors are 40 percent for sheep, 50 percent for cattle, and 60 percent for pigs.
[e]One kilogram = 2.21 pounds.

<u>Note</u>: <u>Kolkhozy</u> account for 30 percent of the farmland in the Far East and 40 percent of the farm-land in Eastern Siberia.

Source: <u>Narodnoe Khozyaistvo SSSR v 1967 god.</u>

vegetables, milk, eggs, and wool are the highest in
the Union. For several commodities (wool, mutton,
and sugar beet), Far Eastern state farm costs are
about double the average for the U.S.S.R. Collective
farm costs are relatively nearer to the Soviet average. In Eastern Siberia, on the other hand, costs
of production are only some 20 percent above the
U.S.S.R. average for most commodities. Here the cost
of livestock products (wool, mutton, and beef) is below average on kolkhozy and also below it for sovkhozy
produced beef and grain. The only product that is
double the average cost for the Soviet Union in this
region is sugar beet. The great cost of producing
foodstuffs in the Far East, and to a lesser extent in
Eastern Siberia, and the region's inability to feed
itself must be of great concern to the economic
policy-makers in Moscow.

The implications of this heavy cost disability
for the agricultural sector can best be illustrated
by an example. Assume that the production of grain
(principally wheat) in the Far East can be justified
only if its cost is less than the cost in the nearest
surplus-producing region (Eastern Siberia) plus
freight costs.[4] Applying this approach to the data
in Table 19 for sovkhozy, and taking a rail transport
cost between Krasnoyarsk and Khabarovsk of 15 rubles
per ton,[5] the resultant delivered cost of Eastern
Siberian grain in Khabarovsk is 20 rubles per ton
(25 percent) below the local Far Eastern cost of production. Unfortunately, Eastern Siberia does not
have sufficient surplus grain to supply all the Far
East's deficit, which means that wheat transported
from even further afield must bear a greater transport cost (see Table 2).

In 1965 the average cost of production for soybeans in the Far East was 110.4 rubles per ton on
kolkhozy and 169.4 rubles per ton on sovkhozy; the
State procurement price of 260 rubles per ton allowed
a surplus in the Far East as a whole of 186 million
rubles in the five years to 1965. About two-thirds
of Far Eastern soybean output is purchased by the
State; the rest is used locally, some of it as a
fodder. U.S.S.R. state purchases of soybeans have

been supplemented traditionally by imports from China
at a cost of 90-100 rubles per ton plus freight,
which is indicative of the relative cost differences
between the two producers.

Industrial crops such as soybean have always
been favored, but, in general, farming in the Far
East still results in a net loss. Even with the much
higher prices announced for agricultural produce in
1965, state farms in the Amur region lost 511,000
rubles--making a cumulative loss for the three years
1963-65 of 13.8 million rubles. Potato production
on sovkhozy in Amur and Khabarovsk territories made
a loss of 992,000 rubles in 1965, and vegetable output also sustained losses of 743,000 rubles in the
Amur, Yakutsk, and Kamchatka regions. Far Eastern
state farm milk procurements in 1965 incurred an
overall loss of 12.1 million rubles (or 13.8 percent);
pork procurements from farms recorded a deficit of
1.2 million rubles. Even the famous fur-breeding
farms of Magadan incurred heavy losses.

In more favored areas, such as Krasnoyarsk,
profitability is satisfactory despite shortcomings
in deliveries of fertilizer and machinery suitable
for local conditions. In 1966-68 the state and collective farms of Krasnoyarsk krai made a net profit
of 206 million rubles as a result of significant improvements in productivity, crop rotations, and animal husbandry.

THE PRODUCTION PATTERN

The adverse climate, low yields, high costs,
and poor profitability have all helped to restrict
agricultural output in Pacific Siberia. As a result,
the Far East "imports" from other parts of the
U.S.S.R. huge quantities of foodstuffs each year, including almost one-half of the milk requirements for
its 5.5 million people, 45 percent of the vegetables
needed, 20 percent of the potatoes consumed (from
Siberia, the Urals, Volga, and Central Chernozem),
one-third of its eggs, and over one-half of its total
meat needs or 105,000 tons slaughter weight (from

Siberia, the Urals, Kazakhstan, Volga, Central Chernozem, and the Ukraine). Grain (including fodder)
imports amount to some two-thirds of consumption;
bread grain shipments alone (largely wheat and wheat
flour) are over 1.25 million tons of which 675,000
tons come from Eastern Siberia, 460,000 tons from
West Siberia, and 85,000 tons from Volga and the
Urals--in about equal quantities. In addition, mixed
feeds from Eastern Siberia total 135,000 tons.[6] Owing to the shortage of milling facilities, about 20
percent of flour consumed is also imported from the
Urals and Volga regions. Most of the Far East's
sugar needs are brought in from Central Chernozem,
the Ukraine, Volga, and--more recently--Cuba; shipments are about 145,000 to 149,000 tons per year. A
high proportion of Far Eastern fruit requirements
are also imported--especially apples from North Korea
and mandarins from China--in quantities exceeding
80,000 tons annually.

     The situation in Eastern Siberia is different
because the local output of grain, meat, and wool
seems to be somewhat in excess of demand at current
prices. Shortfalls do, however, occur in the production of potatoes and vegetables, sugar, milk, eggs,
and fruits. Table 21 is probably a fairly accurate
reflection of demand and supply balances in Pacific
Siberia in view of the U.S.S.R.'s trade policy in
foodstuffs, which has approximated autarky in the
past; thus, the figure for Soviet output per capita
may be taken as a rough magnitude of average per
capita consumption.

     Wheat production in Pacific Siberia expanded
rapidly after 1953, when 9.6 million acres of virgin
and fallow lands were ploughed; by 1959 the output
of wheat had almost doubled. Production then leveled
off to between 3.6 million and 3.9 million tons (or
around 5 percent of Soviet output). Both acreage
and yields tended to stagnate due to poor incentives,
high production costs, and, in the Far East, the lack
of suitable growing conditions and mechanical equipment. In the last few years, however, yields have
improved--particularly in Eastern Siberia where the
dry climate is more favorable. Production in the

TABLE 21

Output of Major Agricultural Products per Capita
(in kilograms)

Agricultural Product	Far East	Eastern Siberia	West Siberia	U.S.S.R.
Arable products				
Grain	165	667	1,110	630
Vegetables	184	317	430	374
Potatoes	58	49	50	73
Technical cultures				
Flax fiber	--	0.2	0.9	1.9
Sunflower seed	--	--	2	19
Sugar beet	14	2	41	230
Livestock products				
Meat and fat[a]	20	42	46	41
Milk	159	262	370	288
Wool	0.1	2.8	1.5	1.7
Eggs	93	101	130	130

[a]Slaughter weight.

Source: A. V. Bolgov et al., Ekonomika Sotsialisticheskogo Sel'skogo Kho-zyaistva (Moscow, 1965), p. 381.

153

late 1960s rose to over 5 million tons, and in 1971
the average yield was probably about 18 bushels per
acre (net barn yield basis).

The most important wheat-producing regions are
the Krasnoyarsk krai and Irkutsk oblast', which together account for two-thirds of Pacific Siberian
output. Here there are 6 million acres under spring
wheat, and yields average a good (for Siberia) 15
bushels per acre, despite the lowest rate of mineral
fertilizer application in the Union. Land is being
diverted out of wheat growing, however, into livestock
uses (annual grasses and fodder maize). One of the
problems of wheat growing in this part of the Soviet
Union is the high percentage of moisture in the harvested grain because of frequent rains and cool
weather during harvesting. Freshly harvested grain
often has a moisture content of 20 percent, sometimes
up to 30-35 percent.

Meat output fares better because of more favorable natural conditions (especially in the sheltered
valleys of Tuva, Chita, and Buryat territories) and
the fact that about 40 percent of production comes
from private plots. About 45 percent of local meat
production is beef, 30 percent pork, 15 percent mutton and goat meat, and 5 percent poultry. A large
livestock complex is being built near Usol'e Sibirskoe;
by 1975 two poultry factories with over 600,000 laying hens will produce more than 130 tons of meat per
year.

Meat production has increased rapidly since 1965,
the terminal year of the Seven Year Plan, which fell
short of its regional target by 23 percent. Between
1965 and 1969 meat production rose from 444,000 tons
to 534,000 tons, but this apparently has been achieved
at the expense of a decline in livestock numbers, especially pigs. There has been a marked increase,
however, in poultry raising for meat. In the remote
areas of Magadan, Yakutia, and northern Kamchatka the
local meat diet is supplemented by venison from nomadic herds of the northern reindeer.

Milk production rose by 18 percent in the Seven
Year Plan, although no real increase was recorded

until 1964. There was a further rise in 1965 and
1966, but through to 1969 output failed to increase
perceptibly. About one-half the milk produced in
Pacific Siberia comes from private plots, but in the
collectivized and state-farming sectors productivity
is relatively low. In the southern Primor'ye, where
the climate is more favorable for grass growth, milk
cows are a profitable activity, but in the rest of
the Far East a loss is sustained.

Butter production mainly comes from Amur Province
and Krasnoyarsk; in 1965 it was 37,582 tons with two-
thirds of it made in Eastern Siberia. Butter output
is growing rapidly and probably reached 45,000-50,000
tons by 1970. Nevertheless, there was a deficit in
meeting local needs by perhaps 20,000 tons--most of
which came from West Siberia (Altai krai).

Nearly three-quarters of the eggs produced in
Pacific Siberia come from private plots. In the
last few years, however, the State has encouraged an
increase in poultry numbers in the socialized sector
of farming despite a shortage of feedstuffs. Feeding
costs are the main determinant of egg production
costs and account for 63 percent of total costs. The
local cost of production varies from 77 kopecks to
1 ruble and 1 kopeck for 10 eggs, and this is very
high in relation to the average unit value (f.o.b.)
paid for shell eggs imported from across the border
in China at 22 kopecks for 10 eggs; these imports
are still occurring.

Wool production in Pacific Siberia amounts to
6 percent of the Soviet total, but most of it is
transported in unprocessed form to the large woolen
mills in Moscow oblast', the city of Moscow, and
Bryansk oblast', which together produce over 50 percent of all Soviet woolen cloth.

In the Far East the wool clip per sheep is the
lowest in the U.S.S.R. and the count is coarse; in
Eastern Siberia yields are above the Soviet average
and the count is finer. About two-thirds of the
wool produced comes from kolkhozy. Chita oblast',
which has over 3.5 million sheep, derives almost one-
half of its kolkhozy gross income from wool and

mutton; in this region sheep-breeding has progressed
rapidly so that 80 percent of the wool produced is
classified as fine or semi-fine, compared with only
25 percent in the early 1950s.[7]

Sugar beet production is exceedingly small in
relation to local population requirements. Output of
beet is about 85,000 tons per year--giving some
12,000 tons of granulated sugar if a yield of 14 percent is assumed.[8] But the factory production of
granulated sugar, almost all of which comes from a
single factory at Ussuriisk (1935) in the Far East,
has averaged 50,000 tons annually--indicating a processing of some 38,000 tons (refined basis) of raw
sugar from beyond the region, possibly from Cuba.
In Eastern Siberia a small factory at Bichura in
Buryat Mongolia was constructed during World War II;
its output is only 2,000 tons per year of refined
sugar. It often is necessary to abandon one-half of
the sown area of sugar beet because the young plants
die in the early part of the growing season and the
shortness of the season does not permit replanting.
Frequently the crop is fit only for livestock fodder.
Also, the harvesting period for beets is critical because it coincides with the harvesting of grains;
the local labor supply is insufficient to handle
both tasks.

The area planted to fruit and berries is not
very large at about 55,000 acres, or 0.6 percent of
the Soviet total. Two-fifths of this acreage is in
the hands of private plot workers. The major producing areas are in Primor'ye, Krasnoyarsk, and Khabarovsk. Even in the more favored part of Primor'ye
the apples grown are of the small ranetka, or cherry
crabapple type (malus robusta), with some varieties
of pippin. Berries are the main fruits grown; and
these tend to be confined to cultivated varieties
of low-growing or creeping berries, which are better
suited to the severe Siberian climate.

Rice is grown in alluvial soils on the west and
east shores of Lake Khanka and in the valleys of the
Daubikhe and Ulakhe to the east. It was originally
grown by Koreans in the 1930s. About 50,000 acres of

rice are sown in the Far East, an increase of 60 percent since 1965.   In 1970 production of rice was
planned to be 140,000 tons, or triple its 1963 output.
One Soviet estimate states that up to 250,000 acres
of land suitable for rice are available in the
Primor'ye and Pri-Amur regions.[9]   In 1971 new rice
plantations were introduced near Vladivostok (Maykhe
Valley) and at Slavyanka.

Honey is an important supplementary sugar crop
(output--6,300 tons annually in the Far East or less
than one-half its 1942 level), and melons and pumpkins
(produced, respectively, in Ussuri-Khanka and Zeya-
Bureya-Amur) also are grown for local needs.   However,
large quantities of canned vegetables have to be
freighted into the Far East to meet shortfalls in
local output; imports are about 35 million cans and
railway freight expenditure costs--one million rubles.[10]   A vegetable canning factory with a capacity
of 5 million cans is being built at Khanka, and another one is to be erected at Suchan.[11]

AGRICULTURE, THE ECONOMY,
AND THE PACIFIC

Agriculture in Pacific Siberia has a precarious
and costly existence in the face of a hostile climate
and an inflexible agricultural system dominated by
sovkhozy.   Beyond the clusters of agricultural activity in the plains around Krasnoyarsk and Irkutsk
and in the valleys of the Zeya-Bureya and Ussuri,
there are only vast expanses of taiga.   The exceptions
to this are hill sheep and cattle breeding in Tuva,
Chita, and Buryat Mongolia and, in the north, small-
scale agriculture along the Yenisei, the Lena (and
tributaries), and the Kolyma.

The expansion of agriculture northward has not
developed a great deal under the Soviets.   The Tsarist
cultivation pattern in the south is still the basis
for agriculture, despite the development of virgin
lands, maize, sugar beet, rice, and soybeans.   Before
the Russians settled this region there were only native hunters and small groups of Manchurian farmers

in the south.   Cultivation started with grants of
wide strips of cultivable land to Cossack settlers
along the Amur and Ussuri rivers.   Large-scale peasant
migration commenced in the early 1900s, but even
then food deficits had to be met by imports of grain
from Manchuria and cattle from Mongolia.   In the
1930s, when peasant settlers were arriving at the
rate of 30,000 per year, the rural population enjoyed
special privileges.   Collective farms were exempted
from compulsory grain deliveries for ten years and
individual farmers were exempt for five years; several
parts of Khabarovsk and Primor'ye districts were also
freed from deliveries of meat and other animal products.[12]

The idea of regional self-sufficiency in food
became very popular with Soviet planners during the
period of the Third Five Year Plan (1938-42).   At
this time the Far East was singled out for special
attention (in view of the Japanese threat in Manchukuo) to achieve self-sufficiency in potatoes, vegetables, and other "bulk foodstuffs."[13]   This aim was
of course never realized.

One of the major problems in the rural economy
at present, especially in Eastern Siberia, is the
seasonal fluctuation in demand for farm labor.   For
kolkhozy, the difference between the months of lowest
and highest employment (January and July) is some
240,500 workers, or 5.7 percent of total civilian
employment.   During the winter these people have to
be given other employment in industries such as forestry or construction work--otherwise, underemployment
would exist in the work force.

In the Far East, capital investments in agriculture during 1966-70 were planned to be 1,172 million
rubles, or double actual investments for 1961-65.
By 1970 annual investment in agriculture was probably
about 360 million rubles, or 1.7 times greater than
in 1965.   A large proportion of this investment went
to farm capital construction works, such as cattle
sheds.   This accelerated rate of investment was necessary because of the increased levels of production
planned for agriculture.   By 1970 grains output was

expected to be 42 percent greater than in 1965 (including a 450 percent rise in rice output), the soybean harvest was to be up by 80 percent, vegetables
by 40 percent, meat (live weight) by 38 percent, milk
by 33 percent, and eggs by 70 percent. On data
available up to the end of 1969, a considerable
shortfall in most of these targets had occurred.
Vegetable production actually fell, and milk output
only rose by 10 percent. The yield of eggs and meat
grew by 57 percent and 32 percent, respectively--both
below plan. Only the grains harvest--up 56 percent
on 1965--exceeded the planned norms. These shortfalls
are illustrative of the difficulties of producing
more food in the region despite a greater allocation
of State investments. Under these circumstances the
output of foodstuffs is likely to remain well below
demands. This has been the case ever since the area
was settled in the mid-1800s. Traditionally, cheap
food imports have come in across the border from
China (especially Manchuria) and Mongolia. But trade
with China declined rapidly in the 1960s.

     It is especially significant in this context
that the long-term development plan for the Far East
and Chita oblast', in 1967-75, stressed the need for
the production of milk, potatoes, vegetables, and,
to a considerable extent, meat to fulfill local demands. But this call for self-sufficiency will not
be met. The agricultural sector of the Pacific Siberian economy will remain heavily dependent upon
imports of foodstuffs. Self-sufficiency by 1975 is
not possible within current economic and physical
restraints--unless, of course, the State is prepared
to pay a crippling price. Production costs are not
likely to fall significantly until the dominant state
farm system is changed in favor of lower-cost collective farming or until special high-yielding strains
are evolved to suit the rigorous climate. Already,
regional price incentives are imposing a high oppor-
tunity cost on the State, compared with the production
responses that could be obtained at less cost from
other agricultural regions in the Union. Given the
costly transportation outlays incurred in sending
foodstuffs long distances to Pacific Siberia from
surplus agricultural regions on the heavily worked

Trans-Siberian railway, it may be comparatively advantageous for the U.S.S.R. to consider a policy of
importing, on a large scale, Siberian food needs
from relatively cheap overseas sources in the nearby
Pacific. In the past China was one such supplier;
in the future there may be trade opportunities for
surplus-food producing countries such as Australia,
New Zealand, and Canada.

                              NOTES

     1. E. Thiel, The Soviet Far East (London:
Methuen, 1957), p. 72.

     2. A. D. Nesterenko, Voprosy Ekonomiki Sel'-
skogo Khozyaistva Dal'nego Vostoka (Khabarovsk, 1967),
pp. 97-99.

     3. P. P. Silinskii, Planirovanie Narodnogo
Khozyaistva v Oblasti (Moscow, 1967).

     4. A. E. Probst in Vestnik Akademii Nauk SSSR,
No. 12, 1963, has stated that specialization can be
justified economically only under the condition:

$$P_1 + \sum T < P_2$$

where

     P_1 is the production cost in the specialized
         region
     P_2 is the production cost in the consuming region
     T is the transport cost between the two regions.

     5. Calculated at 0.34 kopecks per ton/kilometer
over 4,458 kilometers (2,770 miles); derived from
E. G. Meerson and F. V. D'yakonov, "Dal'nii Vostok,"
in Geograficheskie Problemy Razvitiya Krupnykh Ekonomicheskikh Raionov SSSR, ed. V. V. Pokshishevskii
(Moscow: AN SSSR, 1964), p. 410.

     6. D. V. D'yakonov et al., Dal'nii Vostok,
ekonomiko-geograficheskaya kharakteristika (Moscow:
AN SSSR, 1966), pp. 122-23 and 194.

7.   D. I. Kotlyarova, "Perspektivy Razvitiya Sel'skogo Khozyaistva," Prirodnye Bogatstva i Perspektivy Razvitiya Ekonomiki Chitinskoi Oblasti (Chita, 1960), pp. 126-27.

8.   L. V. Opatskii, Razmeshchenie Pishchevoi Promyshlennosti SSSR (Moscow, 1958), p. 97.

9.   D. V. D'yakonov et al., op. cit., p. 206.

10.   Ekonomicheskaya Gazeta, No. 11, March, 1967.

11.   Ibid.

12.   E. Raikhman and B. Vvedensky, The Economic Development of the Soviet Far East (Moscow, 1936), p. 38.

13.   Molotov at the Eighteenth Congress of the CPSU, March, 1939, as quoted in G. D. R. Phillips, Russia, Japan and Mongolia (London, 1942), p. 96. See also Pravda, February 6, 1934, for special provisions in the Second Five Year Plan.

APPENDIX: PRODUCTION AND
EXPORT OF FURS

Furs are a valuable source of export income for
Pacific Siberia. Total Soviet exports of furs and
fur skins (excluding finished articles) have varied
between 50 million and 60 million rubles in recent
years, with Britain taking up to one-half. A substantial portion of this trade comes from the fur
farms and hunting grounds of Pacific Siberia where
more than one-third of Soviet furs are produced.
Yakutia provides about one-fifth of the value of total
Soviet fur exports (mainly squirrel, Arctic fox,
ermine, Arctic hare). Up to 15,000 hunters are employed in this industry.

The main fur-bearing animals of the region are
squirrel, sable, fox (including black and Arctic),
mink, ermine, and Arctic hare; fur seals and sea ot-
ters and beavers are bred on the Commander Islands.
Furs have been a traditional source of trade in Siberia for over 300 years; but, in the Soviet period,
farms, nurseries, and reservations were established,
and hunting has been organized on a collective basis.
On Sakhalin, for instance, there are six state fur
farms that can produce over 200,000 mink pelts a
year. In the wild forest and tundra regions of Magadan and north Yakutia, where most of the fur-bearing
animals have retreated, hunting is regulated in order
to conserve supplies. When the hunting season is
over the furs are delivered to the collective bases
where payment is made according to results.

Some locally caught pelts, generally of an inferior quality, are made up into articles of clothing
at the Chita clothing factories. Fur hats, gloves,
and coats are a necessity in this part of the U.S.S.R.
during the long, cold winters.

Much of the early colonization of Siberia can
be traced back to the fur trade of seventeenth-century
Russia and the fur tributes exacted from the natives
of Siberia. Fur catching is still very important in
the national areas of the Chukotka, Koryak, Taimyr,

and Yevenki peoples (as well as the northern Yaku-
tians), where, together with fishing and reindeer
breeding, this industry provides the main livelihood.

The cooperative fur-trapping organizations have
not been able to guarantee a minimum wage for trappers, and the prices fixed for furs do not reflect
the real cost of trapping in difficult physical conditions. Accordingly, the number of skilled professional fur hunters is declining.

The most valuable Soviet furs come from the Far
East. Kamchatka sable, ermine, and fox are especially
sought after; but, as shown in Appendix Table A.1,
Kamchatka state fur farms (like those of Magadan)
are operating at a loss, whereas the larger Primor'ye
and Sakhalin farms are profitable. There is a high
level of demand for Primor'ye mink from Japan, Britain,
Holland, West Germany, and France, which has enabled
a lowering of costs per pelt through scale economies.
Mink breeding was started in the Primor'ye in 1947;
now there are 15 fur farms supplying mink pelts in a
range of six colors, including sapphire and pearl.

APPENDIX TABLE A.1

Profitability of State Fur Farms in the Far East

Indexes	Primor'ye		Kamchatka		Magadan		Sakhalin	
	1963	1965	1963	1965	1963	1965	1963	1965
Quantity sold ('000 pelts)	252.9	317.3	31.4	70.1	26.2	28.0	168.3	171.4
Returns ('000 rubles)	8,624	12,080	1,005	2,416	336	1,256	6,665	6,735
Costs ('000 rubles)	7,440	9,748	1,419	2,506	1,134	1,325	5,620	6,325
Profit ('000 rubles)	1,184	2,332	--	--	--	--	1,045	410
Loss ('000 rubles)	--	--	414	90	798	69	--	--
Percent profitability	15.9	23.9	-29.2	-3.6	-70.4	-5.2	18.6	6.5

aProfit or loss as a percent of costs.

Source: A. D. Nesterenko, Voprosy Ekonomiki Sel'skogo Khozyaistva Dal'nego Vostoka (Khabarovsk, 1967), p. 229.

Structure of the Sown Area in Pacific Siberia, 1960-67

Type of Cultivation	Eastern Siberia			Far East		
	1960	1965	1967	1960	1965	1967
Total sown area[a] ('000 acres)	17,747	18,837	18,528	5,244	6,158	6,331
Total sown area (percent)	100.0	100.0	100.0	100.0	100.0	100.0
Grains (percent of total sown area)	68.1	66.0	65.7	47.6	41.8	42.1
Spring wheat[b]	39.0	44.0	42.9	30.4	22.3	22.3
Winter rye	1.5	0.7	0.3	0.2	0.2	0.2
Grain maize	--	--	--	0.4	0.2	0.2
Spring barley	6.1	6.4	6.2	4.3	6.1	6.0
Oats	19.0	10.8	13.4	10.8	10.4	10.5
Millet	1.0	0.5	0.4	0.2	0.1	0.0
Buckwheat	0.4	0.6	0.9	1.1	2.1	2.5
Legumes[c]	0.4	2.7	1.4	0.0	0.0	0.0
Technical crops (percent of total sown area)	0.4	0.4	0.3	19.9	34.3	33.3
Sugar beet[d]	0.0	0.0	--	0.4	0.4	0.4
Flax	0.1	0.1	0.1	--	--	--
Soybeans	--	--	--	19.4	33.9	32.9
Vegetables (percent of total sown area)	4.0	3.5	3.3	8.3	6.5	6.4
Potatoes	3.6	3.1	2.9	6.5	5.2	5.1
Vegetables	0.4	0.4	0.4	1.8	1.3	1.3
Fodder crops (percent of total sown area)	27.5	30.1	30.7	24.2	17.4	18.2
Perennial grasses	7.4	4.2	5.3	4.3	2.0	2.0
Annual grasses[e]	9.9	12.7	12.5	10.9	5.0	5.8
Fodder maize[f]	6.9	10.7	10.2	6.5	7.4	8.4
Root crops and melons	0.7	0.4	0.4	0.5	0.3	0.4

[a]All types of enterprise--state, collective, and private.
[b]No winter-sown wheat is cultivated in Siberia.
[c]Mainly peas.
[d]For manufacturing purposes.
[e]Includes (failed) crops sown in the winter and harvested for fodder.
[f]Includes milk-wax stage as well as maize for silage and green fodder.

Source: Narodnoe Khozyaistvo RSFSR v 1967 god, pp. 179 and 182.

8

POPULATION PATTERN, STRUCTURE, AND MIGRATION

One hundred years ago . . . the country
was practically an uninhabited wilderness.[1]

BRIEF HISTORY

Although the Cossacks established a chain of
trading posts and fortified stockades in Pacific Siberia in the 1600s they were created not with permanent settlement in mind but, rather, to facilitate
the levying of tribute and trade in furs from the
native peoples. Some of the local tribes, such as
the Buryats and Tungus, put up fierce resistance to
colonization, but many other more primitive tribes,
such as the Yakuts, were easily subjugated. At first,
settlement was slow and consisted mainly of traders
and trappers and, later, runaway serfs. Then, free
settlers and peasants came in search of new farmlands
and greater freedom than in European Russia. But
the use of Siberia as a place of exile and hard labor for both political and criminal prisoners of the
State gave the region its first large influx of
population.[2]

Large-scale migration into Siberia did not really
occur until the second half of the nineteenth century; prior to that, migratory movements from the
crowded farmlands of European Russia had been directed
primarily southward to the fertile Ukraine and Kuban.

Between 1823 and 1887 some 700,000 exiles were sent to
Siberia, and by 1900 this figure swelled to over 1
million.   Free colonization by peasants on agricultural lands did not make much progress until the
turn of the century, when the completion of the Trans-
Siberian railway made the journey of from 3,000 to
more than 5,000 miles a matter of days rather than
months.*

In the quarter century preceding World War I
a great agricultural migration of free peasants flowed
into the region on the Trans-Siberian railway.   Having been freed from serfdom in 1861 the Russian
peasants left the overpopulated rural lands of Pol-
tava, Kursk, Chernigov, and Voronezh in Europe for
the open spaces of Siberia.   The Government assisted
migrants by special grants and low rail fares.   D. W.
Treadgold has made a detailed study of this remarkable
shift in population and estimates that between 1801
and 1914 the total number of migrants settling in
Siberia was seven million.[3]

Settlement of the area east of Lake Baikal was
particularly slow.   Between 1896 and 1914 over four
million married migrants settled in Siberia, but more
than two-thirds of them stayed in West Siberia and
only one-fifth and one-eighth, respectively, went to
Eastern Siberia and the Far East.   It was not until
after the Russo-Japanese War of 1904-5 that settlement in the Far East became significant.   There was,
however, a large number of settlers who stayed in
Siberia for only a short while and then returned to
European Russia; this was especially true of the un-
married migrants.   Overall, the proportion of migrants to Siberia who eventually returned varied in
the first ten years of this century from between 30
percent and 40 percent to almost 60 percent; dissatisfaction with general living conditions and facilities,
the high cost of essential items imported from the
western industrial cities, and the severer climate

_____

*The Trans-Siberian railway was authorized by
Imperial rescript in 1891 and was completed in 1904;
its cost was over $500 million.

all were contributing factors. Lenin called the
Tsarist settlement policy in Siberia a great failure
(polnyi krakh).

After the Revolution, particularly after 1928,
Soviet migration policy stressed industrial and urban
settlement geared to five-year development plans; the
growth of coal mining and metallurgy in the Kuzbass
was an essential part of this policy. The First Five
Year Plan (1928-32) proposed to settle 780,000 people
in Siberia and the Far East, following the successful
settlement of some 450,000 landless peasants there
between 1925 and 1929. The Soviet era between the
two world wars marked the beginning of settlement in
Siberia away from the thin line of population cling-
ing to the Trans-Siberian railway. Some of this was
accomplished through the coercion of Dal'stroi and
the corrective labor camps. But there were other
Government inducements--such as 20 percent to 30 percent higher wages, tax exemptions for 5 to 10 years,
free food and seed, home-building loans in the form
of one-half the house price as a gift and the other
half lent over 15 years, long-term loans for furniture, and freedom from compulsory deliveries of some
farm products.

One of the effects of this rapid increase of
the population through migration was to reduce the
relative proportion of the native population in Siberia, which fell from 6.6 percent in 1926 to 4.4
percent in 1939. Koreans, Japanese, and Chinese were
greatly lowered in numbers in the deportations of
the 1930s. The Jews, however, increased at this
time because of the formation of the Jewish national
area and the forced transportation of Jewish people
from Europe. By 1939 Russians, Ukrainians, and Belo-
russians made up over 86 percent of the population
of Eastern Siberia, the remainder being mainly native
Yakuts, Buryats, Tuvinians, and Khakass.

THE POSTWAR PATTERN

The invasion of the European parts of the
U.S.S.R. by Germany in World War II and the associated

shift of many important industries to Siberia undoubtedly helped a great deal to consolidate the emphasis already placed on the region in the Third Five
Year Plan. Between 1939 and 1956 the population of
Pacific Siberia rose by 3 million, or almost 40 percent. The expansion was particularly marked in the
Far East, which according to one estimate received
1.7 million immigrants between 1939 and 1950. This
increase occurred largely because of a rise in the
rate of urban migration, compared with the earlier
period with its emphasis on agricultural settlement.
The building of new cities, such as Komsomol'sk, attracted settlers from the older cities to west of
the Urals. The large proportion of young people
among these migrants from European Russia gave Pacific
Siberia the highest rate of population growth in the
U.S.S.R. by the time of the 1959 census.

In the 1960s the population growth in Pacific
Siberia has been helped by renewed Government financial assistance especially through higher regional
wage incentives. But the turnover rate of migrants
(and hence the labor force) has tended to rise. Between the censuses of 1959 and 1970, the total population of the region rose by 1.9 million to 13.2
million (see Table 22). The Far East's rate of
growth (19.6 percent) was above the average for the
U.S.S.R. (15.8 percent), but Eastern Siberia's (15.3
percent) has fallen below it. The climate of Eastern
Siberia is cold, whereas the southern regions of the
Far East have a relatively mild climate--which may
help to account for their differing abilities to retain migrants. The more highly developed urban environment and the greater regional wage incentives
paid are also contributing factors to the attractions
of the Far East. The fastest-growing populations
are in the pioneering territories of Yakutia and
Magadan, where wages can be up to twice those in Moscow. Some of the native autonomous territories also
are growing relatively quickly because they still
have high birth rates. The island of Sakhalin, on
the other hand, is losing population to the mainland
where there are better job opportunities.

In essence, however, the pattern of population
distribution in Pacific Siberia has not changed

significantly from its predominant location near the
Trans-Siberian railway, which was established over
50 years ago. About 70 percent of the towns with
more than 15,000 people are situated within 30 miles
of the Trans-Siberian railway. Some diffusion has
occurred, of course, especially to the industrial
wedge extending from Krasnoyarsk-Minusinsk in the
west to Irkutsk-Angarsk in the east and in the Ussuri
Valley between Vladivostok-Nakhodka and Khabarovsk.
Beyond this highly concentrated corridor of railway-
oriented settlements the only important collection of
cities is in southern Sakhalin. Other sizable urban
settlements are mining towns or regional administrative centers (e.g., Yakutsk, Noril'sk, Magadan, Petropavlovsk-Kamchatskii).

In the whole of Pacific Siberia there are at
present only 16 towns with more than 100,000 people,
and, of these, 8 have 200,000 or more. The major
urban center is Krasnoyarsk, with 648,000 people;
the other three largest cities (Irkutsk, Vladivostok,
and Khabarovsk) all have between 400,000 and 450,000
people. Within this pattern of towns there are no
clearly defined conurbations as such, but the major
urban groupings are as follows:

1.   the Krasnoyarsk cluster, extending west to
Achinsk and east to Kansk--over one million people;

2.   the Abakan-Chernogorsk coal-mining district
--200,000 people;

3.   the Irkutsk-Angarsk-Cheremkhovo chemical,
coal, and aluminum towns along the Angara--900,000
people;

4.   Blagoveshchensk-Svobodnyi and the towns of
the Zeya-Bureya--about 350,000 people;

5.   Vladivostok to Ussuriisk and Spassk Dal'nii
--over 850,000 people;

6.   the towns of southern Sakhalin--200,000 people.

TABLE 22

The Population Pattern
(in thousands)

Population Category	Census 1-15-1959	Census 1-15-1970	Percent Increase 1959-70	Percent Urban 1959	Percent Urban 1970
Eastern Siberia	6,473	7,464	15.3	--	--
Far East	4,834	5,780	19.6	--	--
West Siberia	11,252	12,110	7.6	--	--
U.S.S.R.	208,827	241,748	15.8	--	--
Population by administrative regions					
Krasnoyarsk krai	2,615	2,962	13.3	50	62
Khakass A.O.	414	446	7.7	54	60
Taimyr N.O.	33	38	15.2	61	62
Evenki N.O.	10	13	30.0	20	28
Irkutsk oblast'	1,976	2,314	17.1	62	72
Ust'Ordyn N.O.	133	146	9.8	15	17
Chita oblast'	1,036	1,145	10.5	54	57
Aginsk Buryat N.O.	49	66	34.7	--	21
Buryat A.S.S.R.	673	812	20.7	41	45
Tuva A.S.S.R.	172	231	34.3	29	38
Primor'ye krai	1,381	1,722	24.7	67	73
Khabarovsk krai	1,143	1,346	17.8	74	78
Jewish A.O.	163	173	6.1	72	69
Amur oblast'	718	793	10.5	60	62
Kamchatka oblast'	221	287	29.9	64	76
Koryak N.O.	28	31	10.7	22	34

Magadan oblast'	236	352	49.2	81	75
Chukot N.O.	47	101	114.9	57	69
Sakhalin oblast'	649	616	-5.1	75	78
Yakutsk A.S.S.R.	487	664	36.4	49	56
Population of major towns					
Krasnoyarsk	412	648	57	--	--
Irkutsk	366	451	23	--	--
Vladivostok	291	442	52	--	--
Khabarovsk	323	437	35	--	--
Ulan-Ude	174	254	46	--	--
Chita	172	242	41	--	--
Komsomol'sk	177	218	23	--	--
Angarsk	135	204	51	--	--
Bratsk	43	155	259	--	--
Petropavlovsk	86	154	80	--	--
Noril'sk	118	136	15	--	--
Blagoveshchensk	94	128	36	--	--
Ussuriisk	104	128	23	--	--
Yakutsk	74	108	45	--	--
Yuzhno-Sakhalinsk	86	106	24	--	--
Nakhodka	64	105	64	--	--
Magadan	62	92	48	--	--
Abakan	56	90	60	--	--
Birobidzhan	41	56	37	--	--
Kyzyl	34	52	50	--	--

Notes: A.O. = Autonomous Oblast'; N.O. = National Okrug.

The territories of the Far North (Taimyr, Evenki, Yakutsk, Magadan, and Kamchatka) had a population growth of 37.2 percent, or 367,000, over the 11-year period; the southern relatively well-populated districts rose by 15.2 percent, or 1,570,000.

Source: Pravda, April 19, 1970.

Over 26 percent of Pacific Siberia's population lives
in these six urban clusters--excluding important but
isolated cities such as Khabarovsk, Komsomol'sk,
Ulan-Ude, Chita, and so on, which account for another
14 percent.

The rural pattern of settlement is characterized
by a marked tendency to follow the major rivers into
the interior (e.g., Yenisei, Angara, Lena, and Kolyma).
In the dense <u>taiga</u>, forest clearings are almost always near a river or stream, as these provide the
only convenient means of communication. In the Far
North there are a few fishing villages along the
coast and at the mouth of the estuaries of rivers
(e.g., Chukotka); there are also some nomadic reindeer
herders--who will be completely settled by 1973. The
rural population thickens in the south close to the
Amur and Ussuri valleys and the Shilka and Selenga
rivers nearer to Lake Baikal. It becomes more dense
as the relatively good agricultural plains of the
Yenisei are reached. In these areas the rural population lives predominantly in settlements of between
100 and 500 people.

There is a problem in Pacific Siberia, in common
with many other industrializing regions (both planned
and free enterprise), with the flight of population
from the land. This has become particularly marked
since World War II, with the dismantling of forced
labor colonies, the fairly rapid industrialization,
and the increasing sophistication of facilities in
the cities. In the 1926 census the rural population
of Pacific Siberia was 4.1 million (or 82 percent of
the total); by the 1939 census it had grown to almost
4.8 million (or 61 percent). But in the 1959 census
the rural population had dropped to 4.6 million (41
percent), and by 1970 it had fallen further to 4.5
million (34 percent). Given the excessive labor normally employed on Soviet farms, much of it with a
marginal productivity approaching zero, there is
probably little cause for concern over this trend
from a farm output viewpoint but every reason for
concern for balanced regional development--particu-
larly in that those leaving the farms are the young
and able-bodied.

By the year 2000, the proportion of rural dwellers is expected to be around 25 percent and the number of people living in the Far North, not much more
than 2 million (10 percent of the total); thus, Pacific Siberia's population of about 20 million at
that time will be overwhelmingly urban and located
in the southern areas near the border with China.

STRUCTURAL CHARACTERISTICS

The structure of the Pacific Siberian population
has the characteristics one would expect of a pioneering region. Compared with the norm for the U.S.S.R.
it is relatively young; it has a greater proportion
of males, especially of working age; until recently
the birth rate was significantly higher than the
average for the Soviet Union.

According to the 1959 census,* the proportion
of the Pacific Siberian population under the age of
40 was 76.8 percent, compared with the average for
the R.S.F.S.R. of 70.5 percent. Children under the
age of 10 were particularly numerous, making up 25.3
percent of the total compared with only 21.9 percent
for the R.S.F.S.R.

At the other end of the age scale, 9 percent of
all people in the R.S.F.S.R. were 60 years of age or
older, but in Pacific Siberia they amounted to less
than 6 percent; this is because of a lower expectancy
of life, the severe climate, and a high rate of retirement back to European Russia.

There is also a clear distinction in the male/fe-
male ratio between the R.S.F.S.R. and Pacific Siberia.
Less than 45 percent of the population of the former
was male in 1959, whereas the figure for the latter
exceeded 48 percent. The relative importance of
males in relation to females in Pacific Siberia compared with the R.S.F.S.R. reflects the easier wartime

---

*At the time of writing in late 1971 the regional
details of the 1970 census had not been released.

losses and perhaps, in part, greater numbers of male
deportees.

In general, though, the relatively stronger showing of the male population in Pacific Siberia is to
be expected of a frontier or pioneer region. To illustrate, the remote frontier territory of Magadan
had 56 percent men (cf. 87 percent in 1939 at the
height of Magadan _stroi_ forced labor activities).
The most critical gaps in Magadan were in the age
group 20-24 (5,244 surplus males), 25-29 (5,838),
40-44 (4,144), and 45-49 (5,267); the only age group
in which females outnumbered males was 60 years and
above.[4] The problem of the shortage of marriageable
females is one of the causes of a high labor turnover
in the remoter parts of Siberia.

Table 23 shows the birth, death, and natural increase rates for Pacific Siberia, compared with the
U.S.S.R. average. In 1950 the birth rate in the Far
East was by far the highest in the entire Soviet
Union. This situation reflected the relatively
greater availability of males in the Far East immediately after the war because of the low war losses.

Other contributing factors to the high birth
rate in the Far East were the inflow of young Kom-
somols and rapid expansion of the Far Eastern fishing
industry, which demanded large amounts of young male
labor. (The demobilized Red Army units in the region
were attracted to such jobs.)

By the 1960s the situation had changed completely:
The Far Eastern birth rate was only at the Soviet
average level. Possibly the high divorce rate in
the Far East (reflecting migrant dissatisfaction) is
partly to blame. The pressure on housing and apartment accommodation is another reason for this trend.

If birth rates fall in Pacific Siberia to the
level of those now current in the large cities of
Leningrad and Moscow, and if the death rate remains
at about its present level or a little lower, the
rate of natural increase can be expected to fall from
10 per 1,000 now to less than 5 per 1,000 in the not

TABLE 23

Birth, Death, and Natural Increase Rates
(per 1,000 of population)

Region	Birth Rate			Death Rate			Natural Increase		
	1950	1960	1967	1950	1960	1967	1950	1960	1967
Far East	42.5	24.9	16.7	14.0	6.2	6.4	28.5	18.7	10.3
Eastern Siberia	36.0	27.7	17.2	12.2	6.8	7.1	23.8	20.9	10.1
West Siberia	32.9	26.7	14.8	12.0	6.9	7.2	20.9	19.8	7.6
U.S.S.R.	26.7	24.9	17.4	9.7	7.1	7.6	17.0	17.8	9.8

Note: 1967 is the latest year for which rates are available.

Source: Narodnoe Khozyaistvo SSSR v 1967 god, pp. 40-41.

179

too distant future. This will throw additional
strains on the migration program for Siberia, which,
in order to sustain the planned rate of economic
growth and resource development, needs at least 5
million new migrants between 1960 and 1980.[5] The
development of the lower Angara industrial complex
alone could require an additional 600,000 to 800,000
people. Migration will be critical for future population expansion.

The occupational characteristics of the Pacific
Siberian population are also quite different from
those in the more developed and industrialized regions of the U.S.S.R. For the female population
there are fewer employment opportunities because of
the much poorer development of light industries.
This is important to the combined purchasing power
of families in the region. The textile and shoe industries, traditionally large employers of female
labor, are very weak, and other manufacturing industries are not highly developed. Heavy extractive
occupations (mining, fishing, timber felling) predom-
inate, and even in the U.S.S.R. these industries do
not employ large numbers of women.

THE RATE OF MIGRATION

During the period 1926-59 the population of Siberia and the Far East rose by 12 million of which
some 8 million were settlers from the European regions of the Soviet Union. Perhaps 5 million of
these migrated to Pacific Siberia, particularly to
the Far East, which during that period recorded a
population increase about double that for Eastern
Siberia.* The period 1926 to 1939 was one of particularly intense migration activity: Over 2 million
of the 5 million migrations to Pacific Siberia occurred during that brief time.[6]

---

*Population increase during 1926-59 for the Far
East was 358.3 percent; for Eastern Siberia, 184.2
percent; and for West Siberia, 183.6 percent.

Most of the early Soviet migration to Siberia was directed toward the development of mineral resources and basic industry and the growth of new cities; but there was still some substantial agricultural migration. In the First Five Year Plan (1928-32) the Commissariat of Agriculture of the U.S.S.R. organized the movement of 567,000 farm workers to the Far East. For this purpose state farms were created, and it was planned to double the total cultivated area of the region. Later on, in the 1930s, the Komsomol immigrants built large cities (such as the one on the Amur bearing their name). In World War II there was a large influx of people into the territory from occupied or threatened areas; in 1941 and 1942 Krasnoyarsk krai alone received 84,250 settlers from the Center,* the Urals, West Siberia, the Ukraine, Belorussia, and other parts of European Russia to work in heavy armaments industries.

Since the mid-1950s, however, the immigration rates from other parts of the Union have been at least matched by emigration out of Pacific Siberia. The increases recorded in urban settlement have been achieved to a large extent at the cost of growth in the rural population of surrounding regions and so, according to one commentator, aggravated the already strained labor supply in Siberian agriculture.[7] Government plans for increasing the labor force of skilled people through resettlement subsidies, loans, and higher wages do not appear to have offset the disadvantages of the difficult climate and the higher cost of living because of higher prices for many essential commodities, such as food, and also because of the necessarily greater demand for clothing and heat. The temporary abolition of the special Arctic wage bonuses by Khrushchev did not help matters, and the poor services and facilities, even in the larger cities such as Irkutsk or Khabarovsk, are not attractive to migrants from Moscow or Kiev.[8] The short summers and long dark winters, especially in the Far North, do not provide congenial living conditions, and the lack of work opportunities makes for dissat-

---

*Moscow and eleven neighboring oblast's.

isfied wives; this, together with the distance away
from relatives in European Russia, leads to a high
divorce rate.

V. Conolly cites a case at the cellulose works
at Baikal'sk near Sludyanka.[9] In the summer of 1967
more than 100 workers resigned from a total staff of
about 230; there was no bakery in the town and no
local fruit or vegetable market. The effect of such
an exodus on the factory's output can well be imagined.
One senior Gosplan official in Moscow stated in 1968
that it was recognized that the provision of attractive facilities, especially housing, was important
to solving the migration problem.[10] Some local Siberian officials, however, claim that for migrants
from Europe the severe winters, with prolonged temperatures below -40° C., provide the major deterrent.[11]
On some special priority construction sites (e.g.,
the Bratsk hydro station) the supply and quality of
housing and central heating is certainly much better
than in old Siberian cities such as Irkutsk.

V. I. Perevedentsev has written a very thorough
and well-balanced account of the migration problem
in Siberia.[12] He demonstrates that between January
of 1959 and January of 1964 the migration balance for
Eastern Siberia was -17,000 and that for the Far East
was +24,000; thus, the net situation for Pacific Siberia was +7,000 for five years. Some detailed data
for Eastern Siberia are given in Table 24.

The large migratory loss from Chita oblast' is the
result of a heavy rural and, to a lesser extent, urban exodus--much of it, no doubt, to the industrializing Irkutsk oblast' to the west. In Irkutsk oblast'
itself there is a very large rural out-migration,
some of which goes to the cities of the upper Angara
industrial complex.

Perevedentsev's study for 1959-64 shows that
the regions of surplus labor in the U.S.S.R. are
Volga-Vyatka, Central Chernozem, North Caucasus,
Belorussia, the Ukraine, Moldavia, Transcaucasus, and
Central Asia. There is a shortage of labor in the
Northwest, West Siberia, Eastern Siberia, Far East,

TABLE 24

Migration Balance for Eastern Siberia, 1959-64, by Regions
(in thousands)

| Region | Population | | Increase | | Migration Balance |
	January 1, 1964	January 15, 1959	Total	Natural	
Krasnoyarsk krai	2,854	2,615	239	230	+9
Irkutsk oblast'	2,199	1,976	223	191	+32
Chita oblast'	1,077	1,036	41	105	-64
Buryat A.S.S.R.	752	673	79	77	+2
Tuva A.S.S.R.	202	172	30	26	+4
Eastern Siberia	7,084	6,472	612	629	-17

Source: V. I. Perevedentsev, Migratsiya Naseleniya i Trudovye Problemy Sibiri (Novosibirsk, 1966), p. 37.

and Kazakhstan.   Despite this situation, and its effects on the rational allocation of labor resources
in the U.S.S.R., there are contradictory migratory
movements.   In 1959-64 there was a net migration of
987,000 into the labor surplus areas of North Caucas-
sus, Central Asia, the Ukraine, Moldavia, and Transcaucasus and a net migration of 250,000 out of the
labor deficit areas of West and Eastern Siberia.
These trends occurred despite official policies, publicity, and pressure in favor of migration to Siberia.
Perevedentsev claims that differences in relative
living standards (see Chapter 9) are the main cause;
he suggests the introduction of offsetting public
policy measures such as increased regional wage differentials, more housing construction, grants for
special expenses such as winter clothing, and the
provision of balanced female and male employment opportunities.   Differentiation in the call-up for military service is another suggestion he makes in favor
of labor deficit areas.   He proposes some compulsive
measures, such as forbidding the emigration of workers out of Siberia (especially to labor surplus areas)
and, also, the removal of some obstacles to migration
(some cities are closed to immigrants, and there is
discrimination against the free migration of kolkho-
zniki).[13]

The decision of the September, 1967, Central
Committee Plenum did change wage differentials and
the number of years' work required to receive a pension in favor of the Far East and Far North.   The
directives of the Twenty-Fourth Congress of the CPSU
in 1971 also called for a raising of wage coefficients
for some branches of industry in a number of regions
of the Far East and Eastern Siberia, but none of
these measures have gone as far as Perevedentsev's
guidelines.

Since 1963, the migration of population into
the Far East has increased markedly, whereas the migratory trend out of Eastern Siberia has deteriorated
from that described above.   Calculations show a migration balance for the Far East of +152,000 for 1959-
65, compared with +24,000 for 1959-63, i.e., a net
gain of 128,000 in the last two years of the Seven

Year Plan.[14] The net migration loss from Eastern
Siberia in those two years was -13,000, compared with
-17,000 for 1959-63. Migration records are kept by
registration data from reports to the authorities on
change of residence or place of work. Although under
the Soviet system of internal passports the records
are likely to be accurate, it is not very often that
comprehensive regional data are published. Alternative calculations can be made using population growth
and natural increase rates, but, unfortunately, the
Central Statistical Administration has not released
information on natural growth in the Far East and
Eastern Siberia since 1967. The available information is given in Table 25.

Thus, over the nine years to 1967 the Far East
gained some 204,000 migrants whereas Eastern Siberia

TABLE 25

Migration Balance for Eastern Siberia and Far East,
1959-67
(in thousands)

| Years | Increase | | Migration |
	Total	Natural	Balance
1959-63:			
Eastern Siberia	612	629	-17
Far East	443	419	+24
1964-65:			
Eastern Siberia	168	181	-13
Far East	260	132	+128
1966-67:			
Eastern Siberia	69	155	-86
Far East	171	119	+52
Net 1959-67:			
Eastern Siberia	849	965	-116
Far East	874	670	+204
Pacific Siberia			
total	1,723	1,635	+88

lost 116,000 to give a net balance for the region of
+88,000. It is believed that the trends of 1964-67
continued between January, 1968, and January, 1970
(assuming a natural increase of 10 per 1,000 people),
so that a net loss of 48,000 occurred; however, the
accuracy of the 1970 census figures has probably
thrown the earlier years out so that comparisons are
not very accurate. The Far East gains settlers from
Eastern Siberia and the Center, but Eastern Siberia
loses large numbers of short-term migrants to such
regions as the Ukraine, the Urals, Kazakhstan, and
North Caucasus. About one-quarter of all new arriv-
als are graduates from higher educational establishments and technical and vocational schools who are
compelled by law to work for three years in any job
to which they are assigned. The State spends up to
500 rubles per capita on transport for such migrants,
and the total cost of departures from Siberia has
been put at 2 billion to 3 billion rubles per year.
Agricultural migrants (76,000 in 1966-70) are being
encouraged with a grant of 150 rubles to the head of
the family and an allowance of 50 rubles for each
other member of the family for the purchase of private
livestock.[15]

The main urban inflow in both Eastern Siberia
and the Far East is in the 16-34 age group, which accounts for 90-95 percent of total net movements.
Although this age group is certainly an asset, as it
includes the most energetic and healthy members of
the population, it also includes, unfortunately,
those single people most likely to move from job to
job and so add to the instability of the labor force.
Workers leaving school probably find some initial at-
traction in working on the Komsomol construction
projects, but their enthusiasm wanes.

In itself the migratory movement involves significant losses of work time in traveling to and
from Siberia and, also, in looking for new jobs at
both ends. The rates of urban migration for Siberia
exceed the average for the U.S.S.R. two-fold. Also,
there are the costs to the State of organized recruitment drives, fares, and the upkeep of special
government offices and their staff, such as Glavor-

gnabor (Organized Recruitment Office) and its local
offices.

The future outlook for migration into Siberia is
not hopeful in relation to the likely pace of economic
development. V. V. Pokshishevskii has assessed expected regional manpower needs according to a model
of the future distribution of production.[16] Correc-
tions are made for future regional differences in
the need for labor because of increasing mechanization. Rates of natural increase and labor mobility
are calculated. By this method the migratory influx
required for Siberia and the Far East in the foreseeable future (about 25 years) is put between a low of
5 million and a high of 15 million. In the prewar
and immediate postwar years such a substantial rate
of migration would have been feasible; but now the
net increase for Pacific Siberia would be not much
better than 250,000 over 25 years (based on the performance of the last 9 years), and West Siberia would
sustain an outflow in excess of 1 million.* The best
that can be expected in the Far East, on recent performance, is a gain of 1.1 million. Clearly, policies will have to be implemented to reverse this
trend. One possibility could be to spend more on
people and less on new capital equipment, the installation of which has outpaced the rate of migration
in the region.

Because of the severe climate there will always
be, in the absence of compulsion, a high degree of
population mobility in the Far North of the region.
Increasing mechanization of mining will stimulate
out-migration from such areas. In Magadan oblast',
for instance, about 40 percent of the migrants stay
for less than one year and 20 percent for between
one and two years.[17]

Rural migration of the young to the towns will
continue as the surplus labor inherent in Soviet
farming becomes increasingly evident with progress

---

*In 1959-67 the migratory outflow from West
Siberia was 390,000.

in mechanization. This will occur despite reports
of shortages—mainly seasonal at harvest time—in the
agricultural labor force of the region. The high
cost of Pacific Siberian farming should, in any case,
encourage the Government to look closely at the relative costs of further development here.

The major problem, of course, is migration from
the cities of Pacific Siberia westward to those of
European Russia. Differences in the comparable standard of living (see Chapter 9) can be corrected by
providing more housing per capita than the average
for the U.S.S.R. and equipping those houses with adequate central heating, sewers, and running water.
At present Siberia and the Far East are far behind
in this aspect.[18] Consumer services are also poorly
developed. The cost of providing such amenities must
be weighed by the policy-makers in Moscow against
the critical shortage of skilled labor throughout
the region and the repercussions of a high labor turnover on planning and progress of the regional economy.

NOTES

1. H. K. Norton, The Far Eastern Republic of
Siberia (London: George Allen and Unwin, 1923, p. 18.

2. For a detailed account see T. Armstrong,
Russian Settlement in the North (Cambridge: Cambridge
University Press, 1965); and Yu. Semyonov, The Con-
quest of Siberia (London: G. Routledge & Sons, 1944).

3. D. W. Treadgold, The Great Siberian Migration (Princeton, N.J.: Princeton University Press,
1957), pp. 34-35.

4. Itogi Vsesoyuznoi Perepisi Naseleniya 1959
god—RSFSR (Moscow: Ts.S.U., 1963), p. 72.

5. E. Koutaissoff, "Recent Demographic Trends
in the USSR and Their Possible Implications," New
Zealand Slavonic Journal (Wellington), Winter, 1969,
p. 23; Voprosy Ekonomiki, No. 6, 1961, p. 9.

6. V. V. Pokshishevskii, _Geografiya Naseleniya Vostochnoi Sibiri_ (Moscow, 1962), p. 75.

7. V. Conolly, "Sibirien Heute und Morgen," _Osteuropa_, July, 1968, p. 537.

8. _Planovoe Khozyaistvo_, April, 1966, p. 48.

9. V. Conolly, _op. cit._, p. 538, quoting _Literaturnaya Gazeta_, No. 41, 1967.

10. Interview in Moscow with A. B. Margolin, Gosplan official, September 19, 1968.

11. Interview with P. P. Silinskii, Chairman Irkutsk oblast' Gosplan, September 29, 1968.

12. V. I. Perevedentsev, _Migratsiya Naseleniya i Trudovye Problemy Sibiri_ (Novosibirsk, 1966).

13. One-quarter of the _kolkhoz_ labor force in Belorussia is not needed on the farms, even at the harvest peak in labor requirements. See Perevedentsev, _op. cit._, p. 44.

14. V. I. Perevedentsev, "Sovremennaya Migratsiya Naseleniya v SSSR," in _Narodonaselenie i Ekonomika_, eds. D. I. Valentei _et al_. (Moscow, 1967), p. 103; plus calculations based on _Narodnoe Khozyaistvo SSSR v 1967 god_ using regional natural growth rates.

15. _Pravda_, January 18, 1968.

16. Pokshishevskii, _op. cit._, pp. 63-81.

17. _Naselenie i Trudoviye Resursy Severo-vostoka SSSR_ (Moscow: Nauka, 1968), p. 100.

18. _Zhilishchyi Fond v Gorodakh i Rabochikh Poselkakh RSFSR_ (Moscow, 1963).

CHAPTER

9

**LIVING STANDARDS
AND THE PROBLEM
OF
ATTRACTING SETTLERS**

The shortage of manpower is one of the main factors retarding the development of Pacific Siberia.[1]
In the past, compulsion and coercion were used to
improve the quantity, if not the quality, of labor
resources through such measures as corrective labor
camps and colonies* (especially to develop sparsely
populated areas), special settlements of exile,**
the conditional release of nonpolitical criminals to
settle permanently in Siberia, and the punishment of
free settlers who left their place of work or residence. Pressure was also applied by exempting young
males from military service if they settled in Siberia
and through the creation of Red Army kolkhozy con-
sisting of soldiers demobilized before completing
their military service.*** The abolition of labor

_____

*The chief difference between a camp and a colony
was that the latter was smaller (not more than 5,000
prisoners); it contained prisoners on short-term sen-
tences (less than three years), primarily from local
(oblast') areas.

**The exiles were compelled by law to work as di-
rected in agriculture or at construction sites for
three to ten years.

***With the major reduction in armed forces in 1960
the Soviet Government announced special privileges

camps in the 1950s, and the subsequent reliance by
the Government on voluntary settlement, has brought
in its wake the problem of net migration outflows and
a high turnover of labor throughout the region. In
the absence of compulsion, it is such factors as real
wages, housing, welfare facilities, social amenities,
public transport, ties with relatives in European
Russia, the type and responsibility of work offered,
and the unfamiliar climate that will induce a migrant
to stay or leave. Even for the local Sibiriaks, especially the young, reports of better conditions and
opportunities in European Russia often prove attractive.

The failure to provide satisfactory living conditions has been assessed by some Soviet economists
in the following terms:

> Large scale resettlement in the industrial
> centres of Siberia, the North and the East
> from such regions as the Transcaucasian and
> Central Asian republics, Moldavia, Belorus-
> sia and the western regions of the Ukraine
> cannot be successful because the difference
> in living conditions is too great.[2]

The assignment of students to Siberia after their
graduation from institutions of education is one ad-
mission of failure. Another is the fact that the
unorganized outflow of population from Siberia makes
it necessary to send ever-increasing numbers of new
labor there on an organized basis at great cost. In
September, 1967, a decree introduced wage differentials from January 1, 1968, for workers located in
the Far East and North employed in industries previously not entitled to this type of payment.[3] With a
commitment to full employment, the east-to-west movement of labor from deficit areas in Siberia to surplus areas in European Russia has embarrassed the
Government's aim of rational planned regional development. In the past the socioeconomic base of this
phenomenon has been ignored almost completely.

---

for demobilized soldiers settling in Siberia and
other remote regions.

The costs of a solution are high for the State
not only because of the need to provide high real
wages but also because the cost of providing modern
housing, communal, cultural, and welfare facilities
for one workman in these regions has been put at
about 10,000 rubles.[4] On this basis, it is not surprising that the grandiose plan to resettle approximately six million workers in the East during 1960-80
was abandoned. The cost would have been some 3 billion rubles a year, or an amount equivalent to about
one-half as much again as total State gross fixed
investment in the consumer goods industry.

MANPOWER FLUCTUATIONS

In the U.S.S.R. as a whole, perhaps as a result
of full employment, manpower fluctuations are high.
There are about 3 million changes of job per year,
and the annual loss of working time has been put at
100 million man days.[5] The rate of labor fluctuation
in Eastern Siberia is about 70 percent higher than
the average for the R.S.F.S.R.; this compares with
25 percent for West Siberia.[6]

In an effort to offset this instability, a recruited worker has to conclude a labor contract for
a period of not less than one year; in the Far East
the minimum is two years and for the Far North, five
years. Under the contract the employing enterprise
is obliged to provide the worker with work in his
particular skill (or retrain him if necessary); accommodation at a fixed rent; furniture and household
equipment; meals; social, cultural, and educational
facilities; as well as normal working conditions.[7]
In fact, however, these obligations frequently are
not met by the employer because such infringements
are not considered sufficiently serious to warrant
nullification of the work contract. But in Siberia
the observance of the letter of the contract by the
employer is much more important because it can be
assumed that migration is usually prompted by a
strong desire on the part of the worker to better his
living conditions in one way or another. It follows
that the employer and the local municipal authorities
must create living conditions that will attract

permanent settlers. Much of their ability to do this
depends, of course, on the supply of central funds
to the local budget.

The problem of "vanishing manpower"[8] in Siberia
is best illustrated by the results of a special study
(see Table 26) of settlement in three typical urban
communities of Krasnoyarsk krai.

About one-half of the migrants arriving in the
three cities left before living there for three years.
And between one-quarter and one-third of them emi-
grated after less than one year. The study also
showed that migrants coming from other regions of the
U.S.S.R. are less stable than those from other parts
of Siberia and that people of rural origin stay longer
than urban dwellers. More than one-half the migrants
from western areas returned to the districts they
had come from; some of these were workers assigned
to Siberia for two years under the organized recruitment program. Within the three towns studied the
differences in the proportions of people who settled

TABLE 26

Pattern of Migration in Three Communities,
Krasnoyarsk Krai
(in percent)

Direction of Movement	Achinsk	Nazarovo	Dzerzhinsky
Arrivals	100	100	100
Departures			
Within 1 year	31	29	23
Within 2 years	20	14	16
Within 3 years	10	6	8
Total departures			
in 3 years	61	49	47

Source: V. I. Perevedentsev, "Voprosy Territorial'nogo Pereraspredeleniya Trudovykh Resursov,"
Voprosy Ekonomiki, May, 1962, p. 53.

down are closely allied with relative living conditions. Particularly high rates of labor turnover
were recorded at large industrial sites, such as the
Sorsk molybdenum plant. The permanent movement of
labor back to the Ukraine, Moldavia, North Caucasus,
and Central Asia exceeds the volume of immigration
by 30-40 percent. Most workers leave Siberia before
the expiration of their contracts; S. G. Prociuk
notes that in Krasnoyarsk krai no more than 12 percent
of newly recruited workers actually finish their
labor contracts.[9] This is despite the fact that, because of the shortage of labor, many workers in Pacific Siberia are able to hold much more responsible
positions than they would in European Russia.

The Far East experiences the same kind of problem. The Khabarovsk sovnarkhoz could recruit only
876 college-trained specialists although it had asked
Moscow for 2,100; of these only 767 arrived at their
assigned places of work, and 50 percent of those had
left their jobs within three years.[10]

In 1960, 400 doctors arrived in the Primor'ye,
but over 300 left; 100 geologists arrived, but as
many returned.[11] At a construction site near Komsomol'sk, 354 laborers were recruited in one year, but
this failed to cover the loss of 400 workers. Many
responsible posts in the Far East are being held by
people without even a specialized secondary education, and this affects the quality of work supervision and plan fulfillment. One Soviet newspaper has
stated categorically that "recruitment of workers
for Siberia and the Far East is one of the most in-
tractable problems of the Soviet Government."[12] In
1971 the first secretaries of the Krasnoyarsk Kraikom
and the Yakutsk regional committee of the CPSU complained of labor shortages. As early as 1953 there
were complaints that 63 percent of the workers and
office employees in the Siberian timber industry had
less than three years' service. Twelve years later,
at a conference held in Magadan, it was reported
that not more than 15-20 percent of migrants to the
Far North settled for any prolonged period. At the
Zapsib metallurgical works near Novokuznetsk in West
Siberia, 6,000 workers left the construction site in

1965, one-half of them because there was no suitable living accommodation. It is believed that similar conditions exist for married men at major Pacific Siberian construction sites.

The additional expenditures and dislocation associated with this problem are immense. With an average loss of 30 working days per worker in moving from one place of employment to another the cost has been put at 2 billion rubles per year.[13] V. I. Perevedentsev shows that if the monies spent directly on the organized movement of manpower over the last ten years had been used instead for the construction of housing and the improvement of public utilities and services to attract voluntary labor the population of Siberia now would be at least 300,000 greater.[14] In addition, benefits would have accrued from lower labor turnover, a reduction of expenditures on training and retraining immigrant workers, a more efficient utilization of equipment and machinery, and higher labor productivity.

REASONS FOR DISSATISFACTION

The chief factors prompting an individual to migrate are economic. The term economic includes relative wage and price levels, differences in job opportunities, housing supply and conditions, and the standard of public and cultural services and amenities, including, for example, schools. Demographic factors play a part through differences in the sex and age characteristics of the population, its degree of urbanization, and its structure by social and employment groupings. Ethnic factors also must be considered, such as territorial differences in language, living, and eating habits. Sometimes, as in Siberia, quite different climatic conditions are important as well as regional attitudes (morale) toward migration. All these factors operate together in a complex way, but, generally, one group emerges as the dominant reason for fluctuations in labor turnover.

The Economics Institute of the Siberian Branch of the U.S.S.R. Academy of Sciences has distributed

mass questionnaires among workers leaving industrial
enterprises in Krasnoyarsk and Novosibirsk of their
own volition. These surveys showed that the most
common reasons for leaving a job were dissatisfaction
with the rate of pay, working conditions, and housing
and a desire to move nearer to relatives; this latter
frequently has economic causes. The data in Table
27 is from one such survey by the Academy and embraces a poll of about 4,700 workers who gave up
their jobs in 60 industrial enterprises in Krasnoyarsk
krai. It will be seen that about one-half of those
who quit found other jobs in the same town; of those
who left Krasnoyarsk (49 percent) about one-half left
the krai altogether, mainly to live in cities in European Russia. Dissatisfaction with pay, work, and
housing and the desire to move to relatives accounted
for over 60 percent of the reasons given for leaving
the job. Another 9 percent involved health problems,
aggravated, no doubt, in some instances by the long
and severe Siberian winters. Characteristically,
the majority of those leaving because of dissatisfaction with housing left the city of Krasnoyarsk completely; the same comment applies almost entirely to
those wishing to move nearer to their relatives (obviously a strong motivation) and, also, to those
quitting because of a family illness or because of
the bad climate. On the other hand, the survey claims
that workers leaving because they were dissatisfied
with their wages or the nature of their work found
other (presumably better) jobs in the same city.
This also was the case for those leaving because of
education, worker's health, transportation, or
nursery/kindergarten problems--which seems strange
unless it can be explained by a movement from extreme
suburban to central city location or by the fact that
some factories in Krasnoyarsk provide better facilities (e.g., kindergartens) than others.

Basically, labor movements are to be expected
into those cities of the U.S.S.R. where the entire
complex of living and working conditions more fully
meet the aspirations of the migrant. A net outflow
of labor from a region such as Eastern Siberia,
which is experiencing a manpower shortage, is a
clear indication of that region's backward state in
the provision of such conditions. Soviet sources

admit that living conditions in the labor deficit
areas (Kazakhstan, Siberia, and the Far East) are
lagging perceptibly behind those in the central and
western regions of European Russia where there are
labor surpluses.[15]

In the country areas the reasons for dissatisfaction are primarily the appallingly backward conditions of life in the remote Siberian villages;
settlements with wooden houses, dirt roads, and poor
public welfare facilities are reminiscent of nine-
teenth-century Russian villages. People leaving the
villages are mostly young, and skilled workers are
leaving at a faster rate than unskilled workers because they can easily find jobs in industry. This
leads to a shortage of machine operators, for example,
in Siberian agriculture. The reasons for quitting
the villages are economic and will remain so until
living standards between town and country are more
nearly equalized. The flooding of good agricultural
land by hydro schemes, such as the Bratsk and Krasnoyarsk dams, has also led to rural dissatisfaction
and encouraged a movement of peasants to the cities.
The extreme labor hunger of Siberian towns and cities
has exacerbated rural drift compared with European
Russia.

The harsh climate necessitates additional outlays on food, clothing, heating, and housing. Transport costs are also higher, especially in out-of-the-
way villages in the North; the shortage of suitable
rest homes, health resorts, and sanatoria involves
costly vacations and treatment in Europe. But merely
compensating for such disabilities is not enough:
No amount of recompense will create easy natural conditions in, for example, Magadan or Noril'sk, compared with, for instance, the Crimea. Even a rise
in nominal pay to a very high level will not promote
a stable turnover of labor unless the worker has
good opportunities to spend his income. Siberia
does not have priority in the allocation of scarce
consumer goods, so the special regional wage allowances are saved to be spent when the migrant worker
and his family return to European Russia.

TABLE 27

Reasons for Leaving Job, Krasnoyarsk Krai

Main Reason for Quitting Job	Percent of Total Giving Reason	Selection of Location as Percent of Those Giving Reason	
		Leave Town	Stay in Town
Dissatisfaction with rate of pay	17.5	27	73
Dissatisfaction with type of work	13.9	23	77
Dissatisfaction with housing	11.2	57	43
Remoteness of house from work and poor transportation	4.2	23	77
No place for child in nursery/kindergarten	4.0	18	82
Wish to move to relatives	17.5	96	4
Objectionable climate	0.6	86	14
State of worker's health	4.9	28	72
Illness in family	4.3	73	27
Desire for further education	5.2	37	63
Other reasons	11.3	55	45
Reason not indicated	5.4	71	29
Total	100.0	49	51

Source: V. I. Perevedentsev, "Voprosy Terri-torial'nogo Pereraspredeleniya Trudovykh Resursov," Voprosy Ekonomiki, May, 1962, p. 52.

In 1962-63 wages in Siberia and the North were
only 15 percent higher than in the Center, although
the cost of living there was perhaps twice as high.[16]
E. Manevich stated in 1965 that the retail prices of
milk, sugar, bread, and meat were, respectively, 46
percent, 27 percent, 19 percent, and 13 percent higher
in the Far East and Far North than in the central regions of the U.S.S.R.[17] The overall cost of outlays
on food in the Far North is 37 percent more, reflecting the need for a greater amount of calories as well
as the higher cost of food; consumer goods, including
clothing, cost 38 percent more and the servicing of
appliances is 45 percent more expensive. He put the
total difference in living costs between the southern
regions of Siberia and the Far North at 70-80 percent.
The provision of housing is poor because the housing
construction fund is rapidly depleted by building
costs four times higher per square meter than in the
Center and three times more than in the south of West
Siberia.[18] According to a newspaper survey in 1965-66,
Manevich's figures may be too low; it reported the
cost of living in Siberia to be 2.2 times more than
that of European Russia.[19] The same article remarked
on the frequent disruptions of the supply of fruit,
vegetables, milk, and meat in Siberia.

V. Conolly describes some examples of unsatisfactory working and living conditions in Siberia.[20]
These come from new construction sites where housing,
the supply of consumer goods, food, and general amenities take second place to the building project itself.
The workers on a timber haulage railway in Irkutsk
oblast' near Bratsk voiced the following complaints:

> We work hard but nobody cares about us.
> The food is bad . . . summer is ending but
> we have seen no fresh vegetables. . . .
> There is no meat, sausages or cheese in
> the shop. You have to go more than 100
> km. for a hair cut. . . . There are only
> cold meals . . . the mechanized bakery is
> out of order for the second year. An old
> woman came here with two boxes of tomatoes
> for sale. . . . Why can't our own supply
> organization do the same? Everything is
> available in Taishet . . . but here we

cannot get our boots repaired. Fulfil-
ment of the plan at any price is the aim.[21]

Bricklayers living in the Komsomol' accommodation
near Krasnoyarsk described their living conditions as
follows:

The hostels are poorly built. . . . Over-
alls have to be dried in the rooms on the
radiators . . . bed linen is rarely changed.
The boilers are out of order and . . . there
is no hot water. At night the electric
light goes off . . . and the hostel is
plunged into darkness. We cannot read or
cook any supper on the electric fire . . .
and there are no buffets in the quarters.
The heads of the construction organization
do not worry about our everyday needs.[22]

The Soviet press contains many such examples of des-
pondency and dissatisfaction among migrant workers
in Siberia.

A large number of professional itinerants are
attracted to Siberia. These people work at a new job
only until they have received the Orgnabor ("Organized
recruiting") grant (for males aged 18 to 55, women 18
to 50) in full, generally after three months or so;
they then move to another job and repeat the process.
The internal passport system should provide a check
on such abuses, but, because of critical local shortages of labor, officials and employers are likely to
turn a blind eye. The attitudes of the itinerants are
encouraged by the unreliability of food supplies, the
poor housing and education facilities they encounter,
and the fact that even bed linen, furniture, kitchen
utensils, and soap are hard to come by. S. G. Prociuk
says that a large part of the itinerant work force
consists of workers dismissed for "delinquent behavior"
before migrating to Siberia.[23] Large numbers of such
workers are sent to Siberia, from the cities of the
west, where they continue their disturbing and rest-
less behavior patterns and so add to the instability
of the work force.

There are special reasons for dissatisfaction
among settlers from non-Russian territories, such as

the Ukraine, Baltic states, or Central Asia, because
of the lack of provision of schoolteaching, newspapers, and cultural institutions (clubs, cinemas,
theaters) in their local languages.

Problems such as these must be solved by the central authorities in Moscow if the shock of uprooting
people is to be cushioned and if the return of migrants to their home towns is to be stopped. The dissatisfaction of migrants with poor living conditions
has been responsible for a high labor turnover and the
relatively poor economic performance of the region.
A policy is needed to attract voluntarily to Siberia
the large amount of surplus labor presently living in
the towns and especially the countryside of European
Russia. More sociological studies are needed urgently.
The seriousness of the situation was indicated by
Brezhnev at the Twenty-Third Congress of the CPSU in
1966:

> To develop the economy of Siberia and the
> Soviet Far East faster, a number of social
> and economic measures have to be carried
> through in the next five years. In par-
> ticular, these measures will help to retain
> people already working there and to attract
> new people. This is an important Party and
> State matter.

The main policy act was the provision, in September of
1967, of special regional wage allowances for Eastern
Siberia and the Far East and especially in the Far
North of those territories. The draft directives of
the Twenty-Fourth Congress of the CPSU in 1971 continued this theme by pointing out that it is necessary
to create conditions for the further migration of people to the Far East and Eastern Siberia and to develop
"at a priority rate" housing, social, and cultural
construction to reduce manpower fluctuations.[24] Thus,
the policy-makers' attentions appear to have moved
from higher wages to the provision of a better social
infrastructure for 1971-75. In the meantime, the
critical lack of labor, especially skilled tradesmen,
means that the existing labor force in Siberia works
long hours and is set unusually high work norms.
This in itself leads to dissatisfaction.

PURCHASING POWER AND WAGES

The margin by which the real cost of living in Siberia exceeds that in European Russia is difficult to assess: The superficial cost of living is, on average, perhaps twice as high, as has already been noted--although there are great regional variations, and in the main cities of the southern districts the nominal differential may be only 50 percent or less. Average gross wages are between 30 percent to 40 percent more, and special additional allowances make provision for a doubling of wages, in theory. All this makes it difficult to arrive at an exact assessment of real purchasing power.

N. P. Kalinovskii puts the real wages of workers and office employees in Siberia 10 percent or so below those of the Center.[25] In a later work he shows that real wages in Eastern Siberia are 96 percent of those in the Center (see Table 28), whereas those in the Far East are 12 percent higher than in the Center. For regions of the Far North of the Far East he describes real wages as 22 percent higher than in the Center (the number of workers and employees occupied in the Far North, or equivalent areas, amounts to 43 percent of the total). In the Far East, education, public health, construction work, housing, trade, and catering are the poorest paid occupations; the best paid jobs are in industry, especially the extractive branches, transport and communications, and farming. It is little wonder, then, that professional people in education and health are not attracted here and that turnover in the construction industry is so high. Most teachers from European Russia go back with three years.

The wage coefficients applying to workers in Siberia have varied from time to time since the rate reforms of the early 1930s. In the late 1950s, before the abolition of the Arctic allowances in 1960 by Khrushchev, the approved coefficients were the following:

1.0   central, south, and western regions of European U.S.S.R.

1.1-1.2   parts of North European U.S.S.R., the Urals excluding the north,

TABLE 28

Real and Nominal Wages in Siberia and the Far East
(Center = 100)

Occupation	West Siberia		Eastern Siberia		Far East	
	Nominal	Real	Nominal	Real	Nominal	Real
Industry	118	110	134	108	173	126
Construction	105	97	121	98	143	105
State farms[a]	112	104	128	104	166	121
Transport	106	98	123	100	160	117
Communication	93	86	111	90	158	115
Trade and catering[b]	94	88	112	91	149	108
Housing[c]	97	90	116	94	145	106
Public health	95	88	103	83	135	99
Education	91	85	95	77	119	87
Science	91	84	117	94	159	116
Total[d]	103	96	118	96	153	112

[a]Includes subsidiary farming but not collectives.
[b]Communal catering, also purchasing and supply functions.
[c]And communal services.
[d]Excludes state, economic, cooperative, and communal management.

Source: N. P. Kalinovskii, Narodo-Naselenie i Ekonomika (Moscow, 1967), pp. 149 and 151.

                    south of West Siberia, Kazakh-
                    stan, and Central Asia
          1.2-1.3   remote regions of North Europe,
                    north Urals, south of Eastern
                    Siberia, and Far East
          1.3-1.5   north and remote regions includ-
                    ing Murmansk, and central regions
                    of Siberia and the Far East
          1.5-1.7   Far North of Asiatic U.S.S.R.

The calculation of the differentials was based upon
differences in the conditions of living because of
climatic and natural conditions, differences in the
hardship of work, and variations in the price of consumer goods and servicing. According to Kalinovskii--
and his figures do not differ greatly from Manevich's,
cited earlier--a person in the Far North would have to
spend 41 percent more on food, 47 percent more on
clothing, 16 times as much on heating outlays, and
more than twice as much on transportation (including
holiday trips to European resorts) to attain the same
level of material comfort as in the Center. Further
south, of course, costs are less and, hence, the coefficient is lower: Thus, Kalinovskii says that in the
south of the Far East food costs are only 3 percent
more, clothing no more, heating 80 percent more, and
transport another 25 percent, whereas consumer goods
(and their servicing) are only 5 percent more expensive. The abolition of the special Northern allowance
in 1960 reduced real wages to about the same level as
those in the Center, and, as a result, the turnover
of migrants increased.

     Not all occupations received regional wage coef-
ficients when they were reintroduced in 1967, and it
was not until 1968, for example, that most construction workers were given this privilege--a strange
situation for a region so dependent upon construction
workers. Except in the northern regions, workers in
the light, food, and service industries were exempt
from regional allowances, whereas coalminers received
special wage bonuses.

     A decree of the Presidium of the Supreme Soviet
of February 10, 1960, abolished the coefficients of
wages in the northern territories because it was con-

sidered that the conditions of economic growth there
meant that the continuance of supplements and other
concessions to the basic wages of workers created un-
necessary expenses. It was not until September 26,
1967, that the Presidium officially amended the 1960
decree and introduced a new scheme of hardship allowances.[26]

The new supplements and benefits apply to the Far
North and to similar hardship areas and are in addition to the regional coefficients and long service increments. Payments started on January 1, 1968, for
about 750,000 workers in hardship areas; 350,000 of
these were in the Far East. Previously only production and certain skilled or specialized workers received the Northern allowance, but now all wage and
salary earners in state, cooperative, and public enterprises, institutions, and organizations get it.
The length of service required to qualify for periodic
increments of 10 percent in wages has been shortened
for all workers in hardship areas (about 1.5 million).
In the Chukotka N.O. and North Evenki region of Magadan oblast', the Koryak N.O. and Aleut region of the
Kamchatka oblast', as well as the islands of the Arctic Ocean and adjoining seas (excluding the islands
of the White Sea), wage increases of 10 percent are
granted after the first 6 months' work, instead of after the first 12 months, with further increments of
10 percent for each 6 months thereafter to a maximum
increment of 100 percent, but not exceeding 300 rubles
per month (average wages in the U.S.S.R. are about 120
rubles).* In the rest of the Far North proper the increases are 10 percent after the first 6 months' work,
again instead of after 12 months, with further increments of 10 percent for each 6 months' work thereafter
to a maximum increase of 60 percent (at Noril'sk, 80
percent) and then 10 percent for each complete year's
work. In hardship areas equalized to the Far North,
i.e., the central regions of Eastern Siberia and the
Far East, the rise in wages is 10 percent after the
first year (instead of after two years) with further
increases of 10 percent every year, to a maximum of

_____

*Income tax payable on 100 rubles per month is
8.2 rubles; on 300 rubles per month it is 34.2 rubles.

50 percent. These allowances do not apply to the
southern regions of Pacific Siberia, although in 1969
most workers in Irkutsk and Krasnoyarsk territories
received a special location allowance.

To be eligible for the Northern wage supplements
workers must sign long-term labor contracts of three
years, compared with five years previously under
Clause 5 of the decree of February 10, 1960. On the
Arctic Ocean islands (such as Severnaya Zemlya) a contract of two years is allowed. The bonus to workers
renewing a long-term labor contract is increased to 50
percent of their average monthly earnings, excluding
the regional coefficient, long-service increments, or
special Far North allowance. Lump sum special grants
(edinovremennoe posobie) to graduates of specialized
secondary and higher schools who are assigned to the
North and equivalent areas have been doubled. Also,
workers in the Far North were authorized, from January
1, 1968, to retire, after 15 years' service, at the
age of 55 for men or 50 for women; in areas equalized
to the Far North the same retirement ages apply but a
20-year period of service is required. Since February,
1970, the reduction in the pension for full-time employment of pensioners in the Far East and Siberia has
been liberalized. Workers in the Far North are also
granted an extra 18 workdays of annual leave and leave
without pay to cover travel time to places of vaca-
tion. In 1971-75 increased wages will be introduced
for some regions of the Far East and Eastern Siberia,
and this should enhance the possibility of attracting
more immigrants.

The extension of these privileges to workers in
the Far North and the reintroduction of regional wage
coefficients must have good effects on the labor
force, migration movements, and overall development of
the economy of Pacific Siberia in the long run. The
financial inducements now may be so high as to encourage more people to go there for a short while and
save up surplus money to spend back in European Russia. The new and shorter labor contracts may be ad-
hered to more strictly by employers and penalties for
breaking them policed more strictly; nevertheless,
workers can still sign six-month contracts for seasonal work such as timber floating or fishing. Early

reports indicated that the 20 percent regional coefficients applying to the workers in light, food, and
servicing industries in the Far East and Chita and
Buryat territories were having a beneficial effect.[27]
In Khabarovsk krai the coefficients applied to 150,000
workers whose wages rose by a minimum of 20 percent;
in the Amur oblast' 145,000 men received increases,
and the total annual cost is 27 million rubles. A
significant increase in the demand for consumer products is expected by the local authorities as a result.
In Primor'ye workers and employees are receiving an
additional 45-46 million rubles in their paypackets;
if the other special privileges and nonreturnable
grants set out in the 1967 decree are included, together with free travel, total cost exceeds 100
million rubles.

All this means that purchasing power and standards of living should improve, although a great deal
depends on how the State sets its retail prices in the
region. In the past, higher regional prices have ab-
sorbed a great deal of the higher wages paid, but in
January, 1970, the prices of basic foodstuffs in the
Far East were reduced by 6-10 percent. In 1969 average retail sales turnover per capita in the Far East
and Eastern Siberia were 857.4 rubles and 628.7 rubles, respectively--but it is not known how much of
this can be ascribed to higher prices and how much, if
any, to higher living standards in the Far East.[28]

THE SUPPLY OF GOODS
AND AMENITIES

The supply of many goods, services, and amenities
in Pacific Siberia is unsatisfactory. The network of
distribution facilities away from the major southern
cities is poor, which means that there are frequent
and prolonged breaks in the supply of such necessities
as fresh fruit, vegetables, meat, and bread. Even in
the cities prices for such commodities are well above
the European average: Thus, in the Far East the price
of sugar is 24 percent more; meat, 16 percent more;
bread, 10 percent more; milk, 15 percent more; and
all foodstuffs, 16-18 percent more than in the Ukraine.
In cities such as Irkutsk and Khabarovsk the availability of shoes, clothing, and consumer durables is

far from meeting local demand adequately, even at the
high prices charged.

Most importantly, the great distance of Siberia
from the major manufacturing centers creates problems
of supply, servicing costs, and the need for large
stocks; retail establishments in the Far East carry
stocks sufficient for 130 days turnover, compared
with 107 days in Eastern Siberia, 70 days in West Siberia, and 57 days for the Center.[29]

The provision of housing, both quantitatively and
qualitatively, has been an especially vexatious problem for migrants to Pacific Siberia. In many of the
remote construction sites tents and rough wooden
dwellings have been the norm, but a norm unacceptable
to most settlers except for brief periods. Even in
the large southern cities the situation is poor. Perevedentsev has compared the living area occupied per
capita for newcomers to Krasnoyarsk with old settlers
there.[30] He found that, compared with old settlers,
newcomers arriving in Krasnoyarsk from other towns had
12 percent less living space. Newcomers from towns
subsequently leaving their jobs in Krasnoyarsk had 13
percent less living space when they left than the old
settlers, whereas newcomers from villages leaving
their jobs had 22 percent less room. The latter figure may reflect the simpler living habits of village
people. About 62 percent of the old settlers occupy
municipal or enterprise flats or apartments, but only
20 percent or so of newcomers are so housed, although
their share rises to about 35 percent by the time
they leave their jobs in Krasnoyarsk. Again, the
rural migrants are much worse off in this regard, and
more of them (58 percent) have had to rent privately
or buy their own small houses. Among the people
quitting their jobs in Krasnoyarsk--old and newcomers,
rural and urban in origin--the proportion of hostel
and boarding house dwellers is high and varies from
11 percent to 32 percent.

In priority areas, such as Bratsk, skilled workers can generally get flats almost immediately. But
the additional cost to the local budget of building
houses especially adapted to the prolonged and intense
winter is very high. The average cost of construction

for one square meter (or 10.8 square feet) of housing
in the U.S.S.R. is 140 rubles, but in Magadan it is
344 rubles and in Sakhalin ranges upward from 311 rubles; by comparison, in Belorussia, the Ukraine, and
Moscow costs can be as low as 110 to 118 rubles per
square meter. The thickness of brick walls necessary
to maintain a normal room temperature in a house must
be over 20 percent thicker in Irkutsk and 72 percent
thicker in Yakutsk than in Moscow; this alone is responsible for increasing building costs by between 55
percent and 138 percent.

Overall, the living area available per inhabitant
is 7.5 square meters in the Far East, compared with
7.8 square meters in Eastern Siberia and 8.9 square
meters in West Siberia. There is no reason to believe
that these figures will change much in the short run,
despite large building programs for 1971-75.*

The cost of heating houses is very high. The
heating season (defined as the period with temperatures below 4.5° C. or 40° F.) is 281 days a year at
Dudinka in the Far North and 217 days at Irkutsk, compared with 115 days at Krasnodar in the North Caucasus.[31] The standard amount of fuel required for
heating can be up to four times as much in the Far
North as in the Ukraine.

The chairman of the Irkutsk oblast' Gosplan
points out that people going there to erect new industrial complexes in the wilds of the taiga need good
housing, schools, nurseries, and shops to compensate
them.[32] But the planning of industry, housing, and
public welfare is in the hands of separate agencies
that get out of phase with each other, especially in
their relative rates of construction. Thus, new industrial projects are not provided in time with proper
housing, and the shortage of accommodation makes impossible the task of recruiting adequate working
cadres required to operate the new plants to full

---

*In the Yakutsk A.S.S.R. at least one million
square meters of new housing is to be built in 1971-
75; in Amur oblast' two million square meters will
be built--25 percent more than in 1966-70.

capacity. As a result, the share of workmen with
short-time service (less than three years) in the oblast' is almost three times the national average.
Not only is the amount of housing available per capita
below the Soviet average but the share of amenities in
the houses is poor and many of the dwellings, even in
the oblast' capital Irkutsk, are shabby wooden houses
badly in need of repair, with access from unbelievably
rutted and pot-holed dirt roads. In new towns such
as Bratsk and Angarsk the standard of prefabricated
apartment houses is relatively good. Of the total
living accommodation in Irkutsk oblast' of 7.2 million
square meters, however, only 37 percent of the dwellings are provided with water, 35 percent with sewerage,
37 percent with central heating, and 15 percent with
gas. In the whole of the oblast' about one-third of
the accommodation is rated as 60 percent worn-out, but
in 1966 the total amount of money spent on new housing
was scarcely 89 million rubles, compared with 500 million rubles invested in industry.[33] The housing situation is complicated by the absence of statistical
data on housing availability in rural areas. Too often, also, the erection of other facilities, such as
a railway station, is done by diverting funds from
municipal housing and construction work.[34]

     To continue with the well-documented case of Ir-
kutsk oblast', the schools there are greatly over-
crowded, the construction of new schools is progress-
ing very slowly, and, in general, the shortage of education facilities is acute. In the 1964-65 school
year there were on average only 98 school places per
1,000 population, whereas the norm should have been
between 150 and 160 places. Owing to the school
shortage a three-session or shift system was employed;
in 1965-66, in the town areas, 59.2 percent of the
pupils attended the first session (259,000 students),
39.5 percent attended the second session (173,300),
and 1.3 percent the third session (5,700).[35] Each rural school has to serve an enormous territory of 735
square miles on average, and each rural settlement (of
which there are 3,223) has the equivalent of only 0.49
percent of a school. The number of places available
in kindergartens and nurseries is 46.9 per 1,000 population, whereas the norm should be 70 to 90 places.
The shortage of preschool facilities is hampering the

recruitment of mothers into the work force and is also
a serious problem in Krasnoyarsk krai.[36]

The medical service is not very well provided
for in the oblast'; there are slightly over 1.9 medical staff per 1,000 population, compared with the
R.S.F.S.R. average of 2.1 (this figure includes para-
medical staff).

The number of students in higher schools in the
R.S.F.S.R. is about 16 per 1,000 population, whereas
in Irkutsk oblast' there are only 7.9; similarly, in
secondary special schools the R.S.F.S.R. norm is 14.4
but the number attending in Irkutsk is only 7.4 per
1,000 population. There is an acute shortage of
specialists with higher and secondary specialized
education, and the demand for such people in Irkutsk
oblast' is only 20-30 percent fulfilled.

The Far East does fare somewhat better in education and health facilities than Eastern Siberia. The
number of students in higher and secondary special
schools is 23.2 per 1,000 population in the Far East,
compared with 19.8 in Eastern Siberia (the Soviet
average is 22.8).[37] The number of doctors (excluding
dentists) per 1,000 population is 2.32 in the Far
East, 1.72 in Eastern Siberia, and 1.94 for the
U.S.S.R. as a whole. Similarly, the number of hospi-
tal beds (excluding military hospitals) per 1,000 population is 11.36 in the Far East, 9.16 in Eastern Siberia, and 8.40 for the U.S.S.R. In general, then,
the Far East ranks above the Soviet average, whereas
Eastern Siberia is generally below it. Teachers (and
doctors) normally return home from Eastern Siberia after they have completed their two or three years of
compulsory duty there; they tend to stay longer in
the milder climate of the south of the Far East.

In the entire region of Pacific Siberia there
are only three universities--the Far Eastern University (1956) at Vladivostok, the Zhdanov University
(1918) at Irkutsk, and the Yakutsk University (1926)
--and, consequently, many students must go further
west, to Novosibirsk or Tomsk or even to Moscow. On
the other hand, postgraduate research is fairly well
provided for by the Siberian Branch of the U.S.S.R.
Academy of Sciences at places such as Irkutsk,

Krasnoyarsk, Khabarovsk, Yakutsk, and Vladivostok.
There are higher technical institutes at Vladivostok
(1918), Irkutsk (1960), Komsomol'sk (1955), and
Krasnoyarsk (1956).

The provision of general services--such as municipal transport, repairs to appliances and houses,
water, sewerage and heating systems, dry cleaning,
shoe repairs, barbers, garbage collection, and home
delivery services--is not keeping pace with the
growth in population because of the shortage of labor
and also of spare parts. Again, in Irkutsk oblast'
up to 15 organizations are responsible for carrying
out such services, but in the entire oblast' (which
includes 16 towns, 51 workers' settlements, and 330
rural Soviets) there are only 8 dry cleaners, 1 haber-
dashery repair shop, 14 house repair workshops, and
21 furniture repair facilities.[38] Owing to the shortage of such facilities the volume of this type of
servicing in the oblast' is only 7.9 rubles per capita, compared with the national average of 11.1 rubles;
in the city of Irkutsk this rises to as high as 16.3
rubles; but in outlying districts such as the Chuna
timber complex it falls to a little over 2 rubles,
and in regions like Nizhne-Ilimsk the amount of per
capita servicing is less than 1 ruble per year.

It remains to mention briefly the negative effects of climate on settlers in addition to all the
socioeconomic factors already discussed. Not only
do the long winters mean a much greater outlay in
heating, clothing, and food but also the incidence
of cold-associated illnesses and afflictions, such
as frostbite, tend to be higher. The Institute of
Geography of the U.S.S.R. Academy of Sciences recognizes six physiogeographic regions according to the
requirements of clothing and footwear: The first
zone (tundra and the coastal northeast of Siberia)
and second zone (harsh continental taiga) embrace
the whole of Pacific Siberia with the sole exception
of the Primor'ye and south Sakhalin. The clearest
effect of climate on settlers in Siberia can be seen
in the shorter average length of life. Whereas the
average life expectancy in the U.S.S.R. is 69 years,
it falls to 67 years in the Far East and 66 years in

Eastern Siberia. In separate oblast', krai, and republics the figure is even lower: For example, in
Chita, Irkutsk, Sakhalin, and Buryat Mongolia it is
65 years; in the harsh climate of Kamchatka and
Magadan it goes down to 64 years; and in Yakutia to
63 years. The lowest figure is recorded in the rural
and mountainous Tuva republic where the average life
expectancy is only 58 years. High death rates among
the indigenes of Tuva and Yakutia are related to
poorer health and sanitation services and the generally lower standard of living as well as to climate.

    In conclusion, more investigations should be
done by Soviet authorities on the possibilities of
reducing prices for heating, clothing, food, water,
sewerage, municipal transport, and electric power
rates on a par with those in European Russia. The
regional supply of goods, especially fresh fruit and
vegetables, must be greatly improved, especially in
the winter months. The entire education-health-
public welfare infrastructure needs much more attention. Some regional leaders have been accused of
not endeavoring to secure permanent engineering and
technical staff and of allowing important projects
to be supervised by people without proper technical
training.[39] Aside from propaganda and organizational
agitation, however, there is little the regional
authorities can do to attract settlers when wages
and the local supply of goods and budgetary monies
are determined by the central authorities in distant
Moscow.

    The unstable labor force and relatively poor
standard of living in relation to hardships are at
the heart of nearly all Siberian economic development
problems. Substituting energy-consuming industries
for labor-consuming industries would help matters,
but even now there are neither sufficient people to
develop the resources of the region satisfactorily
nor enough of them to consume the output of local industries. Some planners continue to justify the construction of labor-consuming industries in Siberia
on the principle of the development of evenly distributed productive resources throughout the U.S.S.R.[40]
This attitude can be condoned only if the development

of light industries for female employment is encouraged. The shortage of male labor already gives rise
to idle plant facilities, which account for between
one-third and one-half of lost working time. In the
absence of compulsory migration, the large pools of
surplus (or underemployed) labor in European Russia
can be attracted to the labor-hungry industries of
Pacific Siberia only through such inducements as
superior housing and living conditions (including
educational, health, social, and cultural facilities)
and a better supply of goods and services (in terms
not only of quantity but quality and price as well).
This is a tall order for the Soviet Government in
the face of other pressing priorities, such as agriculture and the supply of consumer goods for the
entire population of the U.S.S.R. It does not seem
likely, in this context, that Pacific Siberia will
get much in the way of really special treatment.

NOTES

1. Speech by First Secretary of Krasnoyarsk
Kraikom at the Twenty-Fourth Congress of the CPSU,
1971.

2. Kommunist, No. 18, 1965, p. 71.

3. Pravda, September 27, 1967.

4. Voprosy Ekonomiki, No. 12, 1966.

5. Bulletin (Munich: Institute for the Study
of the U.S.S.R.), No. 6, June, 1966.

6. V. I. Perevedentsev, Migratsiya Naseleniya
i Trudovye Problemy Sibiri (Novosibirsk, 1966), p. 65.

7. Trudovoe Pravo: Entsiklopedicheskii Slovar'
(Moscow, 1963), p. 39.

8. S. G. Prociuk, "The Manpower Problem in Siberia," Soviet Studies, October, 1967, p. 191.

9. Ibid., p. 195.

10.   Ibid., p. 196.

11.   Sovetskaya Rossiya, November 18, 1961.

12.   V. Conolly, Beyond the Urals (London: Oxford University Press, 1967), pp. 300-1 (citing Trud,
November 12, 1964).

13.   Z. A. Sayonchkovskaya and V. I. Perevedentsev, Sovremennaya Migratsiya Naseleniya Krasnoyarskogo Kraya (Novosibirsk, 1964), p. 87.

14.   V. I. Perevedentsev, "Voprosy Territorial'
nogo Pereraspredeleniya Trudovykh Resursov," Voprosy
Ekonomiki, May, 1962, p. 56.

15.   G. Sorokin, "Stroitel'stvo Kommunizma i
Perspektivnoe Planirovanie," Kommunist, No. 5, 1960,
pp. 60-71.

16.   Prociuk, op. cit., p. 199; the wage levels
reflect in part the abolition, by decree, on February
10, 1960, of the special Arctic privileges.

17.   E. Manevich, "Vseobshchnost' Truda i Problemy
Ratsional'nogo Ispol'zovaniya Rabochei Sily v SSSR,"
Voprosy Ekonomiki, June, 1965, p. 26.

18.   "Stroitel'stvo na krainem severe," Problemy
Severa, Series 10, Moscow, 1964.

19.   Pravda, February 27, 1966.

20.   Conolly, op. cit., pp. 255-56.

21.   Pravda, November 22, 1965.

22.   Trud, June 26, 1962.

23.   Prociuk, op. cit., p. 199; "delinquent behavior" includes breaking work discipline, receiving
a court sentence, unreliability, and dismissal at
the request of the trade unions.

24.   Ekonomicheskaya Gazeta, No. 12, 1971.

25. N. P. Kalinovskii, "Regional'nye razlichiya real'noi zarabotnoi platy rabochikh i sluzhashchikh," in Problemy Povysheniya Urovnya Zhizni Naseleniya Sibiri (Novosibirsk, 1965), p. 43.

26. Pravda, September 27, 1967; Ekonomicheskaya Gazeta, No. 39, September, 1967.

27. Ekonomicheskaya Gazeta, No. 6, February, 1968.

28. Narodnoe Khozyaistvo RSFSR v 1969 god (R.S.F.S.R. average was 655.4 rubles).

29. Ibid.

30. Perevedentsev, Migratsiya Naseleniya, p. 125.

31. Ya. G. Feigin, ed., Problemy Ekonomicheskoi Effektivnosti Razmeshcheniya Sotsialisticheskogo Proizvodstva v SSSR (Moscow: AN SSSR, 1968), p. 94.

32. P. P. Silinskii, Planirovanie Narodnogo Khozyaistva v Oblasti (Moscow, 1967).

33. Ibid.; expenditure on cultural, welfare, and public facilities was over 23 million rubles.

34. BBC Summary of World Broadcasts, Part I, U.S.S.R., November 30, 1967, referring to Bratsk.

35. Silinskii, op. cit.

36. Speech by First Secretary of Krasnoyarsk Kraikom to the Twenty-Fourth Congress of the CPSU, 1971.

37. W. Toshio, "Development of Siberia and the Problems of Labour Force," in A Study on Co-operation in the Development of Siberia (Tokyo: Ministry of Foreign Affairs, Economic Department, East-West Trade Section, October 10, 1967) (in Japanese), p. 49.

38. Silinskii, op. cit.

39. <u>Pravda</u>, October 25, 1969, criticizing Irkutsk <u>Obkom</u> of CPSU.

40. <u>Pravda</u>, October 15, 1969.

10

**SOVIET ATTITUDES
TOWARD
SIBERIAN TRADE**

The geographical location of the Far East,
facing the Pacific Ocean, presents extremely favourable conditions for the development of economic relations with the
countries of the Pacific Basin.[1]

It has not been the policy of the Soviet authorities to encourage autonomous external trade relations by any region of the U.S.S.R. Foreign trade
not only has been looked upon as a state monopoly
but that monopoly is for all practical purposes totally vested in the Ministry of Foreign Trade and
its subsidiary corporations in Moscow. Tendencies
toward autonomy in trade outlook are frowned upon as
contrary to the unified and balanced economic development of the U.S.S.R. as one whole, as potentially
dangerous in terms of local aspirations of more than
a simple trade nature, and as contrary to the general
principles of autarky.

Only three regional trade organizations have
been set up to improve what is mainly barter trade
across the Soviet borders. In 1939 Vostokintorg was
formed as a trading organization specifically concerned with exports to and imports from Mongolia,
Afghanistan, and the Middle East. It now has a turnover of some 160 million rubles per year and has an
office in Baku from which barter trade with Turkey
and Iran is directed on behalf of Azerbaijan, Armenia,

Georgia, and Turkmenia. In 1960 Lenfintorg was established, with an office in Leningrad, to improve
Leningrad oblast's trade in consumer goods with Finland. Its sphere of operations has been widened now
to include Murmansk and Arkhangel'sk oblast's, the
Baltic republics, and Belorussia.[2] In January, 1963,
Dal'intorg, with headquarters in Nakhodka, started
coastal trading activities between the Soviet Far
East and Japan. For the first year the turnover in
coastal trade operations was some 800,000 rubles.
Initially the Primor'ye and Khabarovsk territories
participated, but now the scope has been extended to
include the Sakhalin, Kamchatka, Magadan, Chita, and
Irkutsk oblast's and the Buryat A.S.S.R. Dal'intorg
can represent, in a very limited way, the whole of
the Far East and Eastern Siberia.[3] Turnover in 1964
was 3.2 million rubles, and by 1966 it had reached
9.5 million rubles; it was expected to be about 12
million rubles in 1967, but probably did not exceed
that target until 1969.

Dal'intorg has the status of a vneshnetorgovaya
kontora (V/K), or office, and it will have to expand
its trading relations with other countries and
achieve a turnover well in excess of 30 million rubles before Moscow would even consider elevating it
to the status of vneshnetorgovoe ob"edinenie (V/O),
or corporation. The Ministry of Foreign Trade in
Moscow intends to keep a tight rein over this distant
office so that local aspirations for direct trade
with Japan do not get out of hand. There is a marked
difference in attitude between the Ministry of Foreign
Trade, which still wants to see all significant trade
channeled through Moscow, and Dal'intorg in Nakhodka,
which aspires to as rapid an expansion of direct
trade with countries of the Pacific Rim--especially
Japan--as possible. Dal'intorg is backed up by the
recently established Far Eastern Economic Research
Institute, which is to study the trade policies of
countries in the Pacific area--including Japan,
Canada, Australia, Mongolia, North Korea, and the
countries of Latin America. This institute will provide the research data from which trade decisions
can be made.

TRADING METHODS--A PROBLEM?

The problems that face a basically free enterprise economy in the Pacific region in formulating a
trade policy toward the U.S.S.R. are the following:

1. The great bulk of Soviet trade is carried
out on a bilateral basis, and this makes it difficult
for a country with a multilateral trading policy to
guarantee a tight bilateral balance involving defined
quantities (at previously agreed prices) or to operate special clearing accounts.

2. In the absence of quantitative bilateral
trading arrangements, and with all Soviet export and
import trade being controlled by state agencies, how
can such a country be assured of reasonable access
to the U.S.S.R. market?

3. As there is no necessary or even predictable
relationship among production costs, domestic prices,
and either import or export prices, how can a free
enterprise trader be assured of having a "most favored
nation" tariff access to the U.S.S.R. in exchange for
a similar concession in its own market?

Most of these questions have been answered satisfactorily through the experiences of other market
economies, such as Britain, which have signed mutually
advantageous long-term bilateral agreements with the
U.S.S.R. They have gained a reasonable share of the
Soviet "market" and have only suffered very occasion-
ally from Soviet dumping activities.[4] Generally
speaking, Soviet trade corporations aim at maximizing
their revenues of foreign exchange from export sales
of raw materials and primary produce in order to finance imports of essential producer goods and industrial equipment. The very scarcity of convertible
foreign currency available to the U.S.S.R. from its
international trading operations impels the trade
corporations to get the best possible price for
their exports, within the limits of world competition,
and to finance imports at the lowest price possible

consistent with quality for the particular purpose
required. The overriding requirements of the five-
year plan sometimes have demanded actions of a purely
quantitative nature not bearing much relationship to
prevailing world trade conditions. Usually, however,
Gosplan's requirements for imports, or its planned
surpluses for export, are dealt with through the
Ministry of Foreign Trade and its subsidiary corporations, in the light of reports on world trade opportunities. Even payments for trade exchanges with
other centrally planned economies are broadly based
on world prices in the absence of any other suitable
reference point.

     Long-term quantitative agreements, such as the
U.S.S.R. has with many West European countries, are
a species of barter and as such lend themselves
easily to integration with the Soviet five-year economic development plans. They also fit in well with
the fact that Soviet currency is not freely convertible and so foreign exchange is at a premium, which
makes true multilateral trading impossible. Sometimes, however, bilateral trading lands the Soviet
Union with goods for which it has no urgent use (such
as dates from Iraq) or which have to be processed
in competition with its own locally grown produce
and then re-exported (such as raw sugar from Cuba).
The latter example illustrates the political dimen-
sion of certain Soviet trading activities.

     Despite such difficulties the international di-
vision of labor still has a broad effect, and the
U.S.S.R. continues to export timber and raw materials
and import rubber and factory equipment. Moreover,
the Soviet Union has expressed its interest in active
participation in a new international division of
labor with the rest of the world in order to achieve
the most effective utilization of its productive
resources through international trade.[5] The continuing plans in the U.S.S.R. for a fairly rapid rate
of economic expansion indicate the possibility of a
much higher volume of trade with the rest of the world
than exists at present. This will be especially so
if the international political climate is favorable
and if the U.S.S.R.'s tendency toward greater economic

freedom under the reforms introduced since 1965 is
extended into the sphere of international trade. In
centrally planned economies such as Hungary, Rumania,
Czechoslovakia, and Poland there is already a great
deal of close contact between the foreign trader and
the individual manufacturing enterprises that want
either to export or to import.

This reform has yet to occur in the U.S.S.R.,
possibly because international trade is not so important to the successful operation of its economy.
But the gap between the importer and his supplier
(or the exporter and his customer) is one of the major
causes of delays, inefficiency, and misunderstandings
in the West's trading contacts with the U.S.S.R.
Even in the more liberal East European countries it
is mostly exports that are being freed; imports that
are critical to plan fulfillment are still subject
to extremely centralized control. Most of the Soviet
Union's imports are derived from trade with Communist
Bloc partners under strict bilateral quantitative
trade agreements that assure supplies. A negotiated
reduction in the U.S.S.R.'s tariff rates would not,
of course, bring about an increased volume of imports;
neither, for that matter, would a reduction in the
level of internal prices given continuing controls
over the level of demand.

With the basic differences between market economies and centrally planned economies, reciprocity
in trade can best be brought about by mutual commit-
ments to increase the volume and broaden the range
of their respective imports. The general principle
to be applied here is that an increase in exports
is required, in a planning situation where foreign
exchange is scarce, to permit an expansion of imports.
High priority imports, such as machinery, equipment,
or some raw materials, may be bought by the U.S.S.R.
from abroad without reciprocity, but this policy is
not likely to apply to consumer or luxury goods. For
temperate foodstuffs the long-term Soviet attitude
aims at self-sufficiency, although the effort involved is very great and in the short term there will
be sporadic imports of significant amounts. Although
these amounts will be small in relation to total

Soviet consumption they could be in appreciable quantities for primary exporting nations.

Finally, countries and companies trading with the U.S.S.R. must not only be prepared for long delays in replies to cables (even longer for letters) but they must learn that negotiating with Soviet bureaucracy frequently involves lengthy negotiations --even procrastination--before a contract is signed. For complete factory equipment the discussions and presentation of detailed plans and specifications may take several months, but, if the order is won, the reward at the end can be substantial, as implied in the words of the Birmingham and London chambers of commerce trade mission visiting the U.S.S.R.:

> The fact that the Soviet Ministry of Foreign Trade is prepared to talk about five-year contracts both for buying and selling is a very important and significant step. British industry should be ready to take full advantage of it. It could now be possible for particular branches of industry to plan production ahead and even to expand facilities to accommodate Soviet orders.[6]

If there is no reciprocity in trade, Soviet purchases may well be cut back. In the longer term, however, as the U.S.S.R.'s total trade grows, it is likely that a more multilateral approach to trade will be adopted.

DAL'INTORG AND MOSCOW

The formation of Dal'intorg was an important step forward in Soviet regional trade thinking. It provided the machinery for an expansion--albeit a modest one--in coastal trading with Japan; it recognized the basic disadvantage of Pacific Siberia in relation to distant European Russian markets; and it admitted to the shortage of consumer goods and industrial equipment in the region. But it did not remove the central control of Siberian trade from the Ministry of Foreign Trade in Moscow.

This reflects the vested interests of the Ministry and its subsidiary corporations in channeling
all major trade deals through their hands alone. The
list of products Dal'intorg has to offer is second-
rate. Thus, whereas Dal'intorg can offer timber offcuts or waste for sale, it is Exportles, the central
timber-exporting corporation in Moscow, that handles
all trade in first-class marketable timbers.* The
same applies to exports of fish to the lucrative
Japanese market: The best grades are handled by
Prodintorg in Moscow, whereas Dal'intorg handles such
items as squid, seaweed, and fishmeal.** Some of
this attitude can be explained by the Ministry's desire to see the officers of Dal'intorg have more experience in trading with market economies before the
list of export products becomes more comprehensive.

In 1965 Dal'intorg mounted a commercial exhibition of coastal trade goods in three towns on Japan's
western coast (Niigata, Toyama, and Maizuru). In
the summer of 1966 a Japanese exhibition was held at
Khabarovsk on the banks of the Amur in which some
400 Japanese trading and industrial firms participated; 80,000 people visited it and contracts were
signed for three million rubles. But in each case
the Dal'intorg representatives were backed up by experienced members of the Ministry of Foreign Trade.

The Far East, through the Ministry, handles
about 5 percent of Soviet foreign trade turnover--
about one billion rubles--of which Dal'intorg now
accounts for, at the most, 15-20 million rubles.
Much of the trade handled by Nakhodka (7.5 million
tons in 1971) comes from a region extending further
inland than the Yenisei and includes oil, coal,
chrome ore, rolled ferrous metals, asbestos, cement,
paper-cellulose, canned foodstuffs, machinery, and

----

*Exportles has an annual turnover of some 900
million rubles in timber, paper, and pulp.

**Annual turnover is about 700 million rubles, in-
cluding sugar, edible oils, and dairy products as
well as fish.

equipment that originate in West Siberia, the Urals,
or even European Russia and are destined for markets
in East or Southeast Asia. The weakness of the Pacific Siberian economy precludes the possibilities
for expansion of trade, at least in the short run,
away from basic extractive commodities (such as
timber, fish, coal, and mineral ores), which are produced surplus to local requirements. This is probably
another reason why the Ministry of Foreign Trade is
not actively promoting the activities of Dal'intorg
beyond simple coastal trading operations with Japan.

In the longer term, however, the availability
of products from Eastern Siberia's hydro-electric
industrial plants (aluminum, paper, paperboard, cellulose, and perhaps steel) and the opening up of
huge mineral resources (copper, coal, iron ore, and
oil and natural gas by pipeline from West Siberia
or Yakutia) could make it imperative for Moscow to
have a Siberian trading organization with "local"
experience. This will be particularly so if the
Japanese decide to participate in joint developmental
projects whereby they provide capital and equipment
in return for deliveries, over a period, of the resource being exploited.

From Moscow's point of view it may be desirable,
both economically and politically, for the Far East
and Eastern Siberia to develop their trade with the
Pacific Rim.[7] The limited range of export goods
presently available and the desire to channel most
trade through the Ministry of Foreign Trade must
confine the activities of Dal'intorg for some time.
The huge cost of imports by rail into Pacific Siberia
from distant parts of the U.S.S.R. makes it sensible
to replace them in the long run with cheaper imports
from Pacific countries; however, this cannot be
done, in view of the shortage of foreign exchange,
unless exports, too, are increased by an equivalent
amount.

DAL'INTORG AND JAPAN

Dal'intorg was created as a Soviet regional
trade office to take advantage, within the limits

imposed upon it by the Ministry of Foreign Trade, of
coastal trading opportunities with Japan. Japan is
its raison d'etre. This development reflected a
worsening in traditional trade relationships with
China across the Amur-Ussuri border and the desire
of the Soviets to avail themselves, through local
barter, of the complementary nature of the Siberian
and Japanese economies. Primary products are exchanged for manufactured commodities, and Dal'intorg
was empowered to sign contracts for these items directly with Japanese firms under the terms of the
1966-70 long-term trade agreement.

The Japanese firm first must establish an export credit with Dal'intorg by purchasing something
from it. In turn this action will provide Dal'intorg
with the currency, and the authority, to import on
its own behalf. There is an incentive, too, for
local Far Eastern enterprises to overfulfill their
approved export targets set by Gosplan so that they
can then, through Dal'intorg, gain access to funds
for placing orders in Japan.[8] This, in turn, can
lead to high mark-ups on Japanese products on sale
in the Far East as the local Soviet selling enterprise
seeks to charge what the market will bear in order
to maximize its returns.

Japanese export credits with Dal'intorg, once
established through a purchase, can be used for sales
to the Far East by a third country provided that it
is channeled through the Japanese firm in credit.
This devious way of doing trade also adds substantially to the price.

The major problem the Japanese face in their
relationships with Dal'intorg is finding suitable
Soviet products for sale in Japan. Dal'intorg's timber is poor quality and usually is only suitable for
pulp or particle board; much of the fish is inedible,
and some is converted into meal for re-export.[9] At
the Nakhodka Fishery Trade Fair held May 22-31, 1968,
under the joint sponsorship of Taiyo Fishery Co. of
Tokyo and Ataka & Co. of Osaka, 1,000 tons of fishmeal together with 1,000 tons of whale meat and 12
tons of herring roe were bartered for automatic fish-
packing machines (Mitsubishi), deep-sea buoy manufac-

turing equipment (Ishikawajima-Harima), life buoys
(Sumitomo Electric Industries), and cultured pearls.
These deals, worth $400,000, represented a new type
of barter trade for the fishing industries of both
sides.

The Russians also offered for sale frozen Chum
salmon (400-500 tons), 50 tons of caviar, and 50
tons of sea urchin worth a total of $800,000 and,
in return, were interested in buying fishing nets,
corrugated cardboard for packing canned fish, raincoats, women's dresses, and sweaters. In a more recent deal in January, 1972, Dal'intorg exchanged
pollack fish for fish reconnaissance equipment and
consumer goods.

The western prefectures of Japan are the most
interested in coastal trade with the Far East; and
the small and medium-sized trading companies have
been most active. Unfortunately, trade has not expanded at the rate earlier expected despite conferences of Soviet and Japanese regional authorities.
Under the exchange of notes appended to the 1966-70
Japan-U.S.S.R. trade and payments agreement it was
planned that coastal trade would reach $20 million
by the end of 1970; in the base year, 1966, trade
was $9.5 million. In the event, there was a short-
fall of $5-6 million. The Japan Association for
Trade with the Soviet Union and Socialist Countries
of Europe has complained that Dal'intorg prices are
too high, the range of commodities offered is very
meager, and the powers of Dal'intorg need to be expanded to enable simultaneous signing of both import
and export contracts. There have also been complaints
about the considerable delays, sometimes amounting
to several days, when Japanese vessels waiting to
load cargo have to anchor in the Nakhodka sea roads
because of the lack of adequate port facilities
(more than 500 foreign ships used the port in 1971).

Dal'intorg recognizes the opportunities that
coastal trade with Japan offers for imports of consumer goods and industrial equipment in short supply,
but it is hamstrung by the Ministry of Foreign Trade,

which limits the range of goods it can offer to those
not handled by the central corporations or to commodities in poor demand, suitable only for barter trade.
As a result Dal'intorg's trade is only about 2 percent of all foreign trade turnover handled in the
Far East. The Ministry representative in Nakhodka,
representing the Far East and Eastern Siberia, holds
the power of advising Moscow. Dal'intorg has a certain amount of technical freedom to make limited decisions, but policy decisions are subject to the
Ministry's approval.*

About 60-70 percent of Dal'intorg's trade with
Japan is conducted through three companies--Tokyo
Maruichi Shoji, Progress Trading Co., Ltd., and C.
Itoh. The latter is associated with the other two,
but they all operate separately except for a pooling
of their balances with Dal'intorg.** About two-
thirds of their exports are textile apparel; the
other one-third is fishing nets, marine paints,
ships' fenders, leather shoes, apples, and mandarin
oranges. About 90 percent of their imports are fish
and fish products, the remainder being firewood,
wood pulp, cottonseed oil, honey, potato starch,
marble chips, vodka, and agar-agar. The trade in
clothing, knitwear, and shoes is the most profitable
and offsets losses due to the high prices and poor
quality of the Soviet goods accepted in exchange.

A large shipment of knitted fabrics, motor vehi-
cles, and plate glass for shop windows was delivered
to Nakhodka from Maizuru, Japan, in 1971 in exchange
for canned fish, beef tallow, and honey. This sort
of minor trade could eventually lead to much stronger
commercial links between the two countries.

---

*At present Dal'intorg only has approval to sign
contracts with Japan; direct trade with other countries would require Moscow's approval.

**Tokyo Maruichi Shoji's trade with Dal'intorg in
1972 is expected to be three million dollars.

SIBERIA AND JAPAN: A LESSON
IN SOVIET TRADE INITIATIVE

No two countries could economically be more
in each other's pockets than Japan and the
USSR in the Far East.[10]

In the broader context of trade relations between the Far East and Japan, Soviet sources claim
up to two-thirds of total U.S.S.R.-Japan trade turnover flows through the ports of the Soviet Far East.[11]
This trade probably amounted to some 400 million
rubles out of the 1 billion rubles or so of foreign
trade handled by the Ministry of Foreign Trade in
the Far East.

Until 1961 the Japanese published separate statistics for their trade with the Far Eastern ports
and European ports of the U.S.S.R. These now have
been discontinued, but some of the earlier data is
given in Table 29. Trade with the Far East increased
rapidly after 1959; diplomatic relations were re-
stored in 1956, and the first postwar trade agreement
was signed in 1957. The main items exported to Japan
were timber, coal, and oil; the major imported commodities from Japan were iron and steel, machinery,
synthetic textiles, and, in 1959, four ships.

As early as the mid-1920s the Soviets were dis-
playing a remarkably realistic attitude to trade
contacts between the Far East and Japan. While some
Western commentators of the time pointed to a Soviet
dislike of the Japanese, "which would destroy all
prospects of trade expansion and economic development,"[12] Soviet trade commissars were actively en-
gaged in negotiating the Soviet-Japanese Convention
of January 20, 1925, which includes the following
statement in Article VI:

In the interests of the development of economic relations between the two countries,
and taking into consideration the needs of
Japan with respect to natural resources,
the Government of the USSR is ready to

TABLE 29

Japan's Trade with the Soviet Far East, 1955-61
(in millions of $ U.S.)

Year	Far Eastern Ports, U.S.S.R.		European Ports, U.S.S.R.		Far Eastern Turnover as Percent of Total
	Imports	Exports	Imports	Exports	
1955	2.0	1.6	1.1	0.5	69.2
1956	2.2	0.7	0.7	0.1	78.4
1957	10.8	5.7	1.5	3.6	76.4
1958	18.4	15.6	3.8	2.6	84.4
1959	26.9	19.3	12.6	3.8	73.8
1960	40.0	42.6	47.0	17.3	56.2
1961	58.4	55.0	87.0	10.4	53.8

Source: W. S. Hunsberger, Japan and the United States in World Trade (New York: Harper and Row, 1964), p. 212.

grant to Japanese subjects, companies
and associations concessions for the exploitation of mineral, timber and other
natural resources in all parts of the
territory of the USSR.[13]

Protocol B to the Convention granted specific concessions to the Japanese for working oil and coal fields
in Sakhalin for a period of 40 to 50 years. Japanese
seasonal workers were employed by the Soviets in the
Far Eastern fisheries, especially in the canneries,
until 1933. Throughout the 1920s exports of timber,
fish, coal, and oil from the Far East to Japan accounted for almost three-quarters of total Japan-
U.S.S.R. trade turnover. The development of this
trade in the 1920s and early 1930s led to the following observation by V. Conolly:

> In the exchange of goods and services for
> years what one had to give, the other re-
> quired. If the Russians owned the fishing
> grounds, they had, on the other side, no
> apparatus or proper boats to work them.
> All were supplied by Japan. If they had
> oil and coal in Sakhalin, the equipment had
> also to come from Japan before they could
> extract one ton of material.[14]

The Soviet attitude to trade with Japan cooled considerably with the latter's hostile presence in Manchuria
from 1931 to 1945.

Trade remained small until after the Korean War
and the restoration of diplomatic relations. After
this came the 1956 fishery convention, the 1957 bilateral trade agreement, the 1958 agreement on regular
navigation between Nakhodka and Japanese ports, and
the Soviet participation in the 1958 International
Fair at Osaka. The complementary nature of the resources of Pacific Siberia and Japan has accelerated
this broad development in trade contacts as has the
increasing emphasis upon consumer welfare in the
U.S.S.R. and the signing of long-term trade agreements.*

In Japan's case proximity is paramount. The effect of the latter factor is very simply illustrated
by the example of coal: The cost of transporting
coal from the United States to Japan ranges from
$5.65 to $6.50 per ton, whereas from Nakhodka it
costs only $3.00. The comparison is claimed by the
Soviets to be more or less the same for other goods.[15]

Sometimes the Soviet attitude to the prospects
for Japanese trade with Siberia has been too optimistic. At the 1960 Japanese Industrial Exhibition in
Moscow, Mikoyan held out glowing trade prospects if
the Japanese would make long-term agreements in

---

*Trade agreements were signed between Japan and
the U.S.S.R. for 1960-62, 1963-65, 1966-70, and
1971-75.

connection with a 20-year economic development plan
for Siberia and the Far East that was being drawn up
at that time. More recently, Kosygin has echoed
similar sentiments about the possibility of accelerated development in Siberia and the Far East based
on Japanese needs for raw materials and her ability
to supply industrial and consumer goods.[16]

This brings us to the question of the prospects
for joint ventures in Siberia involving Japanese
capital and equipment and, in return, long-term deliveries of Siberian natural resources to Japan.[17]
Large-scale collaboration in such developmental
projects would mean not only a turning point in
Soviet-Japanese relations but also would be the
first time in Soviet history since the 1920s that
foreign assistance in the exploitation of natural
resources has been sought. The first such agreement
was signed in July of 1968 between V/O Exportles and
the Japanese company KS Sangyo for the exploitation
of timber resources in the Far East. Under this
agreement the Japanese firm is advancing $133 million
credit (to be repaid before the end of 1973) for the
purchase of machinery and equipment for the Far
Eastern timber industry and, also, $30 million for
the purchase of consumer goods. In return the lower
Amur is supplying Japan--for a period of five years,
starting from 1969--with 7.6 million cubic meters
(268 million cubic feet) of lumber and 20,000 cubic
meters (706,000 cubic feet) of sawn timber.[18] Yearly
interest was negotiated at 5.8 percent. The price
of the lumber is adjusted to international price
movements. The consumer goods comprise clothing
(especially from man-made fibers) and shoes, but not
foodstuffs. The machinery being imported from Japan
includes bulldozers, saws, logging equipment, and
other machinery not made in the Far East. In 1971
nearly 30 percent more timber was supplied to Japan
than was originally provided for by contract.

This agreement was supplemented on December 6,
1971, when the Japan-Soviet Economic Cooperation
Committee concluded negotiations whereby the Soviet
Far East will supply 8.05 million cubic meters of
birch wood chips and 4.7 million cubic meters of

pulpwood over 10 years, from 1972 to 1981. In return
Japan will supply $45 million in pulp and chip ma-
chinery and $5 million in consumer goods over the
3 years 1972 to 1974. Negotiations for this particular deal had been going on since June, 1967, and
the delays were typified by intransigence on both
sides. The main disagreement was over prices, which
in the final agreement are based on world prices to
be reviewed in 1977. Both sides will benefit, of
course--the Soviets gain a much-needed pulp and chip
plant, and Japan is assured of a stable source of
supply for her paper industry.

With several of the other projects proposed by
the Soviets the main difficulty has been the enormous
capital costs entailed. One Soviet proposal is to
build a large-diameter pipeline from the Tyumen oil
fields (Anzhero Sudzhensk) in West Siberia to Nakhodka,
a distance of 4,100 miles. Two million tons of
pipes would be involved at a cost of $1.5 billion.
Between 10 million and 12 million tons of oil annually, from a flow of 50 million tons, would be delivered to Japan over a period of about 20 years.
An alternative to this project is a pipeline from
Irkutsk to Nakhodka at a cost of $700-800 million;
construction is to start in the 1971-75 period. The
U.S.S.R. is short of capacity for making wide-diameter
pipelines, and Japan would supply them in return for
oil. At present Japan imports some oil from Sakhalin's 2.5 million ton output. Although it has not
yet agreed to any of the pipeline proposals, discussions are continuing; and in February, 1972 the
Soviets agreed to let a Japanese survey team make a
feasibility study of the Tyumen project.

At the Soviet-Japanese economic conferences
held periodically since 1966, Soviet proposals for
the joint working of gas deposits in Sakhalin and
south Yakutia, the mining of copper at Udokan, coking
coal at Chul'man, and the modernization and recon-
struction of Far Eastern ports have been discussed.
There have even been proposals to deliver electricity
to Japan by high-voltage lines (800 kilovolts direct
current) from a six million-kilowatt thermal power
station to Toyama and Niigata and thence to Tokyo.

(Soviet power could cost 10 percent less per kilowatt-
hour than power generated by a large Japanese thermal
station.)

There have been no suggestions of importing
Japanese labor to work on such ambitious projects.
On the other hand, Japan is, of course, well placed
to supply both capital and markets. Joint commissions
have been studying the feasibility of these proposals
for several years. The Soviet interest is basically
concerned with the supply of machinery and equipment
and long-term economic development, whereas Japanese
interests center around credit charges, repayment
periods, and short-term commercial interests. The
manufacture of engineering machinery is so backward
in the Far East and most of the proposed projects
are so large and remote that massive injections of
outside capital are needed.

The U.S.S.R. is taking the initiative with the
Japanese in discussions on these projects, but the
idea of mutual cooperation in the exploitation of
Siberian natural resources has been given considerable prominence on both sides. In particular, the
following statement in Moscow of N. S. Patolichev
(Minister for Foreign Trade) at the time of the 1965
trade negotiations was widely publicized:

> We are successfully developing and opening
> up the riches of the eastern regions of
> the Soviet Union. We could co-operate with
> you in this matter on advantageous condi-
> tions, on a firm and long-term basis, that
> is if you are interested and wish to do so.[19]

More recently, Japanese talk about cooperation has
become subdued with the realization of the magnitude
of the economic and political issues involved. For
instance, Japan imports about 2.5 million tons of
Soviet crude oil a year out of a total requirement
of some 100 million tons; although this is not a
substantial amount it could become so if a pipeline
was built across Siberia specifically to supply
Japan. This might make Japan dependent on Soviet
goodwill for oil supplies and would certainly invoke

some reaction from the big oil monopolies presently
supplying her.   Until the early 1960s many large
Japanese companies trading with the U.S.S.R. did so
through "dummy" companies to avoid possible adverse
domestic and U.S. publicity.[20]

Control and management of all the proposed projects would be entirely in Soviet hands with the
Japanese role relegated to the subsidiary one of
supplying equipment, machinery, and technical advice;
the lack of control or supervision of their financial
outlays is not especially attractive to the Japanese.

It does not seem likely now that Japan will participate in the exploitation of the Udokan copper
deposits because it would be too expensive, with the
Russians asking the Japanese to raise all or part of
the cost of $1.2 billion.   A railway line of about
340 miles would have to be built across difficult
mountainous country.   An extraction rate of anything
from 20 million to 40 million tons of ore annually
with a copper content of 2 percent has been suggested.
The Soviets claim this is the largest untapped copper
deposit in the world and are now approaching various
West European consortia and even the United States
to develop it.*

The Soviet-Japanese negotiations over the supply
of Sakhalin natural gas also deadlocked at an early
stage over price, production-sharing formula, interest rates, and the terms of deferred payment.   After
six months of protracted negotiations the Japanese
price offer stood at $12 per 1,000 cubic meters, com-
pared with a Soviet asking price of $14.   At the
time of the November, 1966, talks the Japanese proposed an interest rate of 6 percent (for $100 million
worth of pipes over 450 miles, plus $75 million of
liquefying equipment and earth-moving machinery)
over ten years; the Soviet side demanded 5.5 percent.
The Soviet production-sharing formula, whereby

----

*The possibility of developing the Udokan copper
deposits was raised at Commerce Secretary Maurice H.
Stans's visit to Moscow in December, 1971.

one-half of the expected total output of 4.8 billion
cubic meters of natural gas would go to the Japanese
petrochemical industry and the other one-half to
Komsomol'sk for manufacturing into urea, was also
unacceptable. The only significant Russian concession reported was the offer to load the natural gas
in liquid form at Nakhodka instead of at Korsakov,
in Sakhalin, which is icebound in winter.[21] In 1970
a pipeline direct from Okha to Muroran in Hokkaido
(920 miles) was proposed. Deferred payments terms
have been a stumbling block also because the Japanese
Finance and Foreign ministries have looked upon the
U.S.S.R. as an advanced nation that can afford to
pay for its credits; for the Sakhalin project the
offer was up to ten years, including consumer goods
for 20 percent ($20 million) of the total capital
to be supplied. This concession was made because
the project has special implications for the industrial development of Niigata and Akita prefectures.
Just when agreement seemed imminent in 1970 the
Soviets said that the most promising supplies of gas
were from Yakutia and not from Sakhalin and instead
proposed a Yakutsk-Komsomol'sk-Sakhalin pipeline to
deliver 10 billion cubic meters of gas a year. The
Japanese deferred a decision until 1972.

     The Soviet change of mind over natural gas was
based on drastically revised estimates of the gas
reserves on Sakhalin (down from 60 billion cubic
meters to 16 billion cubic meters). The high cost
of production of Sakhalin natural gas may have caused
the U.S.S.R. to reassess its offer. Equally, it
seems likely that the costs involved for Japan to
develop the Yakutian deposits--at present there is
only a short pipeline from Ust' Vilyui to Yakutia and
Pokrovsk--have been weighed against alternative
sources such as Alaska.

     No doubt similar cost calculations caused the
Japanese to defer assistance with the development of
the Chul'man coking coal deposits late in 1970 after
two years of discussions. This coal field would require an access railway of 250 miles as well as mining equipment and housing worth $440 million.[22]
Chul'man, which at present produces only 200,000 tons

a year, contains 1.4 billion tons of coking coal in
a deposit of 3.5 billion tons; a production of 7 million tons a year has been proposed with 5 million
tons for export to Japanese steel mills. The Japanese
can probably get coking coal cheaper from Australia
or the United States at present.

An important breakthrough in Soviet-Japanese
economic cooperation occurred in September, 1970,
when a $70 million agreement was signed for the de-
velopment of Vrangel' port near Nakhodka. Poor port
facilities have created a major bottleneck in trade
between the U.S.S.R. and Japan. Deep-water berths,
bulk loading equipment for timber, wood chips, and
coal, as well as a container terminal will be provided
with Japanese Export-Import Bank credits, which marks
a shift in Japanese credit policy. Nakhodka is already the biggest commercial port in the Far East;
completion of the port at Vrangel' in the 1971-75
plan period at a total cost of some $300 million will
greatly increase the Far East's port facilities* as
well as give Japan quicker access to Siberian raw
materials.

So far, then, despite considerable urging by
the Russians, the Japanese have not signed up for
any large-scale venture in Siberia--other than the
one port and two timber projects worth $280 million
already cited. In the longer term the possibility of
cooperation worth over $3.5 billion with oil, natural
gas, copper, and coking coal is very real. At the
committee stage, talks have also ranged in detail
over prospects for joint exploitation of phosphate
rock near Ulan-Ude, 1.4 billion tons of iron ore at
Rudnogorsk (Irkutsk oblast'), a steel plant at
Taishet, and joint exploration for oil on the continental shelf. One of the factors in favor of joint
operations is the present inability of Pacific Siberia to supply Japan with the raw materials it wants
because of inadequate production capacities. This
was certainly a moving force behind the timber

_____

*The cargo turnover capacity of Vrangel', when
completed, will be 30 million tons per year.

agreement of 1968. By supplying machinery and equipment Japan not only assures itself of some continuity
in supplies but it also offers scope for evening up
the imbalance in its trade with the U.S.S.R.

Japanese caution and expectations on this matter
are perhaps typified in the remark by the Japanese
Foreign Minister, Miki, reporting on his visit to
Moscow in 1967: "It is the Kremlin which is showing
greater zeal than Tokyo in its efforts to improve
relations. . . . The development of Siberia could
well become the 'pipe' linking Japan and the Soviet
Union in the economic field."[23] China has been highly
critical of Soviet plans to develop Siberian resources
with Japanese help, and this may eventually force
Japan to choose between the U.S.S.R. and China as
trade markets; in the short term, however, Japanese
pragmatism will enable both options to be played.

TRADE RELATIONS WITH NEIGHBORING
COMMUNIST COUNTRIES

Traditionally the neighboring countries, now
with centrally planned economies, of Mongolia, China
(especially the northern territory of Manchuria),
and Korea have carried on trade across their borders
with Pacific Siberia. Russo-Chinese caravan trade
through Kyakhta from about the early 1700s bartered
Chinese tea and wool for Russian furs and gold. As
the population of Siberia grew with the great migratory waves in the 1800s the demand for imported
foodstuffs increased. The long land borders with
China and Mongolia gave rise to a considerable transit and barter trade based on regular trade fairs in
the region. Silk, spirits, tobacco, sugar, and textiles were the major imports.

With the construction of the Trans-Siberian
railway, at the turn of this century, the movement
of goods was greatly speeded up, freight costs were
lowered substantially, and the risks of loss or
damage to supplies from European Russia were lessened.
Wheat from West Siberia was railed eastward, forcing
out of the Far Eastern market imports from China.

Nevertheless, imported foodstuffs were still in demand: In 1932, for instance, grain output in the Far East fulfilled only one-third and meat only one-tenth of consumption.[24] Meat, dairy produce, fats, fodder, soybeans, and poultry were all imported from Manchuria before World War II, together with rice and sugar from Japan, wheat from European Russia or Manchuria, salt for the fishing industry from the Crimea, and kerosene from Batumi. The per capita proportion of foreign trade became the highest in the Union--largely because a series of decrees of the Ministry of Foreign Trade permitted freer entry of foodstuffs and manufactured goods. Large quantities of wheat, barley, and millet were imported down the Sungari from northern Manchuria, and the meat combines of Irkutsk processed live cattle imported from Mongolia. Overseas exports of Siberian timber, fish, and furs paid for some of these imports.

Russian exports to China were worth about 2 million rubles a year in the 1870s and 1880s but rose to 5 million or 6 million rubles after the Trans-Siberian railway began operation.[25] By the late 1920s exports to western China (Hsin-kiang) alone were 10.6 million rubles and to Mongolia, 7.7 million rubles--mainly timber, oil, coal, fish, textiles, and metalware.[26] Imports were tea, wool, cattle, and hides worth 13.5 million rubles and 12.1 million rubles from each country, respectively.

Table 30 gives some idea of the postwar trend in bilateral trade with neighboring countries, but specific data on direct trade with Pacific Siberia is not available. Border trade with China flourished in the 1950s but declined drastically in the 1960s. A large part of Soviet trade with China in food, textiles, and building materials went to the Primor'ye, Khabarovsk, and Amur provinces. These regions are short of foodstuffs, clothing, and construction materials, and considerable transport costs must have been saved by purchasing these commodities from China rather than from European Russia. R. O. Freedman states that no data is available on the exact amounts of Chinese trade with the bordering Soviet provinces but quotes a Russian source in 1958 describing the extent of the trade:

> The coal, cement and pig iron supplied the
> USSR by China assures the needs of the Far
> Eastern sections of our country. For the
> satisfaction of the needs of our popula-
> tion, particularly in the Far East, the
> USSR purchases from China in large quanti-
> ties citrus fruits, apples and a number of
> foodstuffs.[27]

Meat, eggs, and vegetables were also supplied by
China, probably in exchange for Siberian timber.

It is interesting to speculate on the significance of the sharp fall-off in trade with China for
the performance of the Pacific Siberian economy.
Some of this trade has been diverted to Mongolia,
North Korea, North Vietnam, and even Japan (e.g.,
apples, leather footwear, clothing). Tea now comes
from North Vietnam, rice and vegetables from North
Korea, more beef cattle come from Mongolia, tobacco
and cement from North Korea. The U.S.S.R.'s trade
with China is now only a fraction of that with Mongolia or North Korea. North Korean pig iron and
rolled steel, window glass, high-voltage insulators,
and such chemicals as hydrochloric acid, calcium
hypochlorite, lead oxide, calcium carbide, and ammo-
nium saltpeter are imported into the Far East in exchange for frozen fish, edible oil, soap, and petroleum products. A railway freight agreement exists
between North Korea and the U.S.S.R., and the 1972
agreement, which was signed in Khabarovsk, provides
for "measures to accelerate the handling of trains
in order to increase the flow of goods traffic between the two countries."[28] The U.S.S.R. is now
North Korea's biggest trade partner and cross-border
exchanges must be of significant regional importance
to the Far East.

Soviet trade with Mongolia is dominated by purchases of wool, livestock, and meat in exchange for
machinery (especially equipment and materials for
complete plants, transport machinery, garage equipment, tractors, and agricultural machinery), clothing,

TABLE 30

Soviet Trade Turnover with Countries Neighboring Pacific Siberia
(in million rubles, f.o.b.)

Country	Turnover 1958	Turnover 1970	1970 Trade Exports	1970 Trade Imports	Major Commodities Exported	Major Commodities Imported
Communist China	1,363.7	41.9	22.4	19.5	Machinery, drilling equipment, tractors, trucks	Meat, fruits, clothing, textiles
Mongolia	100.8	230.9	178.3	52.6	Machinery, oil, metals, tea, sugar, wheat, clothing	Wool, livestock, meat
North Korea	94.6	335.9	207.0	128.9	Machinery, equipment, oil, metals, wheat, cotton, sugar	Minerals and metals, cement, fruit, rice, clothing
Japan	33.9	652.3	341.4	310.9	Timber, oil, coal, pig iron, aluminum, raw cotton, fish, chrome ore	Machinery, equipment, pipes, ships, chemicals, plastics, clothing, shoes
Total as per-cent of U.S.S.R. trade	20.5	5.7	6.5	4.8		

Source: Vneshnyaya Torgovlya SSSR, for several years.

cloth and footwear, oil and oil products, sugar and
confectionery, and wheat. The balance of trade is
over 3:1 in the U.S.S.R.'s favor. A significant proportion of the 1.1 million head of livestock purchased
by the U.S.S.R. in 1969 would have been destined for
slaughterhouses across the border (e.g., at Irkutsk,
Ulan-Ude, Chita, Nerchinsk, or Borzya). Chilled
meat, butter, and leather uppers for shoe factories
are also sent to Eastern Siberia from Mongolia.

Of course, the U.S.S.R.'s attitude toward Mongolia is not one of trade alone. The buffer zone
position of Mongolia, protecting the vital East
Siberian Irkutsi-Angara industrial region against
possible Chinese aggression, is vital. Credits
equivalent to one-third of the total capital expenditure planned by Mongolia for 1966-70 were extended
by the U.S.S.R., which thus remained Mongolia's
principal foreign trade and aid partner, subsidizing
Mongolia's inability to meet her budgetary debts.
In 1971-75 the number of Soviet aid projects in Mongolia will be 120, compared with 81 in 1966-70.

TRADE RELATIONS WITH THE REST
OF THE PACIFIC RIM

There has been no tradition of trade between
Pacific Siberia and other countries of the Pacific
region. Table 31 shows that total Soviet trade with
these countries accounts for only 3.3 percent of the
U.S.S.R.'s trade turnover and has grown very little
since 1958. There are few suitable export products
from the Far East and Eastern Siberia for the Soviets
to sell to these countries. There can be no prospect, for instance, for exports of timber, fish, or
minerals to the west coast of Canada or the United
States because of the complementary nature of local
production in those areas. However, Canadian wheat
and Australian and New Zealand meat have been sent
to the Soviet Far East in recent years, as well as
trial quantities of Australian fruit. In December,
1966, the Soviet Minister for Agriculture, V. Matske-
vich, said that it was sensible in his opinion to
buy some wheat abroad on a continuing basis for the

Far East region.[29] There are also prospects for
timber sales to Australia, but the Japanese market
is larger and much closer to Siberia.

Soviet trade interest in the west coast of Latin
America has developed in the last few years. Trade
agreements have been concluded with Chile (1967),
Colombia (1967), Peru (1968), Ecuador (1968), Costa
Rica (1970), and Bolivia (1970). The value of Soviet
trade with the Pacific Ocean countries of Latin America was only 20 million rubles in 1970, but, according to a member of the Soviet Far East exports council, the prospects for trade between the Soviet Far
East and Eastern Siberia and these countries is very
promising:

> The Pacific Ocean countries of Latin Amer-
> ica are big exporters of a number of goods
> which the USSR regularly buys on the world
> market, such as coffee, cocoa, cotton,
> bananas, tobacco, tin. These countries can
> also provide citrus fruits, pineapples,
> vegetables, wines, tinned meats and consumer
> goods such as clothing, footwear and elec-
> trical appliances. Deliveries from Latin
> America to the Far East and Eastern Siberia
> can effect a significant economy in trans-
> port costs; at present many foodstuffs and
> raw materials are transported to these re-
> gions by road from European Russia over dis-
> tances of 5,000 to 10,000 kilometres.[30]

He said there was ample scope for a return flow of
goods and services from the Soviet Far East and Eastern Siberia--but did not specify what these were.

Soviet trade with Southeast Asia has more than
doubled since 1970, but almost all of this has been
due to war-induced exports to North Vietnam. The
Chinese have hampered the transshipment of Soviet
aid and arms through Chinese territory, and since
the closure of the Suez Canal most Soviet aid has
gone through the Far East. In 1970 about 300,000
tons of dry cargo and a large quantity of oil products
were sent from Nakhodka to North Vietnam.[31] In the

TABLE 31

Soviet Trade Turnover with Other Countries of the Pacific Rim
(in million rubles, f.o.b.)

Country	Turnover 1958	Turnover 1970	1970 Trade Exports	1970 Trade Imports	Major Commodities Exported	Major Commodities Imported
Australia[a]	5.3	61.8	1.5	60.3	Canned fish	Wool, wheat, meat
New Zealand	4.9	19.6	0.7	18.9	Canned fish	Wool
United States	27.7	160.9	57.8	103.1	Chrome ore, furs, gems, tobacco	Raw hides, machinery, staple fiber, chemicals, cellulose
Canada	24.8	125.3	7.5	117.8	Raw cotton, furs, cotton cloth	Wheat, flour, synthetic rubber
Indonesia[b]	34.9	29.5	4.5	25.0	Cotton cloth	Natural rubber
Malaysia[c]	106.2	121.0	7.1	113.9	Cotton cloth	Natural rubber, tin
Thailand	0.3	3.4	2.6	0.8	Cotton cloth, newsprint	Natural rubber
Cambodia	0.4	1.7	0.3	1.4	Medicines, steel	Rice
North Vietnam[d]	16.3	183.2	166.5	16.7	Machinery and equipment, trucks, oil, steel, metals, cables, chemicals, tires, cotton cloth, flour, and medicines	Clothing, shoes, liquors, cigarettes, carpets
Chile	--	0.8	0.5	0.3	Machines	Wool, iodine
Colombia	--	10.9	1.5	9.4	Trucks, buses	Coffee
Mexico	--	1.0	0.7	0.3	Machinery, pig iron	Maize, pepper, beans
Costa Rica	--	6.2	--	6.2	--	Coffee
Ecuador	--	0.8	0.1	0.7	Cement	Cocoa
Peru	--	0.3	0.1	0.2	Sunflower oil	--
Total as percent of U.S.S.R. trade	2.8	3.3	2.2	4.5	--	--

a1959 (U.S.S.R./Australian diplomatic relations were suspended between 1954 and mid-1959).
bTrade turnover reached a peak of 87.5 million rubles in 1962.
cIncludes Singapore.
dTrade started in 1955.

Source: Vneshnyaya Torgovlya SSSR, for several years.

first half of 1971, 350,000 tons of cargo--including
170,000 tons of flour--was shipped to North Vietnam
from Far Eastern ports, compared with 220,000 tons
of cargo from Black Sea ports--which included machinery, equipment, trucks, oil, fertilizers, food, and
clothing. The Far East concentrates on sending raw
materials to North Vietnam, such as timber (40,000
cubic meters in 1971); however, other items, such
as a seagoing tug built at Sovetskaya Gavan', have
also been delivered. Altogether, there are about
20 Soviet ships operating between Vladivostok/Nakhodka
and North Vietnam.[32] Building materials are also exported to North Vietnam, even though they are in
short supply in the Far East.

There has been no public indication of direct
trade contact between other Pacific countries and
the Soviet Far East.* However, the U.S.S.R. has
signed trade agreements with Thailand (1970), Malaysia
(1967), and Singapore (1966) that may lead to some
trade with the Soviet Pacific regions. Mounting
Soviet interest in trade between the Far East and
Pacific Ocean countries is indicated by the establishment in the mid-1960s of an Export-Import Research
Institute at Khabarovsk as a branch of the U.S.S.R.
Academy of Sciences. In 1971 an Economic Research
Institute was created at Vladivostok to study the
trade policies of countries such as Japan, Canada,
Australia, North Korea, Mongolia, and countries of
Latin America. All economic research throughout the
Far East will be coordinated by this latter institute, including the new Pacific Geography Institute
opened on November 1, 1971, which will assess the
natural resources of the Pacific region.[33] It is
believed that these developments are forword indi-
cators of changing Soviet policy attitudes toward
the Pacific.

_____

*India--a country outside the area of this study
--made its first shipment of goods (steel line for
the fishing industry and tea) to the Far East in
December, 1971.

NOTES

1. F. V. D'yakonov et al., Dal'nii Vostok, ekonomiko-geograficheskaya kharakteristika (Moscow: AN SSSR, 1966), p. 115.

2. P. Volin, Literaturnaya Gazeta, No. 22, 1969.

3. Vneshnyaya Torgovlya, No. 9, 1966.

4. See J. Wilczynski, The Economics and Politics of East-West Trade (London: Macmillan, 1969).

5. "Towards a New Trade Policy for Development," Report by the Secretary-General of United Nations Conference on Trade and Development, Document E/Conf.46/3, February 12, 1964, p. 113.

6. Trade Prospects in the USSR: A Survey for Businessmen, Report of the Birmingham and London chambers of commerce, May, 1963, p. 18.

7. Voprosy Ekonomiki, No. 9, 1966, p. 111; Ekonomicheskiye Rayony SSSR (Moscow, 1965), p. 308; BBC Summary of World Broadcasts, Part I, U.S.S.R., September 24, 1971.

8. The American Review of East-West Trade, No. 4, 1968, p. 12.

9. Nihon Keizai Shimbun, June 18, 1968.

10. V. Conolly, Soviet Trade from the Pacific to the Levant (London, 1935), p. 12.

11. Assessment made by V. Kuzenko, Ministry of Foreign Trade representative for the Far East and Eastern Siberia, July, 1967.

12. H. K. Norton, The Far Eastern Republic of Siberia (London: George Allen and Unwin, 1923), p. 126.

13. V. A. Yakhontoff, <u>Russia and the Soviet Union in the Far East</u> (London, 1932), p. 247 and 406.

14. Conolly, <u>op. cit.</u>, p. 50.

15. Y. Shipov, "Economic Relations Between the USSR and Japan," <u>International Affairs</u> (Moscow), December, 1969, p. 90.

16. <u>Ibid.</u>, p. 91.

17. For more details see V. Conolly, "Soviet-Japanese Economic Cooperation in Siberia," <u>Pacific Community</u> (Tokyo), October, 1970.

18. <u>Nihon Keizai Shimbun</u>, August 6, 1968.

19. <u>Vneshnyaya Torgovlya</u>, No. 11, 1965.

20. <u>The Mainichi Daily News</u>, May 16, 1964.

21. <u>The Japan Times Weekly</u>, May 27, 1967.

22. <u>Nihon Keizai Shimbun</u>, August 20, 1968.

23. <u>Japan Quarterly</u>, No. 4, October/December, 1967.

24. <u>Ekonomicheskaya Zhizn'</u>, October 4, 1932.

25. P. A. Khromov, <u>Ekonomicheskoe Razvitie Rossii</u> (Moscow: AN SSSR, 1967), p. 364.

26. J. D. Yanson, <u>Foreign Trade in the USSR</u> (London: Gollancz, 1934), p. 135.

27. R. O. Freedman, <u>Economic Warfare in the Communist Bloc</u> (New York: Praeger, 1970), p. 124.

28. <u>BBC Summary of World Broadcasts</u>, October 29, 1971.

29. <u>Tass</u>, December 27, 1966.

30. A. P. Karavayev, <u>Latinskaya Amerika</u>, No. 1, 1971.

31. <u>BBC Summary of World Broadcasts</u>, October 8, 1971.

32. <u>Ibid</u>., November 12, 1971.

33. <u>Ibid</u>.

11

COMMODITY
OUTLOOK
FOR
PACIFIC TRADE

The Soviet Far East is less subject to
consideration from a purely "Pacific"
viewpoint than is any other of the lands
on the western shore of that ocean.[1]

No regional trade statistics are available for
Pacific Siberia; consequently, some data are here
presented and suggested as reflecting theoretical
opportunities for trade. These figures (see Table
32) are based on the detailed knowledge, gained in
earlier chapters, of the strengths and weaknesses
of the Pacific Siberian economy. As a result, it is
possible to estimate, however roughly, which commodities are in surplus supply in Pacific Siberia (and
so are available for export to interregional or
overseas markets) and which are in short supply (and
so must be met from imported sources, either interregional or overseas). It is necessary to arrive
only at orders of magnitude, not exact estimates, so
that it is then possible to determine the likely
limits of changing Soviet attitudes to Siberian trade
with the Pacific. These can then be related to the
requirements and supply capabilities of other countries located around the Pacific Rim.

The relative freight cost advantage of trading
with the Soviet Far East is an important consideration for most Pacific Rim countries--especially for
Japan, which is only two days' sail away. From

253

Vladivostok to Vancouver in the northeast Pacific is
only 4,800 miles by the shortest sea route, and to
Singapore in the southwest Pacific it is less than
4,000 miles. Even the much longer haul to Sydney
(5,780 miles) is almost identical to the Vladivostok-
to-Moscow rail distance. For a country like Australia, in the southwest of the Pacific Ocean, the Soviet
Far Eastern market is less than one-half the distance
away of major European markets and almost 1,000 miles
closer than the western seaboard of Canada or the
United States.

All this makes for sensible transport geography,
but the crux of the matter lies in the commodities
the Far East and Eastern Siberia can export or need
to import. The huge "imports" of foodstuffs into
Pacific Siberia from other parts of the Soviet Union
already have been discussed.[2] A portion of Siberia's
food needs are supplied by Mongolia, North Korea,
and Manchuria, but there are prospects for major
food-exporting nations in the Pacific, such as Australia, New Zealand, the western provinces of Canada, and the West Coast of the United States,* to
supply some of these Siberian food requirements at a
freight cost advantage over domestic Soviet suppliers.

In terms of current Soviet trade philosophy,
however, these opportunities must be based, at least
to some extent, on reciprocal buying activity by
Pacific region countries--and this is where the
theoretical constructs of trade fall down. Pacific
Siberia is a market of 13 million people that "imports" three-fifths of its food needs, as well as
nearly all its consumer goods and industrial plant
and equipment, but has very little to offer on world
markets other than timber, fish, and some minerals.

----

*In 1972 about 200,000 tons of maize, barley,
oats, and other fodder grains will be exported to
Nakhodka from the United States. This is the first
known delivery of U.S. produce to the Soviet Far East.

TABLE 32

Pacific Siberia--Annual Estimates of Market Surplus
and Deficit for Selected Commodities

Commodity	Unit	Deficit (-) or Surplus (+)	Percent of Market
Wheat and rye	1,000 metric tons	-700	20
Meat[a]	" " "	-125	20
Sugar[b]	" " "	-375	90
Milk[c]	" " "	-730	20
Butter	" " "	-20	40
Cheese	" " "	-10	65
Eggs	million units	-335	20
Apples	1,000 metric tons	-55	n.a.
Citrus fruit	" " "	-25	100
Tea	" " "	-5	100
Coffee	" " "	-2	100
Cocoa	" " "	-5	100
Fish[d]	" " "	+950	90[e]
Sawn timber	million cubic meters	+15	70[e]
Leather footwear	million pairs	-20	65
Woolen cloth[f]	million meters	-20	90

[a]Slaughter weight.

[b]Refined basis.

[c]About 220 gallons per ton, i.e., 730,000 tons =
160 million gallons.

[d]The proportion of edible fish is only 655,000
tons.

[e]Percent of local output "exported."

[f]Cotton cloth "imports" could be as high as 200
million meters.

METHOD

The data set out in Table 32 was derived by se-
lecting fairly homogeneous products, such as foodstuffs, and subtracting Pacific Siberian production
from estimated local demand. This latter parameter
was assessed by first taking the entire Soviet production of the commodity in question, net of international trade,[3] to give a Soviet domestic consumption
figure. Regional consumption for the Far East and
Eastern Siberia was arrived at merely by applying to
the Soviet consumption figure the percentage share
of the Soviet population represented by the Pacific
Siberian market. The results were averaged out over
a period of five years in order to eliminate bias due
to seasonal variations.

The main shortcoming in this approach is that
the calculation of regional consumption assumes that
per capita consumption in Siberia is identical to
the Soviet average. Clearly, this is not the case
for some commodities: Climatic differences result
in varying demands, as do variations in regional purchasing power. Nevertheless, the method was deemed
adequate, especially as several of the "import" estimates so calculated agreed broadly with available
Soviet data.

COMMODITY ESTIMATES

The commodity estimates contained in Table 32
show very clearly the dependence of Pacific Siberia
on "imports" of foodstuffs in return for its "exports"
of fish and timber. It is not possible, of course,
to predict what Soviet trade policies will emerge in
the future as a result of the region's increasing
tendency to import. All that can be said with cer-
tainty is that if the authorities in Moscow wish to
see per capita supplies of these products in Pacific
Siberia at a level equal to the average for the
Soviet Union they must fill the market deficit either
from scarce interregional supplies or from overseas.
Migration and settlement policies discussed in Chapter

9 indicate that Moscow does aim to equate per capita consumption of foodstuffs and consumer goods in Pacific Siberia with those obtaining in the rest of the U.S.S.R.

Some of the commodity estimates in Table 32 have been checked against Soviet sources. One authoritative source states that "imports" into the Far East of meat alone are 120,000 tons.[4] This figure may be compared with that of 125,000 tons given in the table for the whole of Pacific Siberia; Eastern Siberia probably produces a slight surplus of meat. The same source gives Far Eastern imports of sugar as 145,000 tons. Assuming that Eastern Siberia, with a population much greater than that of the Far East, imports proportionately the same quantity of sugar, this would give a total import figure for Pacific Siberia of 385,000 tons, compared with 375,000 tons in Table 32. Bread grain imports (wheat and rye) into the Far East are given as 1,200,000 tons, with 675,000 tons of this supplied by Eastern Siberia.[5] Thus, net imports into Pacific Siberia from West Siberia, the Urals, and Volga were 525,000 tons, compared with 700,000 tons in Table 32. Local grain production fluctuates a great deal, which would be sufficient to explain any differences in the two estimates.

Oil has been left out of these calculations because although the Far East imports about 60 percent of its requirements (over 5 million tons) it is supplied by the low-cost oil fields in West Siberia. For other products--namely ferrous and nonferrous metal manufactures, machinery, and equipment--reliable information is not sufficient to make even an approximate estimate. It is known that the major part of the requirements of these products is "imported" and that for rolled metal this amounts to some two million tons annually.

Two consumer items are given in Table 32--leather footwear and woolen cloth--because they are relatively homogeneous and therefore amenable to the methodology used here. Estimates for clothing consumption are easier to make than those for other commodities because the long and severe winters create a demand for

clothes above the average for the U.S.S.R. The problem here is that not much is known about the relative
usage of fur and padded or quilted cotton clothing.
Similarly, with leather footwear it is likely that
felt and rubber boots are in considerable use in the
winter months.

   The two surplus, or "export," commodities shown
in the table are fish and sawn timber. The live
weight fish catch has been reduced to a usable fish
products basis, and it has been assumed that no more
than 10 percent of that is consumed locally. The
surplus of 950,000 tons is probably "exported" in
the proportion of 655,000 tons of edible fish and
fish products and 295,000 tons of nonfoodstuffs for
meal, fertilizer, and technical end uses. The estimate for sawn timber has assumed average Soviet use
rates per head of population, and, consequently, the
surplus may be too high due to higher than average
local use rates for large construction projects.
Sawmill capacity is, however, the only real limiting
factor to sawn timber output in this part of the
U.S.S.R. It is known that the surplus of lumber
transported out of the region each year is equivalent
to over 20 million tons (25 million cubic meters).
More than one-half of this was in round log form--
approximately 13 million cubic meters;[6] a large part
of the balance would be sawn timber.

   No estimates have been made for plywood, paper,
cardboard, or cellulose. These commodities are in
short supply in the U.S.S.R. Nevertheless, some of
the pulp from Bratsk has been exported, inter alia,
to Japan; but the major source of Japanese imports
of pulp and paper is still the island of Sakhalin--
especially the Poronaisk mills, which supply un-
bleached sulphite pulp. One Western authority has
said that the industry there "is now being more actively developed by the Soviets with an eye to Pacific markets, in the first place in Japan and
Australia."[7] Cuba, North Korea, and Mongolia are
also probably supplied from this source. For the
future, there may be good prospects for cord pulp
sales from the Baikal'sk mill and the second stage
of Bratsk.

FOODSTUFFS

Considering the information listed in Table 32, it is apparent that, among the major food surplus-producing countries of the Pacific Rim, Australia, New Zealand, Canada, and the United States could supply some of the import requirements of Pacific Siberia. Clearly, all kinds of questions--both economic and political--arise for Soviet policy-makers; for instance, the high costs of farming in the Far East must be set against the availability of foreign exchange to finance food imports from hard currency areas.

The problem of convertible currency is a very real one; in the mid-1960s Soviet purchases of wheat from Canada, Australia, and the United States were financed in part by sales of gold on the London and Paris exchanges. Normally, however, the U.S.S.R. seeks to use surplus sterling earned from its trade with the United Kingdom to buy Australian and New Zealand wool and Malaysian rubber.[8]

A multilateral clearing arrangement for Pacific Siberian trade with all Pacific Rim (non-Communist) countries would provide an alternative solution; any imbalance could be settled by extra deliveries of goods in the following year.[9] (Alternatively, import surpluses could be financed by swing credits or overdrafts at low interest rates.) Triangular deals would provide another approach whereby, for instance, Australia could import Far Eastern fish products and pay for them by sending foodstuffs to Japan, which in turn would complete the triangle by sending the Far East an equivalent amount of specified machinery or consumer goods. Another method would be to provide financial switch-dealing through private trading banks in, for example, Japan with a Japanese importing firm buying a clearing balance earned by a New Zealand foodstuffs exporter to the Far East--which must be spent in the U.S.S.R. on Soviet goods. The discount might be 5 percent, or more; and by this means the Japanese firm obtains relatively low-cost imports from the U.S.S.R., but

the reseller of the clearing balance in New Zealand
loses financially.[10] These are theoretical examples
that would demand radical changes in the trade policy
of some of the countries concerned.

From the U.S.S.R.'s point of view bilateral trade
minimizes the need for foreign currency transactions,
and imports can be used to facilitate exports. This
is particularly important where, as the Japanese have
discovered, the Soviet product is not of the high
quality necessary to compete on world markets. For
foodstuffs, which in most cases are in surplus supply
internationally, the U.S.S.R. could use its bulk purchasing ability to obtain either favorable entry
conditions for its exports or to finance its imports
under generous credit terms. A portion of the Pacific
Siberian food market could be extremely important to
the United States, Canada, Australia, or New Zealand,
and the U.S.S.R. might well apply leverage to get a
quid pro quo for its exports. (For example, the
U.S.S.R.-Canada trade agreement, starting with the
1960 Protocol to the 1956 agreement, provides for a
2:1 ratio for Soviet-Canadian purchases.)

We have dwelt on the subject of the possible
mechanisms of trade here because trade in foodstuffs
seems to be relatively promising in the long run.
Clearly, however, any complex multiangular deals or
unwieldy credit operations will not maximize the
benefits to be derived from trade with the Soviet
Far East and, indeed, may well discourage the interest
of private trading companies. The initial aim could
be quite modest. A 10 percent share of the food imports listed in Table 32 would give a Pacific Rim
country annual exports of 70,000 tons of wheat,
12,000 tons of meat, 3,000 tons of butter and cheese,
and 8,000 tons of fruit.

There are no very obvious export markets for
Far Eastern fish and fish products in the Pacific
except Japan and Australia. The west coasts of
Canada, the United States and Latin America, or New
Zealand and the Pacific islands are not very likely
prospects. Some of the countries of Southeast Asia
could emerge as markets in the longer run, but a more

likely prospect is for the U.S.S.R. to help these
countries to catch more of their own fish with the
aid of Soviet fishing vessels and equipment. Japan
already absorbs 50,000 tons of Far Eastern fish each
year and could take much more; the Australian market
for imported fish is around 40,000 tons. Most Pacific
region countries are already well acquainted with
Soviet Far Eastern canned crab and salmon, and this
should help the market acceptability of fish products
generally, although the quality of Soviet goods would
have to be improved.

FOREST PRODUCTS

There is no very obvious market for Pacific Siberian forest products in the west coasts of Canada,
the United States, or Latin America; New Zealand itself is an exporter of softwood timber, pulp, newsprint, and kraft paper. There may well be a growing
market for Siberian newsprint (the Krasnoyarsk mill
is the only large producer at present) in Southeast
Asia, but for most forest products Japan is the only
very large market.

Lumber exports to Japan are limited only by the
productive capacity of the machinery installed in
Siberia. The natural resource itself is of the highest quality. One-fifth of Japan's timber imports
come from the U.S.S.R. and this will increase if the
Japanese undertake to provide more machinery and
equipment to the Soviet Far East to assure themselves
of continuing supplies of lumber. At present, exports to Japan of Soviet forest products consist, in
value terms, of more than 90 percent round logs and
less than 10 percent of sawn timber (coniferous species), pulp (sulfite and sulfate), and paper. The
round logs are predominantly for sawing for house
frames; about one-quarter to one-third comprise pulp-
ing logs and construction timber. Round log shipments to Japan have risen rapidly from 1.8 million
cubic meters in 1963 to 7.0 million cubic meters in
1970. Japan is now the biggest market for this commodity. The main species supplied are fir, pine,
larch, cedar, aspen, and poplar; June-August is the

busiest shipment period. Most of this timber comes
from Pacific Siberia (with an increasing amount from
the Far East, including one million cubic meters from
the Amur area)* and the rapid increase in sales to
Japan demonstrates the region's latent export capacity.
The potential for increased exports of forest products is large; in the long run they will expand rap-
idly--especially as supplies from the West Coast of
the United States tend to diminish.

     Australia offers a small but lucrative market
for forest products. At present, imports are worth
about $200 million and, at current prices, will rise
to over $500 million (or 10 million cubic meters)
by the year 2000. In view of its geographical location, the Soviet Far East should be able to compete
on the Australian market with Canada or the United
States.** Imported softwoods have a much wider industrial use than native Australian hardwoods, and,
consequently, much of the expected future increase
in demand will be for softwoods.

     Softwood timbers may be in acute short supply
on world markets by the end of the century as increasing income levels and house-building activity
in many Asian as well as Communist and Western countries lead to greater demand. This is where Pacific
Siberia, with about 70 percent (50 billion cubic
meters) of the U.S.S.R.'s reserves of timber, can
assume a dominant position on the world timber market.

                          MINERALS

     Japan is, as already mentioned, keenly interested
in Siberian mineral developments not only because of

_____

     *In 1971 the Soviet Far East delivered 1.4 mil-
lion cubic meters of timber to 12 large Japanese
companies, an increase of 40 percent over 1970.

     **Australia imported small quantities of Siberian
timber in 1960, 1964, and 1965, but the presentation,
grading, and freight of the shipments left much to
be desired.

their relative proximity to her economy but also because of her dependence on imports of minerals to
sustain expanding export industries competing on
world markets. Continuity of supplies at favorable
prices is of the utmost importance to her. The political aspects of supply have probably restrained
Japan, so far, from joint mineral ventures in Siberia.
Japan does not want to be too dependent upon any one
particular supplier. The politically unstable Middle
East, for instance, supplies nearly all of Japan's
oil, and Siberian oil would provide a welcome diver-
sity in supplies. The United States would not like
to see Japan become too economically dependent upon
the U.S.S.R., and this may influence Japanese policy
in the short run. More recently, however, the United
States' high-handed policy to Japan in both political
and economic affairs will probably cause some reas-
sessment in Japan's international policies. In the
long term the cost of investment in the huge Siberian
mineral ventures, rather than political considerations, may deter Japan. Japan has, after all, a
long history of involvement in the exploitation of
Soviet Far Eastern resources and is more aware than
most of the difficulties involved.

The United States itself may now be interested
in the possibilities of exchanging machinery and
equipment for Siberian natural gas or copper. These
subjects were discussed by Commerce Secretary Stans
when he visited Moscow in December of 1971.

For some other countries of the Pacific, interest in Siberia lies in the potential threat it poses
to their traditional, or emerging, mineral and metal
export markets in Asia or Europe. It is not hard to
imagine Eastern Siberian aluminum ingots, using electricity generated at a projected cost of 0.032 kopecks
per kilowatt-hour at Sayan-Shushenskoe,[11] competing
with the Canadian product in a market situation that
is already oversupplied. In 1969 the U.S.S.R. emerged
as the largest source of dealer supplies of nickel
due to world shortages caused by strikes at the Sud-
bury, Canada, mines. An estimated 7,000 to 11,000
tons of Soviet nickel moved through dealers' hands.
Some of this must have come from Noril'sk, which is
the largest producer in the U.S.S.R. The periodical

withdrawal of the U.S.S.R. from the free market for
nickel certainly has been a factor in the continued
tightness of supplies, and this could be used to good
advantage by her in the future.

There is also a long-term potential threat from
Pacific Siberian exports of coal, iron ore, and copper to Japan in competition with Australian supplies.
With all three of these minerals it will take the
U.S.S.R. some time to move into large-scale production
for export. Nevertheless, the long-term threat is
there, and the relative freight cost advantage between
the Far East and Japan may offset any additional
costs of extraction inland. The U.S.S.R. could, in
any case, take a policy decision to export at, or
just below, the prevailing world price, irrespective
of costs or profit margins. Queensland coal and
Hamersley iron ore soon could be in competition on
the Japanese market with Chul'man coal and Angara-
Ilim iron ore; copper from Udokan could displace some
of the supplies from Mount Isa on world markets.
There is no sign of such a threat at present--and
Japan has signed neither production-sharing agreements nor supply contracts--but the future situation
will bear careful watching. Japanese demand for most
minerals is expected to increase very rapidly in the
1970s, but the presence of an additional large sup-
plier--the Soviet Far East--could encourage the
Japanese to keep prices from other sources, such as
Australia or the United States, from rising.

The poor quality of nepheline deposits in Eastern Siberia, and the high costs of freighting reasonable quality bauxite in from the Urals, may mean that
Australia could be asked by the Soviets to export
alumina from the rich Weipa deposits for use by the
Shelekhov, Bratsk, and Krasnoyarsk aluminum refineries.
It was estimated in Chapter 6 that the shortfall in
alumina supplies to Eastern Siberia may exceed one
million tons a year. If Australia was to supply a
significant share of this market, the Soviets would
probably demand a quid pro quo--such as hydro-electric
or mining machinery or even oil. Alternatively, the
Soviets could seek bauxite from Indonesia or Malaysia.
As part of the Five Year Plan for 1971-75 a big petro-

chemical complex is to be built near the port of
Nakhodka, "from where tankers will carry oil products
to Sakhalin, Kamchatka and continental ports, and
for export."[12] The complex will specialize in the
production of high-grade gasoline, kerosene, diesel
fuel, and primary products for synthetic materials.
Siberian oil will thus have a direct outlet to the
Pacific. By the mid-1970s the U.S.S.R. may start applying pressure on its trading partners in the region
for sales at competitive prices.

MACHINERY AND CONSUMER GOODS

The lack of homogeneity within any particular
group of these manufactures makes it very difficult
to estimate the size of the "import gap," even though
it is known that the major part of local demand is
satisfied by imports from other regions of the
U.S.S.R. It was seen (see Table 32) that local output of leather footwear satisfies only 35 percent,
and woolen cloth only 10 percent, of regional demand.
Again, the Japanese are actively seeking sales of
these products, whereas other countries in the Pacific
region do not seem to be aware of the opportunities.
The Japan Chemical Fibre Association set up a special
committee to ensure the timely and orderly flow of
exports of consumer goods, mainly textiles and footwear, worth $30 million under the terms of the 1968
joint venture timber agreement.[13] Payment was on
deferred terms of 18 months.

It is known from reports in _Pravda_ that the
availability of woolen sweaters, pullovers, woolen
underwear, felt boots, sheepskin, and even fur coats
in Siberia is far from sufficient.[14] Timber-cutting
workers cannot buy woolen gloves or mittens that
last more than a day or two. There is a shortage of
rubber boots and waterproof clothes for fishermen
and of reindeer hide or sheepskin clothing and footwear suitable for hunters. In Vladivostok, there is
a clothing factory called the Vladivostok Production
Union of Sewing Enterprises. Among its suppliers
are the Kansk cotton fabric _kombinat_ and the Sverdlovsk
textile _kombinat_, as well as manufacturers of labels

in Leningrad and Moscow.[15] Deliveries of cloth to
this factory are often greatly delayed and their
quality is inferior; accordingly, there are frequent
stoppages in production, and supplies to the Far
Eastern market are erratic. There are good opportunities for the Japanese textile industry in Pacific
Siberia as well as for other simple consumer goods,
including crockery, soaps, razor blades, shoe polish,
and the like.

Nearly two-thirds of all machinery requirements
are imported (Eastern Siberia produces only one-
quarter of its machinery needs). There is some manufacture of metal-cutting machines, industrial presses,
woodworking, agricultural, and mining machinery, and
marine engines in Pacific Siberia, but a great deal
of it is highly specialized production for "export"
to other parts of the U.S.S.R. or even overseas.*
Most heavy machinery, including equipment for the
timber and mining industries, is imported, as are
precision machine tools and the complete range of
machinery for the hydro-power generating and pulp,
paper, and paperboard industry, as well as equipment
for the fishing industry. Even cement kilns are
brought in from European Russia. The main centers
of machine building, at Krasnoyarsk, Irkutsk, Komsomol'sk, and Khabarovsk, are completely unable to meet
the demands of local industry; there are long delays
in obtaining suitable equipment from the western regions of the country. The cost of freighting machinery into Siberia often exceeds the cost of transporting the raw materials required for their manufacture several times over. This is a region where the
construction of roads, railways, settlements, factories, dams, and large industrial complexes puts a
premium on the supply of heavy machinery, but the
shortage of skilled workers will make it difficult to
improve the situation for many years.

There are good prospects for exports of machinery from countries such as Japan or the United

---

*The Amurlitmash factory at Komsomol'sk exports
foundry machines to Eastern Europe, Cuba, Iran, and
France.

States. There has been some interest in Japanese
cement kilns for the Far East because the U.S.S.R.
is switching from the wet to the dry process. Fin-
nish, Swedish, West German, and American machinery
and equipment was installed at the Bratsk pulp and
paper mill (300,000 tons bleached sulfate pulp), including a board mill (140,000 tons white paperboard)
and paper-making machinery (100,000 tons of printing
paper). The suggestion has been made that the purchase of machinery from Japan be offset against deliveries of pulp under a production-sharing scheme.

The Soviets have also expressed an interest in
Japanese coal-mining machinery. In 1968 Mitsui,
Mitsubishi, C. Itoh, and others examined the prospects
of developing the South Yakut (Chul'man) coking coal
deposits by offering, on credit, $400 million of
mining equipment plus the materials necessary to construct a railway to connect Chul'man with the Trans-
Siberian railway.[16] No agreement was reached, but
in 1970 four Japanese steel companies (including Nip-
pon Steel Corporation) examined the project; although
a decision was delayed until more accurate feasibility
studies could be made, it appears this project may be
finalized in the next few years.[17]

Other opportunities for machinery exports exist
in supplying the Far Eastern fishing industry with
items such as fish-canning and -processing equipment,
cleaning and packing machinery, fish detectors and
navigation aids, equipment for fishing vessels, factory ships, and the like. In 1969 Satsuki Kai, representing 36 Japanese trading, fishing, and industrial
firms, signed a $4-6 million two-year agreement ex-
changing such machinery and equipment for Soviet fish
products.[18]

TRANSIT TRADE

With the closure of the Suez Canal, and considering the great cost of exporting products to Asia
from Europe, there has been an interesting development
in Europe-U.S.S.R.-Japan rail transit trade. In the
long term this trade may increase European awareness
of the Pacific Siberian market. The V/O Soyuzvnesh-

trans organization in Nakhodka reported a tripling
of rail transit trade for the two years ended 1969.[19]
Japan, Austria, Belgium, West Germany, Britain, Italy,
the Netherlands, Iran, Finland, and East European
countries such as Bulgaria, Czechoslovakia, and Rumania are involved. Vessels carrying container cargo
eventually will have a shuttle service between the
Nakhodka terminal to the Trans-Siberian railway and
Japanese ports; separate wharves are being allocated
now for transit cargoes. Another container-handling
area is to be built in Vrangel' Bay.[20]

The Russians have cut railway transport charges
so that rates on the Trans-Siberian railway route
are about 20 percent cheaper on the average than alternative sea routes, although this varies with
cargo.[21] In addition, transportation has been speeded
up from the 40-50 days previously required to 30 days
transit time between Japan and West Germany and 25
days to Northern Europe. The main items transported
this way are highly processed goods such as instru-
ments, business machines, other machinery, and a
considerable amount of canned foodstuffs. Early in
1969 Soyuzvneshtrans signed a Japanese agency contract with Nissin Transportation and Warehousing Co.,
which at that time was handling between 50 and 100
tons of transit cargo a month; Soyuzvneshtrans expected this figure to triple by the end of 1969.[22]
The Soviet authorities are encouraging a greater interest in transit trade both in Japan and Europe.
In 1971 the National Freight Corporation in London
announced a new freight route between Britain and
Japan via Siberia; it will deliver goods in 30 days
at "significant economies over more conventional
freight routes."[23]

Freight to the Middle East takes five days less
than the usual sea and overland routes. Soviet rail
freight rates depend on cargo weight so that bulky
but relatively lightweight goods, such as automobiles,
can be economically sent across the U.S.S.R. to the
Middle East from Japan.

Another prospect for transit-type trade would
be the opening up of a Japan-Europe shipping service

along the northern sea route. From Yokohama to London this way is 4,000 nautical miles shorter than via the Suez Canal and 5,000 miles shorter than via the Panama Canal. The Mitsui OSK Line Ltd. showed some interest in such an Arctic sea route in 1968; but the navigation season is limited to only three summer months (even then, icebreakers are necessary), and not much cargo can be picked up or unloaded en route because of the sparse population in northern Siberia. A regular shipping service from Japan would, however, have considerable impact on the economic development of northern Siberia and would assist in cutting the final cost of items delivered there. The Soviets may be prepared even to offer substantial trade access elsewhere in Pacific Siberia in return for such a shipping service, which would relieve them of delivering some 10 million tons of cargo per year for workers in the North.[24]

A PACIFIC TRADE OUTLOOK

Opportunities do exist for an expansion of mutually beneficial trade between Pacific Siberia and some of the countries bordering on the Pacific Ocean. The development of this trade is still in its formative stages, but there is a danger that Japan, with a long history of commercial contact with the Soviet Far East, will come to dominate Pacific Siberia's trading operations in the Pacific region. Over the last five years or so, in particular, Japan has built up an extensive expertise in trading operations with the Soviet Far East. With Soviet encouragement, it has set the pace in the non-Communist world for exploiting direct trade opportunities with the eastern regions of the U.S.S.R. As a result, a considerable number of Japanese companies are greatly experienced now in the peculiarities of Soviet regional trade, and they may attempt to act as intermediaries for the Soviets. (In October, 1971, for instance, the first cargo of alumina from Japan arrived at Vanino; the bauxite from which the alumina was made must have come from Australia, Indonesia, or Malaysia.)

The most significant outlook for Japan is the development of production-sharing arrangements with

the Soviets in Siberia. In the past, the export
branches of the Pacific Siberian economy were inadequately developed; this is still largely true, but
the situation could change rapidly under the impetus
of production-sharing arrangements with Japan. The
first of these, concerning timber, has been relatively
successful since its signing in mid-1968, and another
followed in December, 1971. The idea that this could
be the easiest way for the U.S.S.R. to enter the boom-
ing Japanese raw materials market--while at the same
time developing its own sparsely populated and capi-
tal-hungry territories in Siberia--seems to be gain-
ing favor, albeit cautiously, in Moscow.

     The Japanese, on the other hand, see prospects
for exports of machinery, equipment, consumer goods,
footwear, and clothing while at the same time ensur-
ing themselves of long-term supplies of raw materials
from a nearby source. So far, the production-sharing
negotiations have been prolonged--mainly because of
the sheer size of the projects envisaged by the Soviets and their demands for favorable financial conditions. The advantages of a close (almost off-shore)
raw material base for Japan are clear; equally clear
is the long-term threat of the development of such
production-sharing ventures to Australian, U.S., and
Canadian mineral exports to Japan, to Middle Eastern
oil sales to Japan, to Canadian and American timber-
marketing activities, and even to the newly developed
sales of Alaskan natural resources to Japan.* None

-----

     *Japan purchases from Alaska liquefied natural
gas, and Japanese firms have substantial oil leases
in the Bristol Bay area. A Japanese company has
built a pulp mill at Sitka; its output is shipped to
Japan for processing into paper and paperboard.
Another Japanese firm owns a sawmill for spruce and
hemlock exports in squared log form. The Alaska
Pulp Co. also has agreed to export 350 million board
feet of lumber to Japan. Trial shipments of coal
have been sent to Japan for evaluation from the
Prince William Sound area. Japanese fish-processing
plants buy a major part of the catch of Alaskan fishermen and crab catchers.

of these markets is presently in any danger from substantial Siberian competition, but the long-run potential is there.

A great deal will depend upon the development of
normal bilateral trade relations between the U.S.S.R.
and countries bordering on the Pacific Ocean. The
U.S.S.R.-Japan trade agreement, for instance, has
been used as the commercial framework within which
the development of trade with the Soviet Far East was
fostered. Proximity between the two regions as well
as Japan's ability to exchange imports of raw materials for exports of machinery and consumer goods
played a dominant role. The weak state of trade relations between the U.S.S.R. and other Pacific countries (e.g., the United States) or their relative
smallness and distance from Soviet territory (e.g.,
Australia and New Zealand) explains why regional
trade with Pacific Siberia has not developed. Trade
relations with Canada are much more cordial, but
basically the two countries are too complementary for
trade to be very large.

Some new trade initiatives from Moscow are required, and this is inextricably linked with the de-
sirability of a more rapid rate of economic growth
in Pacific Siberia. As long as China claims part of
Soviet territory in the Far East, she probably will
exploit the weak development of the Pacific Siberian
economy by irritating the Russians with the knowledge
of that weakness. Border trade with China probably
will never again regain its former importance, and
the U.S.S.R. may be seeking to supplant it with imports from other Pacific countries. The main difficulty to be overcome is finding complementary Pacific
Siberian export products that (1) would be acceptable
quality-wise on sophisticated Pacific markets and
(2) can be handled by Dal'intorg as distinct from
the distant and central bureaucratic corporations in
Moscow. Trade associations established in Pacific
countries specifically to represent the interests of
merchant houses and export-import companies doing
trade with Pacific Siberia would be an important

first step. A direct shipping service, without transshipment in Japan, would also help to keep costs down.*

Unfortunately, the U.S.S.R.'s basically autarkic
approach has not allowed it to realize the opportunities for greater economic development of its eastern
regions that could occur through trade. At present
the U.S.S.R. is giving priority in its allocation of
scarce foreign exchange reserves and credits to large
industrial plants in European Russia, such as the
Fiat/Tolyattigrad automobile factory and the Kama
River truck plant. Unless the Soviet Union decides
that the development of Pacific Siberia through international trade is important enough to warrant
special allocations of foreign exchange for import
requirements, it is not likely that trade relations
with any Pacific country except Japan will improve
very rapidly in the 1970s.

The point remains to be made, however, that
more direct foreign trade could assist the Pacific
Siberian economy greatly. The principles of comparative advantage would tend to encourage an exchange
of exports of Siberian minerals, timber, and fish
for imports of foodstuffs, machinery, and consumer
goods. Such imports would not replace local regional
production but, on the contrary, would provide a
welcome supplement. The inflow of attractive foreign
trade goods earned from the efficient specialization
of the region would (1) tend to reduce and stabilize
labor turnover, which has been the major factor retarding orderly economic growth in the past, and (2)
reduce, through the relative cheapness of sea transport, the total freight bill for the region and relieve some of the pressure on the more heavily worked
parts of the Trans-Siberian railway.**

----

*The Soviet Far Eastern Line already operates be-
tween Japan and Canadian and U.S. Pacific coasts.

**The completion of the 2,000-mile Mid-Siberian
(Baikal-Amur) line from Ust'-kut to Komsomol'sk will
ease the traffic pressures but not the costs; in any
case, completion will not occur before 1980 or 1985.

In the longer run, the planned acceleration in the economic growth of Pacific Siberia will lead to a diversification of the present limited range of export possibilities. Benefits from expanded trade activity, if the Soviet Government allows it, will accrue and have a multiplier effect on the whole complex of economic activity. The limited labor resources of the economy will lead Moscow to place more emphasis on capital inputs, mechanization, and higher productivity per worker and, logically, to a greater interest in imports to satisfy regional needs for labor-intensive products--such as textiles and clothing. Exports may be promoted more vigorously through the creation of regional production complexes that would operate with economies both in investment and production.[25] Current Soviet academic interest-- which normally pre-dates official policy thinking by some years--in the Pacific region and the growth of Pacific research institutes in the Soviet Far East indicate a growing awareness of the Pacific as a whole and of the benefits to be derived from commercial contacts with the countries of the region.

NOTES

1. W. Mandel, The Soviet Far East and Central Asia (New York, 1944), p. xi.

2. In 1963 Far Eastern imports of grain and meat amounted to one million tons. A. B. Margolin, Problemy Narodnogo Khozyaistva Dal'nego Vostoka (Moscow: AN SSSR, 1963), p. 145.

3. See for example Vneshnyaya Torgovlya SSSR za 1969 god, pp. 48-49, where some 50 commodities are assessed in this way.

4. F. V. D'yakonov et al., Dal'nii Vostok, ekonomiko geograficheskaya kharakteristika (Moscow: AN SSSR, 1966), p. 194.

5. Ibid.

6. Voprosy Ekonomiki, No. 8, 1966, p. 52.

7. V. Conolly, Beyond the Urals (London: Oxford University Press, 1967), p. 310.

8. See J. Wilczynski, Multilateralization of
East-West Trade (Australian and New Zealand Association for the Advancement of Science, Fortieth Congress, Section G, January, 1968, Christchurch, New
Zealand); the Sterling Area has been treated by the
U.S.S.R. as a convenient multilateral zone where
trade deficits with some countries are offset by
trade surpluses with others.

9. Ibid.

10. For details of West European switch deals
see The Economist, January 14, 1967, pp. 143-44.

11. V. A. Shelest et al., Problemy Razvitiya i
Razmeshcheniya Elektroenergetiki v Srednei Azii (Moscow, 1964), p. 118; comparable projected costs are
0.040 kopecks for Ust'-Ilim, 0.045 kopecks for Bogu-
chansk, and 0.047 kopecks for Krasnoyarsk. Lower-
cost electricity will be generated only at Nurek and
Nizhne Rogunsk on the Vakhsh River in Tadzhikistan.

12. Novosti Information Service Bulletin, No.
8290, August 13, 1969; as of January, 1972, the Soviet
Far Eastern tanker fleet consisted of more than 40
ships, although most were small (less than 12,000
tons).

13. Nihon Keizai Shimbun, May 7, 1969. The
products involved include shirts, sweaters, raincoats,
other synthetic clothing, and footwear.

14. Pravda, March 28, 1969, quoting I. Kirianov,
their Krasnoyarsk correspondent; at Yeniseisk, the
largest sawmilling center in Siberia, there is an
acute shortage of furniture--even of simple stools,
tables, and bookcases.

15. Ekonomicheskaya Gazeta, No. 1, January, 1968.

16. Nihon Keizai Shimbun, August 20, 1968.

17.   Ibid., July 24, 1970.

18.   Ibid., January 21, 1969.

19.   Novosti Information Service Bulletin, No. 8791, December 12, 1969.

20.   BBC Summary of World Broadcasts, Part I, U.S.S.R., October 29, 1971.

21.   Nihon Keizai Shimbun, April 8, 1969.

22.   Ibid.

23.   East-West Trade News, October 21, 1971.

24.   BBC Summary of World Broadcasts, October 29, 1971.

25.   Tass News Agency, Moscow, September 6, 1971.

SELECTED BIBLIOGRAPHY

NEWSPAPERS AND PERIODICALS

Soviet Sources

Ekonomicheskaya Gazeta. Moscow: Central Committee of the Communist Party of the Soviet Union (weekly).

International Affairs. Moscow: Znanie (monthly).

Izvestiya. Moscow: Presidium Supreme Soviet (daily).

Lesnaya Promyshlennost'. Ministry of Forestry (three times weekly).

Planovoe Khozyaistvo. Moscow: State Planning Commission (bi-monthly).

Pravda. Moscow (organ CPSU; daily).

Problemy Severa. Moscow (irregular).

Vestnik Moskovskogo Universiteta--geografiya. Six issues a year.

Vneshnyaya Torgovlya. Moscow: Ministry of Foreign Trade (monthly--available in English).

Voprosy Ekonomiki. Moscow: Institute of Economics (monthly).

Voprosy Geografii Sibiri. Tomsk (irregular).

Vostochno-Sibirskaya Pravda. (Organ Irkutsk oblast' CPSU; daily).

Western Sources

BBC Summary of World Broadcasts. London (weekly).

China Trade Report. Hong Kong (monthly).

Far Eastern Economic Review. Hong Kong (weekly).

Nihon Keizai Shimbun. Tokyo (weekly--available in
     English).

Soviet Geography Review and Translation. New York:
     The American Geographical Society (monthly).

Soviet Press Translations. University of Washington
     (bi-weekly).

Soviet Studies. University of Glasgow (quarterly).

The American Review of East-West Trade. New York:
     Symposium Press (monthly).

USSR and the Third World. London: Central Asian
     Research Centre (ten times yearly).

                    SOVIET STATISTICAL ABSTRACTS

Itogi Vsesoyuznoi Perepisi Naseleniya 1959 god--RSFSR.
     Moscow: Ts.S.U., 1963.

Narodnoe Khozyaistvo Amurskoi Oblasti v 1963 god.
     Khabarovsk, 1965.

Narodnoe Khozyaistvo Buryatskoi ASSR. Ulan-Ude, 1963.

Narodnoe Khozyaistvo Irkutskoi Oblasti. Irkutsk,
     1967.

Narodnoe Khozyaistvo Khabarovskogo Kraya. Khabarovsk,
     1957.

Narodnoe Khozyaistvo Krasnoyarskogo Kraya. Krasno-
     yarsk, 1958.

Narodnoe Khozyaistvo Magadanskoi Oblasti. Magadan,
     1960.

Narodnoe Khozyaistvo Primorskogo Kraya. Vladivostok,
     1958.

Narodnoe Khozyaistvo RSFSR, "Statistika." Moscow,
     annually.

Narodnoe Khozyaistvo Sakhalinskoi Oblasti. Yuzhno-
    Sakhalinsk, 1960.

Narodnoe Khozyaistvo SSSR, "Statistika." Moscow,
    annually.

Narodnoe Khozyaistvo Tuvinskoi ASSR. Kyzyl, 1962.

Narodnoe Khozyaistvo Yakutskoi ASSR. Yakutsk, 1964.

Promyshlennost' SSSR. Moscow: Ts.S.U., 1964.

Sel'skoe Khozyaistvo SSSR. Moscow: Ts.S.U., 1960.

Transport i Svyaz' SSSR. Moscow, 1967.

Vneshnyaya Torgovlya SSSR. Moscow, annually.

BOOKS, PAMPHLETS, AND MONOGRAPHS

Soviet Sources

Aleksandrova, T. A. Vostochno-Sibirskii Ekonomiche-
    skii Raion. Moscow, 1962.

Atlas Irkutskoi Oblasti. Moscow and Irkutsk, 1962.

Australiya i Okeaniya (istoriya i sobremennost').
    Moscow: AN SSSR, 1970.

Bandman, M. K. Krasnoyarskoe Priangar'e. Novosibirsk,
    1962.

Bardin, I. P., ed. Problemy Razvitiya Chernoi Metal-
    lurgii v Raionakh Vostochneye Ozera Baikala.
    Moscow, 1960.

Belikov, I. F., and I. G. Tkachenko. Soya v Primor-
    skom Krae. Vladivostok, 1961.

Bobrievich, A. P., et al. Almaznye Mestorozhdeniya
    Yakutii. Yakutsk, 1959.

Bratskaya G.E.S.   Vol. I (1955-60) and Vol. II (1961-
    66).   Irkutsk: Vostochno-Sibirskoe Knizh. Izd.,
    1967.

Butiagin, I. B., et al.   Razvitie Energetiki Sibiri.
    Novosibirsk, 1960.

Dal'nii Vostok, fiziko-geograficheskaya kharakteris-
    tika. Moscow: AN SSSR, 1961.

Dolzhnykh, V. N.   Industriya Pribaikal'ya i Effektiv-
    nost' ee Razvitiya.   Irkutsk: Vostochno-Sibir-
    skoe Knizh. Izd., 1967.

D'yakonov, F. V., et al.   Dal'nii Vostok, ekonomiko-
    geograficheskaya kharakteristika. Moscow: AN
    SSSR, 1966.

Energeticheskie Resursy Yakutskoi ASSR. Yakutsk, 1962.

Geografiya Naseleniya Vostochnoi Sibiri. Moscow:
    AN SSSR, 1962.

Geografiya Primorskogo Kraya. Vladivostok, 1963.

Granik, G. I.   Transport Magadanskoi Oblasti.   Maga-
    dan, 1960.

_____.   Transport Severo-vostoka Yakutskoi ASSR.
    Yakutsk, 1958.

Grishin, A. K., and I. I. Konoplev.   Zeiskii Gidrouzel.
    Blagoveshchensk, 1959.

Il'inskaya, S. A., and L. P. Brysova.   Lesa Zeiskogo
    Priamur'ya. Moscow, 1965.

Istoriya i Kul'tura Narodov Severa Dal'nego Vostoka.
    Moscow: Nauka, 1967.

Ivanis, A. N.   Rybnaya Promyshlennost' Dal'nego
    Vostoka. Vladivostok, 1963.

Ivanov, A. A.   Ekonomika Proizvodstva Soi na Dal'nem
    Vostoke. Alma-Ata, 1963.

Ivanov, B. V. "Konferentsiya po razvitiyu proizvodi-
    tel'nykh sil Vostochnoi Sibiri," Izvestiya Sibir-
    skogo Otdeleniya Akademii Nauk SSSR. Moscow,
    1958.

Karasev, I. P., et al. Geologiya i Neftegazonosnost'
    Vostochnoi Sibiri. Moscow, 1959.

Klopov, S. V. Gidroenergicheskie Resursy Basseina
    Amura. Blagoveshchensk, 1958.

Kogan, I. L., and R. I. Faershtein. Voprosy Razvitiya
    Ugol'noi Promyshlennosti Magadanskoi Oblasti.
    Magadan, 1959.

Kondavkov, K. G. O Napravleniyakh Razvitiya i Razmesh-
    cheniya Promyshlennosti Yakutskoi ASSR. Yakutsk,
    1962.

Konferentsiya po Razvitiyu Proizvoditel'nykh sil
    Vostochnoi Sibiri. Moscow: AN SSSR, 1958.

Konoplev, I. I. Dal'nevostochnaya Baza Chernoi Metal-
    lurgii. Khabarovsk, 1966.

_____. Promyshlennost' Amurskoi Oblasti v Razvitii.
    Blagoveshchensk, 1963.

Krotov, V. A. Osnovnye Problemy Ekonomicheskoi Geo-
    grafii Vostochnoi Sibiri. Moscow-Irkutsk, 1964.

_____, et al. Vostochnaya Sibir'--ekonomiko-geo-
    graficheskaya kharakteristika. Moscow: AN
    SSSR, 1963.

Lesa Dal'nego Vostoka. Moscow, 1969.

Loginov, V. P. Puti Povysheniya Effektivnosti
    Razvitiya Gornoi Promyshlennosti Severovostoka
    SSSR. Moscow, 1962.

Malagin, A. P. Magadanskii Ekonomicheskii Raion.
    Magadan, 1957.

Margolin, A. B. Problemy Narodnogo Khozyaistva
    Dal'nego Vostoka. Moscow: AN SSSR, 1963.

Materialy 1-i Khabarovskoi Kraevoi Nauchnotekhnicheskoi
    Konferentsii, Mart 1965 god. Khabarovsk:
    Ts.B.T.I., 1966.

Materialy po Ekonomike Sel'skogo Khozyaistva Yakutii.
    Moscow, 1957.

Matveev, A. K. Ugol'nye Mestorozhdeniya Dal'nego
    Vostoka i Perspektivy ikh Razvitiya. Moscow,
    1958.

Mazover, Ya. A. Toplivno-Energeticheskie Bazy Vostoka
    SSSR. Moscow: AN SSSR, 1966.

Mishchenko, I. G., and E. A. Ur'eva. Rol' Sibiri v
    Ekonomike Sel'skogo Khozyaistva Strany. Moscow,
    1961.

Naselenie Irkutskoi Oblasti po Dannym Vsesoyuznoi
    Perepisi na 15-1-1959 god. Irkutsk, 1961.

Naselenie i Trudoviye Resursy Severo-vostoka SSSR.
    Moscow: Nauka, 1968.

Naumov, G. V. Zapadnaya Yakutiya. Moscow, 1962.

Nesterenko, A. Proizvoditel'nost' Truda i Sebestoi-
    most' Produktsii v Sel'skom Khozyaistve Amurskoi
    Oblasti. Blagoveshchensk, 1963.

_____. Voprosy Ekonomiki Sel'skogo Khozyaistva
    Dal'nego Vostoka. Khabarovsk, 1967.

Nikolaev, N. I., and N. M. Singur. Perspektivy
    Razvitiya Ekonomiki Dal'nego Vostoka. Khabarovsk,
    1968.

Nizovoe Ekonomicheskoe Raionirovanie Sibiri i Dal'nego
    Vostoka. Irkutsk, 1962.

Novak, A. G. Tselinnye Zemli Dal'nego Vostoka.
    Vladivostok, 1963.

Ozhigov, E. P. Khimiya na Dal'nem Vostoke. Vladivo-
    stok, 1965.

Parmuzin, Yu. P. Severo-Vostok i Kamchatka. Moscow:
    Mysl', 1967.

Penzin, I. D. Gorodskie Poseleniya Yuzhnoi Chasti
    Dal'nego Vostoka. Moscow, 1965.

Perevedentsev, V. I. Migratsiya Naseleniya i Trudovye
    Problemy Sibiri. Novosibirsk, 1966.

Pokshishevskii, V. V. Yakutiya, Priroda--Lyudi--
    Khozyaistvo. Moscow: AN SSSR, 1957.

Pomus, M. I. Osnovnye Voprosy Ekonomicheskoi Geo-
    grafii Sibiri. Moscow, 1964.

Popov, V. E. Chernaya Metallurgiya Sibiri. Moscow,
    1960.

_____. Ekonomika Ugol'noi Promyshlennosti Sibiri.
    Moscow, 1960.

_____. Problemy Ekonomiki Sibiri. Moscow, 1968.

Pozdnyakov, L. K., and V. I. Gortinskii. Lesa i
    Lesnye Resursy Yuzhnoi Yakutii. Moscow, 1960.

Preobrazhenskii, V. S., ed. Voprosy Geografii
    Zabaikal'skogo Severa. Moscow, 1964.

Prirodnoe Raionirovanie Tsentral'noi Chasti Krasnoyar-
    skogo Kraya i Nekotorye Voprosy Sel'skogo
    Khozyaistva. Moscow, 1962.

Problemy Nauki na Severo-vostoke SSSR. Magadan, 1967.

Problemy Razvitiya Chernoi Metallurgii v Raionakh
    Vostochnee oz. Baikal. Moscow, 1960.

Problemy Razvitiya Promyshlennosti i Transporta
    Buryatskoi ASSR. Moscow, 1958.

Problemy Razvitiya Promyshlennosti i Transporta
    Yakutskoi ASSR. Moscow, 1958.

Promyslovye Ryby Magadanskoi Oblasti. Magadan, 1959.

Pyat'desyat let Sovetskomu Primor'yu. Vladivostok,
    1968.

Razvitie Ostraslei Narodnogo Khozyaistva Irkutskoi
    Oblasti. Irkutsk, 1957.

Razvitie Proizvoditel'nykh Sil Vostochnoi Sibiri--
    Transport. Moscow: AN SSSR, 1960.

Razvitie Proizvoditel'nykh Sil Zapadnoi Yakutii v
    Sviazi s Sozdaniem Almazodobyvayushchei Promy-
    shlennosti. 3 vols. Yakutsk, 1958-59.

Rokhlin, M. I. Chukotskoe Olovo. Magadan, 1959.

Rudykh, V. M. Gorod Bratsk. Irkutsk: Vostochno
    Sibirskoe Knizh. Izd., 1968.

Rybakovskii, L. L. O Sozdanii Postoyannykh Kadrov
    na Sakhaline. Novosibirsk, 1961.

Sakhalinskaya Oblast'. Yuzhno-Sakhalinsk, 1960.

Severnoe Olenevodstvo. Moscow, 1961.

Severo-Vostochnyi Ekonomicheskii Raion. Moscow, 1965.

Shimaniuk, A. P. Sosnovye Lesa Sibiri i Dal'nego
    Vostoka. Moscow, 1963.

Shitikov, A. P. Nash Ordenonosnyi Khabarovskii Krai.
    Khabarovsk, 1967.

Sholnikov, M. G. Angaro-Eniseiskaya Problema. Mos-
    cow, 1958.

Shul'man, N. K. Reka Zeya i ee Budushchee. Blagovesh-
    chensk, 1962.

Shvarev, V. A., ed. Dal'nii Vostok za 40 let Sovet-
    skoi Vlasti. Komsomol'sk: AN SSSR, 1958.

Sibirskii Geograficheskii Sbornik. 5 vols. Moscow-
    Leningrad: AN SSSR, 1963-67.

Sistema Vedeniya Sel'skogo Khozyaistva v Tuve. Kyzyl, 1960.

Slavin, S. V., ed. Problemy Razvitiya Proizvoditel'-nykh Sil Magadanskoi Oblasti. Moscow: AN SSSR, 1961.

Smagin, V. N. Lesa Basseina Reki Ussuri. Moscow: Nauka, 1965.

Soveshchanie Rabotnikov Sel'skogo Khozyaistva Dal'nego Vostoka i Yakutskoi ASSR. Khabarovsk, 1961.

Spiridonov, B. S. Ekonomicheskie Osnovy Kompleksnogo Ispol'zovaniya Kedrovykh Lesov Sibiri. Moscow, 1968.

Starikov, G. F. Lesa Severnoi Chasti Khabarovskogo Kraya. Khabarovsk, 1962.

Stepura, P. P. Primor'e Promyshlennoe. Vladivostok, 1962.

Tarasov, G. L. Territorial'no-ekonomicheskie problemy razvitiya i razmeshcheniya proizvoditel'nykh sil Vostochnoi Sibiri. Moscow, 1970.

_____. Vostochnaya Sibir'. Moscow, 1964.

Tatarnikov, P. A. Spetsializatsiya v Mashinostroenii Dal'nego Vostoka. Moscow, 1962.

Tokarev, S. P. Uskorennoe Razvitie Promyshlennosti v Vostochnykh Raionakh SSSR. Moscow, 1960.

Tsymek, A. A. Lesoekonomicheskie Raiony Dal'nego Vostoka. Khabarovsk, 1959.

Turetskii, V. S. Resursy Uglei Primor'ya i Priamur'ya i Sovremennoe Ispol'zovanie Ikh. Vladivostok, 1962.

Uchenye Sel'skomu Khozyaistvu Dal'nego Vostoka. Vladivostok, 1965.

Udovenko, V. G. <u>Voprosy Razvitiya i Razmeshcheniya
    Proizvoditel'nykh sil Dal'nego Vostoka kak
    Osnovnogo Ekonomicheskogo Raiona</u>. Moscow: AN
    SSSR, 1958.

Volchkov, A. K. <u>Baza Sibirskoi Metallurgii</u>. Krasno-
    yarsk, 1961.

<u>Voprosy Ekonomiki Dal'nego Vostoka</u>. Vladivostok, 1965.

<u>Voprosy Ekonomiki Stroitel'stva i Proizvodstva
    Stroimaterialov v Vostochnoi Sibiri</u>. Irkutsk,
    1966.

<u>Voprosy Ekonomiki Ugol'noi Promyshlennosti Vostochnoi
    Sibiri</u>. Blagoveshchensk, 1959.

<u>Voprosy Geografii Priamur'ya</u>. Khabarovsk, 1967.

<u>Voprosy Lesnogo Khozyaistva Sibiri i Dal'nego Vostoka</u>.
    Krasnoyarsk, 1959.

<u>Vorposy Prirodnogo Raionirovaniya Dal'nego Vostoka v
    Sviazi s Raionnoi Planirovkoi</u>. Moscow, 1962.

<u>Voprosy Razvitiya Transporta Irkutskoi Oblasti</u>.
    Irkutsk, 1960.

<u>Voprosy Sel'skogo i Lesnogo Khozyaistva Dal'nego
    Vostoka</u>. Vladivostok, 1961.

<u>Voprosy Trudovykh Resursov Dal'nego Vostoka</u>. Khaba-
    rovsk, 1963.

Vorob'ev, V. V. <u>Goroda Yuzhnoi Chasti Vostochnoi
    Sibiri</u>. Irkutsk, 1959.

Vstovskii, L. <u>Lesnoi Eksport na Dal'nem Vostoke</u>.
    Vladivostok, 1964.

<u>Yakutiya za 50 let v Tsifrakh</u>. Yakutsk, 1967.

<u>Yuzhnaya Chast' Dal'nego Vostoka</u>. Moscow: Nauka,
    1969.

SELECTED BIBLIOGRAPHY 287

Zakharov, G. A. Osobennosti i Perspektivy Razvitiya
Metalloobrabatyvayushchei Promyshlennosti Maga-
danskoi i Kamchatskoi Oblastei. Novosibirsk:
AN SSSR, 1962.

Zolotarev, S. A. Lesa i Pochvy Dal'nego Vostoka.
Moscow, 1962.

Zolotaya Kolyma. Moscow: AN SSSR, 1963.

Zubkov, A. I., and B. B. Gorizontov. Promyshlennye
Uzly Krasnoyarskogo Kraya. Moscow: AN SSSR,
1963.

Western Sources

Algvere, K. V. Forest Economy in the USSR. Stock-
holm: Royal College of Pharmacy, 1966.

Armstrong, T. Russian Settlement in the North. Cambridge: Cambridge University Press, 1965.

Bukshtynov, A. D. Forest Resources of the USSR and
the World. Jerusalem: Israel Program for Scientific Translations, 1960.

Conolly, V. Beyond the Urals. London: Oxford University Press, 1967.

_____. "Soviet-Japanese Economic Cooperation in
Siberia," Pacific Community (Tokyo), October,
1970.

Gregory, J. S. Russian Land Soviet People. London:
Harrup, 1968.

Hooson, D. J. M. A New Soviet Heartland? Princeton,
N.J.: Van Nostrand, 1964.

Ikeda, H. The Economic Development of Siberia. In
Japanese; Tokyo, 1964.

Kirby, E. S. "The Soviet Far East," International
Affairs (London), January, 1971.

_____. The Soviet Far East. London: Macmillan,
1971.

Kolarz, W. The Peoples of the Soviet Far East. London: George Philip & Son, 1954.

Krypton, C. The Northern Sea Route and the Economy
of the Soviet North. London: Methuen, 1956.

Levin, M. G., and L. P. Potapov, eds. The Peoples
of Siberia. Trans. Chicago: University of
Chicago Press, 1964.

Stanley, E. J. Regional Distribution of Soviet Industrial Manpower: 1940-60. New York: Praeger,
1968.

Studies on the Soviet Union. Vol. I, No. 4: "Hand-
book issue on Siberia and the Soviet Far East--
geopolitics, population, economics." Munich:
Institute for the Study of the USSR, 1962.

Suslov, S. P. Physical Geography of Asiatic Russia.
London: W. H. Freeman & Co., 1961.

Swianiewicz, S. Forced Labour and Economic Develop-
ment: An Enquiry into the Experience of Soviet
Industrialization. London: Oxford University
Press, 1965.

Thiel, E. The Soviet Far East. London: Methuen,
1957.

Treadgold, D. W. The Great Siberian Migration.
Princeton, N.J.: Princeton University Press,
1957.

Tupper, H. To the Great Ocean. London: Secker &
Warburg, 1965.

Wilczynski, J. The Economics and Politics of East-
West Trade. London: Macmillan, 1969.